D0871492

The Italian Stage
From Goldoni to D'Annunzio

by
Marvin Carlson

McFarland & Company, Inc.
Jefferson, N.C., & London
1981

Also by Marvin Carlson:
The French Stage in the Nineteenth Century (Scarecrow, 1972)
The German Stage in the Nineteenth Century (Scarecrow, 1972)

Library of Congress Cataloging in Publication Data

Carlson, Marvin A   1935-
  The Italian stage.

  Bibliography: p.
  Includes index.
  1. Theater — Italy — History. 2. Italian drama —
19th century — History and criticism. I. Title.
PN2683.C3   852′.009   80-10554
ISBN 0-89950-000-5

Manufactured in the United States of America

Contents

Introduction   v

I Eighteenth-Century Foundations   1
    The Search for Comedy   1
    The Search for Tragedy   14
    The Musical Theatre   24

II French Occupation   33
    Milan and the Royal Company   35
    Venice, Naples and Rome   45

III Restoration and Romanticism   50
    The Revival of Naples   52
    Milan and the Romantics   57
    Florence and Niccolini   68
    Turin and the Compagnia Reale Sarda   74

IV The Risorgimento   86
    Mazzini and Modena   87
    The Reale Sarda   98
    Verdi and Milan   107
    Verdi, Naples and Rome   114

V The International Era   124
    Ristori   126
    Salvini   137
    Rossi   149
    Verdi's Later Years   155

VI Realism   161
        Morelli and Bellotti-Bon   162
        The Dialect Theatres   169
        Verismo   175
        Duse and D'Annunzio   192

Conclusion   201

Bibliography   203
        General   203
        Eighteenth Century   206
        Early Nineteenth Century   208
        Late Nineteenth Century   211

Index   215

Introduction

For most of the theatre-going public of the nineteenth century, Italy meant only one thing — the opera — an impression easy enough to understand. The achievement of Italy in this genre, from Rossini's *Barbiere di Siviglia* in 1816 to Puccini's *Tosca* in 1900 (with Bellini, Donizetti, Verdi, and others of only slightly lesser stature between), surely ranks with the golden ages of any of the arts and not surprisingly served and still serves to eclipse the considerable achievement during this period in other aspects of the Italian theatre.

When Goldoni was born, at the beginning of the eighteenth century, the opera was already well established, but a significant tradition of spoken drama, even faintly comparable to that long since developed in France, England, and Spain, simply did not exist. In its place was the ancient but still flourishing improvised commedia dell'arte and an occasional literary tragedy, rarely read and quite likely never performed. Under the inspiration and the leadership of Goldoni Italian writers finally began, despite many obstacles, political, cultural, and linguistic, to build their own dramatic repertoire.

Thanks to Goldoni's genius, the bases for a comic repertoire were laid first, though he encountered much resistance in his own lifetime from advocates of the older improvised style. The most successful of these, Carlo Gozzi, even managed for a time to rival Goldoni in popular success. The serious drama faced even greater difficulties, with no great dramatist like Goldoni to develop it and hampered by a determination in most authors to cling to classic rules and models despite the public's indifference to such matters. Riccoboni attempted the establishment of an Italian tragic theatre early in the eighteenth century, and others followed him, but not until the appearance of Alfieri, late in the century, did Italy gain a group of plays which, with the comedies of Goldoni, could be considered the basis for a national repertoire. As the nineteenth century opened, Goldoni and Alfieri were almost universally accepted as the two pillars which must support the further development of the Italian spoken theatre.

The concern which necessarily dominated all else in nineteenth century Italy was the political unification of the peninsula and the creation of the Italian state. As the century began, this goal seemed remote indeed, though the patriotic dream was strongly present in the dramas of Alfieri. In 1800 Italy was a battleground between the great powers of Europe, led by France on one side and Austria on the other. Within a few years the French had become masters of most of the peninsula, a position they retained until the fall of Napoleon. These years gave Italy a taste of political unity, albeit under foreign domination, and provided relatively settled conditions for the encouragement of the theatre. Milan became for the first time an important theatre center, home of the first state-supported Italian theatre in modern times, the Compagnia Reale Italiana, founded in imitation of the Comédie Française. Young playwrights appeared, continuing the tradition of Goldoni and Alfieri, but they were generally forced to accommodate themselves to French taste and to avoid possible political references, since censorship was strong.

When the French left they were replaced by the Austrians, who divided Italy into a group of small, politically reactionary states under Austrian influence. Political repression became stronger than ever and uprisings in 1820, 1831 and 1848 brought no relief. Romanticism, the great international movement of the period, dominated Italian letters, but was naturally dominated there in turn by the political situation. Italian romanticism was interwoven with the Risorgimento, the movement toward national freedom and unity. Thus the great romantic writers in Italy were not isolated visionaries, as they were often elsewhere in Europe, but spokesmen for the Italian people, and recognized and revered as such by their countrymen. They were, as a rule, less interested in new artistic forms and subject matter than in political and social freedom and the creation of an Italian consciousness. The opposition to classicism was not nearly so strong nor so clear in Italian romanticism as it was north of the Alps.

The major dramatists of this period were naturally severely restricted by censorship, and some of their most popular works were known largely in only a printed form because of the impossibility of public presentation. Still, the less suspect opera and those dramas and comedies which did not arouse official suspicion received warm support. The old Italian system of touring companies continued, but the best troupes now settled in individual cities, provided with permanent homes and state subsidies. The Reale Italiana, left without support by the departure of the French, was invited to become a royal company in Naples, and other Italian courts, large and small, followed this example. The most famous company of the period was the Reale Sarda, established in Turin in 1820, which lasted until 1855 and served as the example for the government-supported *Stabile* theatres of the twentieth century.

By mid-century this system of support was disappearing as the pressures for freedom and unity grew and the existing states became more unstable and repressive. Gustavo Modena, the greatest actor of this period but involved like most artists then in the political struggle as well, sought in vain during the 1840s for support for his troupe of promising young comedians. Forced into the traditional pattern of touring, with a constantly changing company, he nevertheless set the standard for the new realistic mode which the great Italian actors of the next generation displayed around the world. In dramaturgy, the influence of the French romantic plays of Hugo, Dumas, and De Vigny could be seen in the rise of the spectacular historical drama. The leading dramatist in this style was Paolo Giacometti, who provided most of the plays associated with the great actress who appeared at the Reale Sarda during its final years, Adelaide Ristori.

With Ristori the Italian stage entered a new era, for she was the first Italian actress since the renaissance to attempt and to gain an international reputation. Europe had long been accustomed to welcoming Italian artists. Rossini had made Paris a second home for Italian opera, bringing there the greatest composers and singers of the century, and Verdi was by now an international figure. But the spoken drama was another matter, and the scope and success of Ristori's tours was without precedent. Once she had shown the way, the international star became a major part of late nineteenth-century theatre history and with Ristori, Rossi, Salvini, Duse and a number of touring artists whose fame was second only to these giants, Italy contributed more than any other country to the international circuit.

By 1871 the peninsula was finally united as an independent nation, but the fulfillment of the dreams of the Risorgimento did not bring an era of success or prosperity to the theatre. On the contrary, amid the stresses of building a new nation, the theatre was often neglected, and state support, already declining before unification, now disappeared almost entirely. The leading actors remained on almost permanent tours outside Italy, where both they and their productions received better support, and those who remained at home returned to the ancient though highly unstable system of touring, the *compagnia di giro*.

A few minor attempts were made to provide state support for the theatre in the 1870s and 1880s by establishing dramatic competitions, taking public subscriptions, or allowing a troupe the free use of a building. The most important of these efforts was the Città di Torino, a semipermanent company in Turin which had rent-free use of the former home of the Reale Sarda for half of the year. Some of the best actors of the period were associated with this company, including the young Eleanora Duse. Still, for the most part Italian theatre remained in the hands of the traditional traveling companies, with constantly changing personnel and a disinclination to attempt new works.

Fortunately for Italian playwrights of the time, a few directors appeared to challenge this tradition and actively seek new dramas. First Alamenno Morelli and Luigi Bellotti-Bon in the 1870s and then in the early 1880s Virginia Marini, Ermete Zacconi, Flavio Andò and Ermete Novelli created an atmosphere receptive to the works of the Italian verists and to the new drama of Ibsen and others now being translated into Italian. The plays of such dramatists as Verga, Bracco, Butti and Giacosa offered by these companies created the long-sought modern Italian repertoire. When a reaction to these strongly realistic works came at the end of the century, most notably in the poetic dramas of D'Annunzio, these directors were receptive to that as well. They introduced to Italy plays by the new generation of European dramatists being produced elsewhere in the independent theatres and contributed to those theatres works by the new Italian playwrights. As the century ended Italy had demonstrated that, though it still lacked a single permanent theatre, it was no longer only the land of opera but in actors and playwrights of the spoken drama could hold its own with any of the leading theatre nations of Europe.

I

Eighteenth-Century Foundations

The Search for Comedy

In painting and sculpture, architecture and poetry, the heritage of Renaissance Italy to the rest of the world was immense and brilliant, but the theatre's part in that great movement was far more modest and even somewhat ambiguous. No great Italian playwrights appeared; indeed the major legacy of the Italian Renaissance to European dramaturgy was a system of ornate and artificial rules which it was the occupation of playwrights and scholars throughout Europe for generations to debate, to explicate and ultimately to circumvent, defy and then ignore. The sterile and pedantic literary tragedy and erudite comedy of Renaissance Italy was not replaced, as it was in Spain and England, by a rich and living new drama, perhaps because the weight of the past lay too heavily on Italian writers, or perhaps because the disunity of Italy prevented the appearance of a great national drama.

On the other hand the unwritten comedy, the largely improvised commedia dell'arte, apparently absorbed most or all of the theatrical energy and imagination of the culture. This, though scorned by scholars, spread throughout Europe and left its mark everywhere on popular entertainments and even on the developing literary comedy outside of Italy. Most notably in the works of Molière can be seen the exuberance and theatrical imagination of the commedia used as the basis for a living literary theatrical tradition. Clearly the materials were present for an Italian author to achieve for Italy what Molière had done for France, to establish a tradition both popular and literary upon the foundations so plentifully provided by the commedia. Still, this proved extremely difficult in Italy. There the commedia was far more firmly entrenched, with both actors and public much less likely

1

to accept so radical a change as a shift to a set drama with memorized lines. The commedia was popular in Paris—Molière himself shared his theatre during most of his career with a commedia troupe—but several generations of playwrights before Molière, culminating in the great Corneille, had educated both actors and public to appreciate written drama as well. Moreover, Molière's France was the highly centralized France of Louis XIV, Molière's Paris its undisputed literary and cultural capital. Italy possessed no such tradition, and no such center. It was therefore not until almost a century after Molière, and inspired perhaps as much by the French playwright's example as by the commedia itself that at last an Italian Molière appeared in Carlo Goldoni. His center of activity was, not surprisingly, Venice, the city in Italy at that period which came nearest to serving as the cultural and theatrical capital.

When Goldoni was born in Venice in 1707, that city was enjoying one of the many glorious pauses in its long and luxurious decline. Venice had become the pleasure capital of Europe, and governmental restrictions on lavish expenditures for parties, dress, and jewelry had little effect; small wonder when expensive fans and muffs and periwigs costing more than twelve ducats were banned "except for masquerade" at a time when the masquerade was a central manifestation of Venetian life. The mask and cloak opened all pleasures to all classes in Venice and masked figures filled the gaming houses and theatres, the fairs and fêtes, as they fill the canvases of Pietro Longhi. A constant stream of visitors added to the color and holiday atmosphere—young gentlemen on the grand tour and leading members of European society: the Queen of Poland in 1705 and the King of Denmark in 1709.

Venetian music was enjoying a golden age. Vivaldi was violin master at the Pietà, Galuppi director of music at the Incurabili. Sung Mass at St. Mark's lasted up to five hours and musical services at the hospitals were packed with admiring audiences. Opera, which had first been offered in a public theatre in Venice in 1637, was in the year of Goldoni's birth available to the Venetian public in no less than eight theatres (some of which offered spoken drama and commedia as well)—San Cassia, San Salvador, SS Giovanni e Paolo, San Samuel, San Angelo, San Giovanni Grisostomo, SS Apostoli, and San Fantin. It should be remembered that at this time London and Paris had to be content with two theatres each.

Goldoni from his earliest years was immersed in this highly-charged artistic atmosphere. His grandfather's house, where he first lived, was a regular gathering place for actors and musicians, the frequent location of private operatic and theatrical offerings. Goldoni's father presented him with a complete marionette theatre at the age of four and according to his own testimony he began reading the plays in the family library at the same time.(1) At the age of eight he composed his first comedy, much to the delight of his parents, and not long after enjoyed his first taste of actual performance in Perugia, where his father had been appointed medical advisor. Apparently as a reward for young Carlo's achievements at school, the elder Goldoni allowed him to participate in an amateur performance for the entertainment of the Perugian aristocracy. Since Perugia was within the Papal States of central Italy, women were not allowed on stage, and the young Goldoni was given the leading female role and a pompous prologue, written by the aristocratic patron of the entertainment. In his *Memoires* Goldoni recalls the old-fashioned hyperbolic rhetoric of this prologue with amusement:

> Most benign heaven, filled with the most dazzling rays of your sun, we come like butterflies who, on the weak wings of our expressions, take flight toward your radiance, etc.(2)

The elder Goldoni was willing enough to indulge his own and his son's interest in the theatre with harmless activities of this sort, but the suggestion of a theatrical career for young Carlo would have scandalized him. The much more respectable, if scarcely more financially secure profession of the law was his selection. Carlo dutifully pursued his studies in Padua (reading plays and attending the theatre whenever the opportunity presented itself), achieved his degree and set up a practice in Venice. He found that Venice had 240 lawyers, ten or twelve of the first rank, some twenty in the second, and the rest with little hope of attracting clients. At this critical time his father died and Carlo, perhaps in desperation or perhaps because released from the parental eye, turned to literature. He produced a moderately successful almanac, and then turned to the theatre. His taste was for comedy, but he knew neither actors nor audiences would be interested, so he produced a lyric tragedy, *Amalasonte*, which he carried to Milan in hopes of having it accepted at the opera there.

Such a move a century or so later would have indicated that Goldoni was willing to try his fortune in the opera capital of Italy, but this was far from the case in 1732. Naples and Venice were the great music centers of the early eighteenth century, and Milan was, relatively speaking, a cultural backwater. While Venice boasted eight theatres, Milan had only one, the Teatro Ducale, though it was a large and impressive one, with five ranks of boxes. There was no permanent company at this theatre; performers there were primarily touring lyric and ballet troupes, with occasional companies of actors doing prose works and commedia. When Goldoni arrived, an opera company was in residence, with several members of his acquaintance. They gained him a reading, but could not gain acceptance for his opera, which was apparently poor indeed. The rejected author destroyed his manuscript and turned from literature to service in the diplomatic corps.

Still Goldoni remained in contact with the world of the theatre, striking up an acquaintance with one of the great montebanks of the Italian stage, Bonafede Vitali, who under the pseudonym l'Anonimo was then selling patent medicines in Milan with the aid of a troupe of commedia actors. In Lent of 1733 the company which had been performing at the Teatro Ducale left for an engagement in Germany and Vitale's troupe took over the theatre. Goldoni submitted to them a comic interlude, *Gondoliere veneziano*, which was presented with modest success, and promised them a more substantial and serious work for the following season, when they expected to be in Venice. This tragi-comedy, *Belisario*, was a great success at San Samuel in 1741, applauded, says Goldoni, even by the connoisseurs who recognized its faults, since:

> seeing the superiority which my piece had over the farces and ordinary puerilities of the commedia, they looked forward from this first experiment to a continuing series of equal merit which would open the way to the reform of the Italian stage.(3)

That promise, if apparent, was not so easily or rapidly fulfilled as Goldoni suggested, for another six years passed before he became a full-time playwright or concerned himself particularly with theatrical reform. In the interim he served as consul in Genoa, then practiced law in Pisa and Florence. He wrote some thirty plays during the years, with varying success, but they were almost entirely within the standard genres of the time—tragedies and tragi-comedies in the neoclassic manner, opera libretti, commedia scenarii with at most the love scenes written out and the rest left to the invention of the players—little, in short, to expand the boundaries of the Italian stage.

Then in 1747 his career entered a new era. He was contacted by the theatrical manager Girolamo Medebac (1706-1781), who proposed to lease a theatre in Venice for five or six years provided Goldoni would serve as his playwright in residence. Goldoni accepted and returned to Venice as the official dramatist of the Teatro San Angelo, one of three then devoted to comedy. The fall season began in October and lasted until the Christmas holidays, the winter season began after Christmas and extended until Lent, and there was a two-week spring season during the Feast of the Ascension. During the summer the companies left Venice to tour on the mainland. When Goldoni arrived in Venice, spectators were still occasionally seated on stage, but like Voltaire in France and Garrick in England, he achieved the abolition of this practice.

The spectators in the pit and those in the boxes were clearly distinct groups, but either would be thought a great trial to producers today. The more well-to-do patrons of the boxes tended to view the theatre not as a source of esthetic pleasure but only as a fashionable place of social assemblage. A traveler of this period remarks that when the theatre season opened in the major cities, the salons closed, since each important family rented boxes at the leading theatre and

> the ladies hold so-called *conversazione* in their boxes, where spectators of their acquaintance pay them little visits.... The taste of these people for spectacle and music is shown more by their attendance than by any attention they pay to them. After the first performance, where there is moderate silence, even in the parterre, it is not considered in good taste to pay attention to the stage except for the most interesting passages. The major boxes are well furnished and brightly illuminated. There one gambles, or more often simply chats, seated in a circle within the box.(4)

Indeed, the boxes were provided with shutters so that those who sought to conduct their social affairs in private, or who wished to avoid the possible distraction of the performance, could shut themselves away in their elegant cubicles. This, however, was rarely done, since an important part of the occasion was public display. Young men of wealth could flaunt their mistresses and members of the aristocracy could see what other people of their social position were present and decide which boxes to visit during the evening.

The parterre was far more attentive to the play, though it made the lot of the actor if anything more difficult. Its inhabitants were the common folk, a noisy, turbulent, brawling and demanding group. Wooden benches were provided for them in the fore part of the theatre and an occasional guard appeared if they became too boisterous, but the pit remained nevertheless in constant movement and commotion. The benches were insufficient for the crowd, and directly in front of them an empty space was provided for "women suffering from an incontinence of urine,"(5) hardly encouraging audience members to come close to the stage. Further back, they were subjected to the spitting and the dropping of orange peels, candle ends and other debris from the boxes, so it is little wonder that they remained in constant turmoil. Nevertheless they maintained a running commentary on the happenings on stage. If the actors pleased, they were rewarded with steady applause, cheers, and encouraging cries: *"Siestu benedeta! Benedeto el pare che l'ha fato! Ah! Cara, me buto zozo!"* ("Blessed by thou! Blessed be he who fathered thee! Darling, I throw myself at your feet!")(6) If the actors did not please, they were subjected to whistles, stamping, and missiles of every description. Baked apples and pears, sold just outside the entrance to the theatre, were the most popular, but during every entr'acte (and each program had several, when officials would pass through the audience collecting admission money) girls would sell other foods — oranges, cakes, anisette, fritters and chestnuts.

Still it was this difficult public which Goldoni must satisfy, and in his case the task was made particularly hard by his wish to please them and at the same time to wean them away from the commedia, which had hitherto provided the mainstay of their theatrical entertainment. His first attempts were indifferently received, but before the end of the first season he produced three works which were both great successes and important contributions toward the new Italian comedy: *I due gemelli veneziani*, in which Darbes, the popular Pantaloon, achieved his first triumph without a mask; *La vedova scaltra*, which contained masks but which was Goldoni's first successful "national comedy," based on contemporary Venetian life rather than on the stock situations of the commedia; and *La putta onorata*, his first realistic portrait of the common people of Venice. The audience in the pit was delighted to see itself represented realistically on stage, and Goldoni revelled in their delight:

> In this comedy there are scenes of Venetian gondoliers, traced from nature, and very diverting for those who know the language and manners of my country. I wished to reconcile myself with this class of servants who deserve some attention and who were not pleased with me. The gondoliers of Venice were allowed entrance to the theatre only when it was not full; they could not come to my comedies; they were forced to wait for their masters in the street or in their gondolas; I myself heard them apply to me a few very droll and comic names. I had set aside for them some places in the corners of the theatre. They were enchanted to see themselves represented on stage and I became their friend. (7)

In the small world of Venetian letters, Goldoni's sudden success inevitably inspired certain manifestations of literary jealousy. When a revival of *La vedova scaltra* opened the 1749-50 season at the San Angelo, the rival San Samuel opened with a parody, *La Scuola delle vedove,* by a prolific if uninspired Jesuit author, Pietro Chiari (1711-1785). Wearing the inevitable Venetian disguise, a full cloak, a white vizor, and a three-cornered hat, Goldoni attended the rival production and was furious to find it not a parody at all, but a thinly masked plagiarism: "One actor would recite several phrases from my original, another would respond 'nonsense, nonsense.' They would repeat some clever sayings, some jokes from my piece, then cry in chorus, 'rubbish, rubbish.' "(8)

This thin effort, and the applause it received, drove the angry Goldoni to write an "Apologetic Prologue" which, against the advice of his friends, he had published and distributed throughout Venice. Goldoni was clever enough to recognize the so-called parody's weakest point, at least in the eyes of the authorities, its unsympathetic treatment of the various foreigners which appeared in it. The response doubtless exceeded the author's expectations. Large crowds were attracted to both plays and the Venetian government, fearful of offering any insult to the tourists who were so important to the economy of the city, not only closed Chiari's play but instituted theatrical censorship in Venice for the first time.

This series of events by no means silenced Goldoni's critics; if anything it heated their anger. For another ten years the supporters of Chiari and of Goldoni carried on a war of pamphlets, plays, and pastiches in the coffee-houses and theatres of the city. Goldoni's free admission of gondoliers to the San Angelo was called a trick for gaining their support, and his comedies were dismissed by many members of elegant society as rough and crude productions for the masses. Goldoni, it was said, had a greater knack, but Chiari took more pains. By the end of his second Venetian season Goldoni felt the need of a powerful gesture to gain a clear supremacy. Accordingly, in the traditional prima donna's speech closing the season, he had Theodora Medebac promise that he would produce the unheard-of total of sixteen new comedies the following season.

This bold undertaking indeed focussed the attention of the Venetian world on Goldoni and the San Angelo. Though both his health and his creative ability were stretched to their limits, Goldoni fulfilled his promise, creating sixteen new works, all but two of which were successful. The first work in this remarkable series was *Il teatro comico*, which Goldoni himself characterized as "less a Comedy in itself than a foreword to all my Comedies."(9) In the second scene Goldoni proudly recalled his boast and even listed the titles of the sixteen upcoming works. The following scenes included a play-within-a-play and a free-wheeling defense of Goldoni's new style. The commedia dell'arte, one character remarked, was rightly losing its popularity: "People are bored with always seeing the same thing and always hearing the same words. The audience knows what Harlequin will say even before he opens his mouth."(10)   The original purpose of comedy, argued a later passage, had been lost:

> Comedy was created to correct vice and ridicule bad customs.... But when comedies became merely ridiculous, no one paid attention any more, because with the excuse of making people laugh, they admitted the worst and most blatant errors. But now that we have returned to fish comedies from nature's *Mare Magnum*, men feel their hearts touched again. They can identify with the characters or passions and discern whether a character is well observed and developed, and whether a passion is well motivated.(11)

Goldoni remained with Medebac at the San Angelo from 1748 until 1753, but the desire for a better salary, more freedom in the publication of his plays, and a larger and more prestigious theatre led him then to sign a contract with Antonio and Francesco Vendramin, the aristocratic proprietors of the Teatro San Luca. One of his last works for Medebac was *La locandiera* (1753), doubtless the best known and most popular of his "new comedies." The San Luca remained his base for the next decade, and some of his best works were created there, but Goldoni's working conditions proved generally less favorable than he had hoped. The larger size of the San Luca encouraged its actors to strive for broad effects, and Goldoni spent several seasons working out a compromise between their declamatory habits and his more delicate and intimate style. For a time he was forced to write popular but undistinguished potboilers like *La sposa persiana* (1753) simply to keep his hold on the public. Chiari, who had followed Goldoni at the San Samuel, regularly wrote rival plays during these years to counter each success, such as *La schiava chinese* in imitation of *La sposa persiana*. With *La massère* (1755), Goldoni successfully negotiated a return to his favorite subject, contemporary Venetian life.

Two years later, with his reputation spreading throughout Italy, Goldoni was invited to Rome by Count Rezzonico, nephew of the Pope Clement XIII and patron of Rome's Teatro Tordinona. Rome could not claim to be the rival in theatre of either Venice or Naples, but it was not far behind them, and Goldoni gladly accepted the invitation. When he arrived in Rome, in 1756, the city possessed eight theatres, the Alberti, the Argentina, the Tordinona, the Capranica, the Valle, the Granari, the Pallacorda, and the Pace. The leading house was the Argentina, erected in 1732 and considered one of the most beautiful in Italy. Theatres in Rome were generally open from January 7 until the beginning of Lent only, and during this period the Argentina was accustomed to presenting two *opere serie* by such composers as Gluck and Galuppi. The Argentina's leading rival was the Alberti, and beginning in 1755 the two theatres alternated years for major operatic spectacles, to avoid the problems of direct competition.

All of the Roman theatres were built in the elongated horseshoe shape, with a seated parterre and ranks of surrounding boxes, six in the Argentina, Alberti, and Capranica, five in the Tordinona and Valle. The central box in the center rank was reserved for the Governor of Rome, and those about it leased for the season by the Roman Princes for their families and friends. Generally those of higher rank obtained the best boxes (the ones from the first to the fourth rank facing the stage) and in case of conflict, lots were drawn. Having obtained a box, the owner would then furnish it to his taste at his own expense and use it not only as a place to watch the opera but as an auxiliary salon. The Abbé Richard reported:

> Since the performance is rather long and recitatives make up two thirds of it, the theatre would be extremely boring if the custom had not been established of paying visits to acquaintances in their boxes, especially to the ladies, for the purpose of engaging in conversation. This attention is a social obligation. The talk is rather loud, until the instant when arias or other familiar parts of the spectacle require attention. Refreshments are served and the whole is like any social gathering. But in general the boxes at Rome are too small to have gaming tables in them, as I have seen elsewhere in Italy. (12)

The Roman theatre also differed from those elsewhere in Italy in being darkened for performances. The central chandelier was drawn up into the ceiling and candles were forbidden in the boxes, so that the stage gained unusual focus there.

Doubtless this practice was pleasing to Goldoni, but much in the Roman theatre he found alien and discomforting. The Tordinona, to which he was invited, ranked next after the Argentina and Alberti in prestige, and predated both of them. It was Rome's leading house for comedy and tragedy and Goldoni's *L'amante militare* (a masked comedy created for Medebac in 1751) had enjoyed a great success there in 1755. By way of preparing themselves and their audiences for Goldoni's arrival, the Tordinona company performed another of his works in 1758, *Il vecchio bizzarro*. Goldoni thus naturally expected to find a company receptive to his style and his reforms, and he was stunned to find them tradition-bound and unregenerate, fully prepared to present his new works playing in both the traditional masks and the Neapolitan dialect that were totally uncongenial to the dramatist. Moreover, according to the law of the Papal States, all female roles had to be taken by men, and Goldoni was offered a barber's boy and a carpenter's apprentice for the female roles in *La vedova spiritosa*, the work he had brought with him for his Roman debut.

From their first encounter, Goldoni and the Tordinona actors realized that their partnership would be difficult, and each tried to compromise as much as possible. Goldoni reworked and shortened his play; the actors struggled with the unfamiliar task of memorizing their roles. Still, despite their best efforts, the performance was a disappointment for both. "Heavens! What exaggerated declamation! What awkward movements! No truth, no intelligence," observed the suffering author. "The public became impatient; they demanded Puncinella, and the play went from bad to worse."(13) Goldoni fled the theatre long before the performance was completed.

The production was, by any standard, a total failure, but the conventions which helped to make it so were not easily discarded. A decade later a French traveler was appalled to find many of the same oddities corrupting a production in Rome of Crébillon's *Rhadamiste et Zénobie*:

> It begins with a combat of more than a hundred persons; the soldiers often return to the stage, even mounting a siege and capturing a position; and although the original piece is highly tragic throughout, Polichinel is added, who fears the fighting, does a thousand *lazzi* and often parodies the leading actor of the piece. Much amusement is also provided by Zenobie's nurse, an old woman (represented by a man with a black beard and a white wig of lamb's wool) who expresses her fear that her charms will be violated and who takes all possible precautions to avoid any insolent advances.(14)

Fortunately, another Roman theatre, the Capranica, provided Goldoni with a more satisfying experience. Here each of the previous three seasons had featured one of his comedies, and this season *Pamela nubile* held the stage from the December 26 opening until the Mardi Gras closing. The Capranica actors were a delight and solace to Goldoni, and at their request he wrote a sequel, *Pamela maritata,* which they premiered the next season. Fortunately Goldoni was by then on his way back to Venice, for it was a clear failure. A traveler viewing a revival of the work in 1769 found it simply grotesque: "The actor who played the young and lovely Pamela, although very intelligent, was so alien to the character that he was playing, that one could not accept him: youth, grace and beauty could not be represented by nervous features, a thick black beard, large feet and thick arms."(15)

Goldoni hoped to follow his Roman visit with a tour to Naples, but his aristocratic employers in Venice, dissatisfied with the works he had left for them, summoned him back. Reluctantly he returned, to face a far more serious literary rivalry than that mounted by the rather foolish Chiari, and one which had already begun to develop before he departed for Rome. This was his famous confrontation with Carlo Gozzi (1720-1806).

The literary and intellectual world of Venice at mid-eighteenth century was divided into two fairly distinct camps. There was a conservative group, determined to shore up the crumbling Venetian political system and pledged to protect the purity of the Italian tradition in arts and letters, and a liberal group which challenged the old order with ideas provided by Rousseau and Voltaire. In the theatre the liberals, enamored of French thought, not surprisingly scoffed at both commedia dell'arte and the pompous early Italian tragedies, and turned to the fashionable contemporary *drame* and *comédie larmoyante* sentimental and socially-oriented domestic drama. Both groups naturally had their journals and their literary societies, and one of the leading conservative organizations was the Accademia dei Granelleschi, founded about 1747 with the expressed goal of preserving a purity of style in Italian letters.

In the quarrel between Goldoni and Chiari, which provided much entertainment for the Venetian theatre world in the early 1750s, the Granelleschi remained neutral, for they found the bombast and rant of Chiari as offensive as the careless and colloquial style of Goldoni. Gozzi, who emerged as the leader of the Granelleschi, summarized in his memoirs the deficiences he observed in both authors. He admitted an abundance of comic motives, truth, and naturalness in Goldoni, but condemned him for "poverty and meanness of intrigue; nature copied from the fact, not imitated; plebeian phrases of low double meaning" and so on. Further, as a writer of Italian, except in the Venetian dialect, he found Goldoni "not unworthy to be placed among the dullest, basest, and least correct authors who have used our idiom." Chiari fared even worse, as a writer "the most turgid, the most inflated of this century," with "a brain inflamed, disordered, bold to rashness, and pedantic; plot dark as astrological predictions; leaps and jumps demanding seven-league boots; scenes isolated, disconnected from the action, foisted in for the display of philosophical sententious verbiage."(16)

In a mock almanac, written "in strict literary Tuscan," *La tartana degl'influssi per l'anno bisestile 1757*, Gozzi excoriated both Goldoni and Chiari as dealers in chaos, two charlatans who kept the public in an uproar to line their own pockets. Goldoni, stung, replied in an occasional poem which challenged Gozzi to provide evidence for his attacks:

> He who does not prove his assertions and argument
> Acts like the dog who barks at the moon.

The literary quarrel thus launched continued for another five years, much to the delight of the Venetian public, in a snowstorm of pamphlets, epistles, poems and plays spreading across literary Europe so that in Paris Voltaire came to Goldoni's defense and in London Guiseppe Baretti, a member of Johnson's circle, championed Gozzi. In Venice Goldoni and Chiari, united by this common enemy, forgot old grievances and lauded each other's work to the skies. The climax of the battle came in 1761 when Gozzi, in response to Goldoni's repeated charges that he was simply a carping critic who would never dare enter the lists as a playwright competing for popular support, created the first and most famous of his theatrical "fables" *L'amore delle tre melarance.*

In this work, Gozzi boldly returned to the traditional masks which Goldoni had removed from the stage, giving Pantalone, Tartaglia, Truffaldino, and Brighella leading roles in a largely improvised, fantastic recreation of an old fairy tale, filled with Aristophanic jibes at Goldoni and Chiari. The brilliant commedia troupe of Antonio Sacchi, for whom Goldoni had written his greatest work in the old style, *Il servitore di due padrone,* offered the work at the Teatro San Samuel. It was an immediate, overwhelming success and Goldoni and Chiari were for a time quite eclipsed. The triumphant Gozzi followed this with three more fables the next season, *Il corvo, Re cervo,* and *Turandot,* with little diminishment of popular enthusiasm. In two seasons, Baretti reported, Goldoni was utterly stripped of his theatrical honors. This boast is hardly correct, for Goldoni offered five new works at the San Luca during the first of these seasons, and three during the second, with considerable success, but the clear preference of the public for his rival's works may well have seemed a repudiation to him, as it certainly did to Chiari. The latter gave up writing comedies in the new style entirely after 1762 and retired to the country.

At about the time Gozzi was scoring his first and greatest triumph with *L'amore delle tre melarance* Goldoni was offered a contract from the manager of the Comédie Italienne in Paris, and although the popular story that Gozzi's success literally drove Goldoni from Venice is surely somewhat exaggerated, the shift in public enthusiasm to his rival's work was doubtless an important consideration in Goldoni's decision to accept the new post. The Vendramins, who apparently now considered him an author of rapidly fading attractiveness, were willing enough to cancel the remainder of his ten-year contract with them, and in the spring of 1762 Goldoni and his family left Italy, never to return.

Gozzi now reigned supreme in the Venetian theatre. After the departure of Chiari, the Sacchi company moved to San Angelo, and there offered six more fables between 1762 and 1765. The Vendramins, finding it difficult to compete with these novelties, invited Gozzi to write for them at the more prestigious and centrally located San Salvador. Gozzi insisted upon maintaining his ties with Sacchi, so in 1770 the Vendramins severed their ties with Goldoni's old company and employed the Sacchi troupe instead. The displaced Goldonians settled at the San Angelo and avenged themselves somewhat by winning Cesare Darbes, a popular Pantalone who was one of the pillars of Sacchi's company. They were also fortunate enough to attract as a resident playwright the young Elisabetta Caminer (1751-1796), who gained a striking success in 1770 with her verse translation of Falbaire de Fenouillot's *L'Honnête Criminel (L' onesto colpevole)*. During the following years she provided the San Angelo with a stream of popular translations of contemporary French sentimental comedies and dramas from Arnaud, Beaumarchais, Mercier and Saurin.

Gozzi, finding the vogue of fable plays diminishing, countered this new rivalry with a series of attractive translations of Spanish intrigue plays, and Sacchi was able to replace the departed Darbes with the popular Giovanni Battista Roti. He also engaged an attractive new leading lady, Teodora Ricci (1750?-1794?), with the result that Lessing, touring Italy in 1775, noted that the Sacchi company was generally considered the best in Italy.(17) Ricci's popularity was considerable, but she was not an unmixed blessing for the company. Vain, capricious and cynical, she eventually precipitated a major scandal by carrying on a more or less open affair with Gozzi (her husband resolutely ignoring the whole thing) and subsequently with a secretary of the Venetian Senate, Antonio Gratarol. These intrigues became public property in 1777 when Gozzi created a character in *Le droghe d'amore* (adapted from Tirso da Molina) which was widely taken to be a caricature of his rival. The actor Vitalba stressed the resemblance by dressing as Gratarol and the Venetian public, delighted by the scandal, flocked to the San Salvador. Gratarol attempted in vain to have the play suppressed, or at least censored, but he had powerful enemies among the Venetian aristocracy who were pleased to use Gozzi as a means for humiliating the poor secretary. Finally Gratarol left the city, renouncing his obligations as civil servant, an act which placed him under penalty of death should he return, and took up residence in Stockholm. There he published a *Narrazione apologetica* in 1779 attacking Gozzi and the general political corruption of the Venetian republic, a document which caused so much embarrassment in Venice that Gozzi, who wished to answer it, was forbidden to provide it with that further publicity. When the French occupied Venice in 1797 and proclaimed freedom of the press, Gratarol's *Narrazione* was among the first works published, and then Gozzi hastily rushed his own memoirs into print as his defense.

After the departure of Gratarol, the Sacchi company gradually disintegrated. Quarrels divided the actors, Gozzi withdrew as a dramatist, and leading players began to seek employment elsewhere. The Vendramins sought another, more stable company for their theatre, and the remnants of the Sacchi company took refuge once again at the smaller San Angelo. Gozzi wrote two further works for them for the 1786 season, but found the company restricted in funds and actors so that the plays had to be given to rival troupes at San Salvador and San Giovanni Grisostomo. After that season Sacchi left Venice for the Teatro Falcone in Genoa, a theatre where the San Samuel Company had earlier toured very successfully with works by Goldoni. Goldoni was now much in demand in Genoa, but there was little interest in the older mask tradition which was Sacchi's specialty. Discouraged once again, he left Genoa in 1788 to sail to Marseilles and died on the voyage. Some said that the great tradition of the commedia died with him.

The Search for Tragedy

In the close-knit theatrical world of Venice, Gozzi's triumph over Goldoni and Chiari seemed unqualified and definitive, but this impression proved illusory. After Goldoni's departure, each new fable by Gozzi was greeted with rather less enthusiasm, and within a decade, as we have seen, he had given up such works to turn to adaptations of Spanish comedies of intrigue. Outside Venice, as the works of Goldoni gradually drove the old improvised comedies from the stage, Gozzi's challenge passed almost unnoticed. Only in Germany, where he was seen as an experimental precursor of romanticism, did Gozzi's plays attract much attention by the end of the century. Early in the next century Sismondi observed, understandably if a bit unfairly:

> It does not appear that Gozzi's plays were ever represented upon other theatres than those of Venice, nor do they, in truth, represent the national spirit of the Italian people. We almost feel inclined, on their perusal, to refer them to a German, rather than an Italian origin.(18)

The ideal of a literary drama was gradually acknowledged throughout Italy, and Goldoni was generally recognized as the most important contributor to this, but the process was a slow and gradual one. The power of Goldoni's realism was widely enjoyed from the very beginning, but as the author himself observed in Rome, this did not necessarily guarantee that his comedies would be at first presented in a manner strikingly different from that of more traditional pieces. A traveler in Florence in the 1760s reported that "the comedies of Goldoni are presented with much truth and in the most straightforward style," but the actors required "only one or two rehearsals to prepare themselves; they never bother to learn their roles and are thus prompted from beginning to end. These people are natural actors and to gain truth in their playing they require only a general idea of the plot."(19)

This observation is all the more striking in Florence, a city where one might expect a more enlightened appreciation of Goldoni's reforms. Here the poet Giovan Battista Fagiuoli (1660-1742) initiated the revolution in comedy which Goldoni completed by introducing characters and situations into the masked plays and by forbidding puns and ad libitum jokes. His first play, *Gl'inganni Iodevoli* (1706), was offered the year before Goldoni's birth and his last, *Gli sponsali in maschera* (1738), when Goldoni was midway through his first contract in Venice. According to Riccoboni, Florence was one of the few cities in Italy where the audiences listened to the actors with respectful silence,(20) and Goldoni was quickly accepted there as a popular favorite. During his busiest years in Venice he was also under commission to provide plays for Florence and it was to the Florentine publishing house of Paperini that Goldoni turned when he could not get his plays published to his satisfaction in Venice.

The campaign to create a serious drama of literary merit was carried on during these same years, although no single dominant champion arose there as Goldoni did in comedy. The Renaissance tradition of neoclassic tragedy inspired a few works in each generation from Trissino's *Sofonisba* (1515) to Carlo Dottori's *Aristodemo* (1657). At the end of the seventeenth century the actor Pietro Cotta (d. 1720) gained great success in Venice with *Aristodemo* and in Bologna with tragedies by Corneille and Racine, but was unable, as he dreamed, to establish a permanent repertory of serious drama. Cotta's project, however, in turn inspired the young Luigi Riccoboni (1676-1753), who between 1706 and 1715 attempted with some success to renovate the Italian repertoire. He began with Corneille and Racine, then offered Trissino, Tasso and the more recent French-inspired Alexandrine tragedies of the Bolognese Pier Martelli (1665-1727). He was encouraged in this endeavor by the Veronese scholar and poet Scipione Maffei, who also provided him with the best Italian tragedy of the period, *Merope*, performed by Riccoboni with great success in Modena in 1713 and at Venice's Teatro San Luca in 1714. *Merope* was so widely published and produced that Riccoboni could boast that in ten years he had "established tragedy in Venice."(21) His attempted similar reform of comedy fared less well. Riccoboni approved of the commedia, but hoped to supplement it with more regular comedies in the French manner. His attempts with Regnard, Molière, and Corneille were not well received, so he turned to Ariosto's *La scolastina*, hoping that Ariosto, like Trissino, might inspire interest in more modern Italian works. The San Luca audience remained indifferent, and the discouraged Riccoboni, like Goldoni a generation later, took refuge in Paris.

The little impetus that existed for the establishment of a serious drama was channeled in the early eighteenth century into reform of the opera. Since its invention in Florence in the late 1500s, opera had spread rapidly through Italy and then throughout Europe. The vogue of the form was enormous by the end of the next century, but as opera grew in popularity, it steadily declined in literary merit. The libretto was for the most part simply an excuse for gorgeous scenery, elaborate staging effects, and dazzling displays of virtuoso singing. A reaction began at the end of the seventeenth century led by the famous Arcadian Academy, established at Rome in 1690 to develop a national neoclassic literary tradition as successful and popular as that of the French. The first president of the Academy was Giovan Crescimbeni (1663-1728) who in *La belleza della volgar poesia* (1700) blamed the opera for bringing about "the downfall of the art of acting, and as a consequence also the demise of the true and good sort of comedy and of tragedy itself." This had come about by mixing of genres for the sake of novelty, indifference to the classic rules, interruption of dramatic action by arias, and debasement of poetic language as the more "natural" rhythms of music replaced traditional poetic structure. Fortunately, he felt, as the new century began Italy was opening her eyes, and though she had not "reclaimed true comedy," certain authors were at least creating "entirely serious melodramas" in tragic style with a minimum of arias. The major credit, he suggested, went to the Venetians Domenico David and Apostolo Zeno. In Rome itself Felippo Merelli had gone a step further, translating French tragedies such as Corneille's *Stilicon* without music for production at the private theatre of the Collegio Clementino.(22)

The other pillar of the Academy, Gian Gravina (1664-1718), published five tragedies in Naples in 1712, followed by a critical defense, *Della tragedia*, which took an essentially neo-Aristotelean position, insisting for example on strict adherence to the unities, but allowing music in tragedy provided it were well integrated. The success of such efforts was dryly summed up by Voltaire:

> The taste [for tragedy in Italy] had been entirely extinguished for nearly a century when Pier Martelli decided he could revive it by substituting certain techniques of French tragedy for the bizarre and romantic intrigues that Italians borrowed from the Spanish; but he was no more fortunate than the first poets of his nation had been when they tried to adapt the Greek manner to their theatre. Gravina wrote on the principles of art as a man of enlightenment, but at the same time created pitiful tragedies.(23)

Thus, despite the great success of *Merope*, acknowledged as an important play even by Voltaire, the revival of spoken tragedy seemed at this time most unlikely. The reforms begun by Zeno in the opera had to serve as Italy's only signficiant attempts in this generation at a serious theatre. These reforms were developed further in the works of Pietro Trapassi (1698-1702), or Metastasio, a young poet discovered and encouraged by Gravina, who also provided him with a suitable classic name. Inspired by Gravina, Metastasio created a classical tragedy, *Guistino*, in his fourteenth year, and his first opera, *Didone abbandonata*, at twenty-six. It was an enormous success in Venice, in Rome, and then throughout Europe, set to music by many of the leading composers of the period. He was called to Vienna as Zeno's successor there and produced a stream of libretti which soon made him the leading theatrical poet of his time. He succeeded in elevating the text to a position of importance as Zeno's generation of critics had demanded, not only by purifying it of comic elements and similar non-classic extravagancies but also by creating poetry and plots which were interesting in themselves, even without music. During the mid-eighteenth century, the libretti of Metastasio, presented as straight dramas, provided the leading serious theatre in Italy.

Maffei's followers on the other hand seemed incapable of in-fusing their neoclassic experiments with life. The French classic tradition they viewed with a mixture of suspicion and fascination. Thus Antonio Conti (1677-1749) called French tragedy "the purest

and most flourishing'' in Europe but expressed concern over its
"rhymed dialogue, many confidants, and love-stricken heroes."(24)
This concern led Conti to be one of the first continental European
dramatists to consider Shakespeare as a possible model. His first play
was *Giulio Cesare* (1726), in the preface to which he defended looking
to the English as well as to the French and Spanish. English comedies
and tragedies, he noted, were "filled with chance happenings like the
Spanish, but with much more natural and graceful characters."
Shakespeare, "the Corneille of the English" was admittedly "far
more irregular" than Corneille, "but equal to him in the grandeur of
his ideas and the nobility of his sentiments." Unhappily none of these
qualities were captured by the cold and oratorical *Giulio Cesare* nor by
the six other original tragedies and translations from Voltaire which
followed.

The Jesuits, interested in theatrical undertakings since the
founding of their order, joined with the learned societies in the attempt to revive serious theatre, but with no greater success. Alfonso
Varano (1705-1788) created five tragedies, the second of which,
Giovanni di Giscala (1754) has been called the best Italian tragedy of
the mid-eighteenth century, but this is small praise, since the work is
only slightly less hollow and artificial than its fellows. Saverio Bettinelli's (1718-1808) works were the most popular of the Jesuit offerings, several of them produced with modest success at the Collegio
San Luigi in Bologna and the Collegio dei Nobili in Parma. His *Gli
eroi ateniesi* (1758) was one of the few Jesuit dramas to attain presentation at a public theatre, San Giovanni Grisostomo in Venice.
Looking back over his career in his *Discorso sul teatro italiano* (1771),
Bettinelli suggested to his fellow poets that individual feelings and
national history should be the basis of tragedy and that the French
should be taken as models for lively dialogue and variety of character,
the Greeks for heightening of moral and political ideas.

In 1770 the Bourbon Duke Ferdinando of Parma founded an
annual competition for dramatic works which made that city during
the next decade the center of such experimentation. The winning plays
were presented in the Teatro Ducale erected in 1688, but given a new
auditorium by Ferdinando in 1760 and considered one of the most
beautiful in Europe. The Abbé Richard described it shortly after its
opening:

> It is oval in form, large enough to hold 1400 spectators. The stage is
> vast and deep, and capable of mounting a spectacle which needs many
> actors and machines or a very deep perspective. At the bottom of the
> oval are ranks of benches in the antique style which rise to the height

of the second boxes in ordinary theatres; above these benches is a row of boxes formed by a gallery ornamented with simple columns, equally spaced supporting arches surmounted by a lovely architectural corniche; above these boxes is another rank of benches, smaller than the one below but still capable of holding many spectators.(25)

Another traveler reported in 1769 that no opera had been presented in the Teatro Ducale for over thirty years, because of its enormous expense. In fact, opera was occasionally offered but the theatre clearly favored the spoken drama: Maffei, Goldoni, and the libretti of Metastasio. Troupes like those of Battaglia and Medebac were always welcome here. Few locations could have been better suited to Duke Ferdinando's new project, but the state of Italian serious drama was such that little of significance emerged from his competitions. Sismondi reports that five tragedies received the first prize but that within half a century they were all almost forgotten. Indeed, he was able to discover the names of only four of them: *Zelinda*, by Count Orazio Calini, *Valsei* (subtitled *The Hero of Scotland*) by Don Antonio Perabò, *Conrad* and *Roxana* by Count Ottavio Magnocavallo. All of these Sismondi dismisses as "rather an imitation of the softness of Metastasio, than any real attempt at true tragedy."(26)

Clearly the Italian *tragedia erudita* needed a reformer parallel to Goldoni in the commedia dell'arte, an artist to give unity, power, and psychological depth to what had become a predictable and often sterile form. At last such an artist appeared, and although he was not premiered at Parma, such was the literary reputation of that state that he sought there the advice and encouragement he needed to launch his dramatic career. Early in 1775 Padre Paciaudi, Parma's ducal librarian, received a letter from the young Count Vittorio Alfieri (1749-1803) enclosing a sonnet with which the Count proposed to enter the field of literature. The sonnet was undistinguished, but Paciaudi must have been pleased nevertheless to find another potential contributor to the new cause—a young author who seemed interested in turning from the standard eighteenth-century francophilia to develop something of literary merit on an Italian base. Paciaudi called this rather indifferent effort "good, pithy, forceful, and sufficiently correct," and judged that it augured well for a literary career. He also urged Alfieri to consider Giovanni Delfino's tragedy *Cleopatra* as a possible model for further literary experiments.(27)

Alfieri took this advice and soon dispatched to Paciaudi the first act of a projected *Cleopatra tragedia*. Paciaudi was still encouraging, but rather more guarded. He praised the "intelligence, fecund imagination, and judicious handling" of the work, but was disturbed by the badly turned lines, incorrect usage of words, and poor spelling. This time, in addition to previous Italina treatments of the subject he urged Alfieri to consult the *Ortografia italiana* and the *Avventimenti grammaticali.*(28) With these comments in mind, Alfieri reworked the entire manuscript and submitted it to Girolano Medebac, who was then performing at the Teatro Carignano in Turin.

We last encountered Medebac and his company in Venice in the 1750s, where they premiered the early works of Goldoni, then, after 1753, the rival offerings of Chiari at the Teatro San Angelo. In 1760 the troupe left that city to tour with great success to Modena, Bologna, and Milan with neoclassic tragedies, the operas of Metastasio, the comedies of Goldoni and commedia dell'arte. The growing popularity of the rival comic operas, especially in Milan, caused Medebac to return to Venice in the early 1770s. He settled his company at the Teatro San Giovanni Grisostomo, where he struggled with only moderate success against the highly popular Spanish intrigue plays of Gozzi at the San Luca and the translations of French *comédies larmoyantes* by Caminer at the San Angelo. His one major success was Voltaire's *Semiramide* in 1773, due in large part to his actress Maddalena Battaglia (1728-1803). The following year Maddalena and her husband Carlo took over San Giovanni Grisostomo from Medebac, who resumed his tours across northern Italy, appearing in Turin just when the young Alfieri was completing his new play.

Few critics in his own time or since have had much positive to say about Alfieri's first play, and the dramatist himself condemned it roundly in his autobiography. For its premiere he was circumspect enough to pair it with an original after-piece, *I poeti*, in which he undercut criticism by exposing both himself and his tragedy to ridicule. The plays were received with warm applause on two nights and called for on a third, but the young poet recalled the work. The production had opened his eyes to defects he had not seen before and revealed to him how much he still must learn before creating a significant drama. "Every verse," he admitted, "as it came from the actor made me bitterly critical of the whole work, until I viewed it all as quite worthless—as nothing more than a spur to produce the works still to come."(29)

One indeed wonders a bit at Medebac's willingness to mount the work and at its enthusiastic reception, but perhaps both may be in large part explained by considerations outside the field of esthetics. Alfieri was a member of one of Turin's best known families, with strong ties to the artistic, cultural, and political life of the city. His uncle Benedetto, Turin's leading architect, had in fact designed the theatre where *Cleopatra* premiered, and Medebac could surely expect that the playwright's name alone would guarantee a certain enthusiasm. A first literary effort by a native son, presented in his uncle's theatre, would have every chance of the most sympathetic hearing, and this is apparently what the work received. Fortunately Alfieri was not blinded by this warm response, and began at once to consider how to avoid the defects of this work in his next.

Before proceeding to that work, however, we might pause for a brief look at the Carignano, where *Cleopatra* was performed, one of the largest and generally considered one of the most beautiful theatres in Italy—an outstanding example of Italian theatre architecture of this period. The first Teatro Carignano was destroyed in 1752 and Turin's leading architect, Benedetto Alfieri, was commissioned to build a new hall on the same site. The shape was the standard horeseshoe, with six ranks of boxes, the proscenium framed by pairs of huge corinthian columns and containing a main curtain painted by Bernardino Galliari. The Abbé Richard, visiting the theatre a decade after its opening, provided a useful comparison between its stage and machinery and those of contemporary French theatres:

> A beautiful feature, scarcely known in France, is the great depth [105 feet] of the stage [with a 24-foot-deep court to the rear that also could be used], where everything necessary for the play can be placed with an ease that gives a true impression of the thing represented—especially in scenes showing the assembly of a senate, encampments, of armies, perspectives beyond the subject. This advantage is most particularly to be observed in ballet, when the largest chorus can move about without confusion and provide every advantage that one could have in this type of spectacle. There are few machines for changing the scenery; when it must be shifted, the wings slide in on grooves one behind another, and a man is required for each. One rarely sees flying machines, few descents of the gods; when Jupiter or Venus must descend from the heavens the curtain is lowered, the divinity stands upstage in a group of clouds as if he had descended, and when the curtain rises, the god steps away from all this aerial apparatus and moves downstage. While he is performing, the clouds and chariot are taken off and the divinity leaves through the wings to find another way back into the heavens.(30)

The success of *Cleopatra* was a great encouragement to Alfieri, but it clearly showed him how much he had still to learn about the theatre and even about the Italian language. While this play was being prepared for presentation he had completed two others, *Filippo* and *Polinice*, both in French. His attempts to convert them into Italian were condemned by his literary friends and Alfieri embarked on a campaign to gain real proficiency in Italian. He vowed to stop reading or speaking French, and to avoid further Piedmontese corruption he departed for Tuscany, home of the literary language. Here he reworked his first plays, wrote an *Antigone* in Tuscan prose, and filled his mind with lines of Petrarch, Dante and Tasso. The *Antigone* was rewritten in verse after Alfieri's return to Turin and read before La Sampaolina, a leading literary society, to warm praise. The author himself was still far from pleased and resolved to return to Tuscany to continue polishing his style. Accordingly, he gave up his Piedmontese citizenship the following year and established himself in Florence. His literary output steadily increased, and the first publications of his plays appeared, but with little immediate effect on the Italian stage.

In Rome during the Carnival of 1781 he saw posted at a minor theatre his *Oreste* and attended the performance, only to be appalled by what he saw. Scenes were totally rewritten or mercilessly cut and at the conclusion Orestes, instead of killing his mother, reconciled himself with her to the warm applause of the audience. The furious author leaped from his box onto the stage and began arguing with the actors. When the audience protested, he stepped to the footlights and introduced himself. The actors apologized and the management promised to restore the tragic ending, but they knew their audiences better than Alfieri did and one can only assume that these vows were soon forgotten after his departure.

Alfieri remained known at this time essentially as a literary rather than a theatrical figure and the main "performances" of his works were in fact readings in aristocratic salons. Alfieri himself particularly favored the Roman salon of Maria Pizzelli and one of his auditors there, the young Vincenzo Monti, was inspired by Alfieri to become one of the leading dramatists of the next generation. Alfieri's new tragedies, with their small number of characters, extreme simplicity of action, and rough blank verse which ran counter to the tradition of that written for singing, were still too alien to attract much attention from professional producers, but the dramatist was able to interest a group of aristocratic amateurs in Rome in producing his *Antigone* in 1782. This group was in the habit of performing rather poor French translations at the palace of the Spanish Ambassador Duke Grimaldi (the palace which gives its name to Rome's Piazza di Spagna). In their performance of Thomas Corneille's *Le Conte d'Essex* Alfieri was struck by the acting potential, if not by the achievement, of the Duchess of Zagarolo as Elisabeth. Accordingly, he assigned her the part of Antigone while the playwright himself took the role of Creon. The work was very well received and this encouraged Alfieri to publish *Antigone*, along with *Filippo, Polinice* and *Virginia*. They were printed in Siena to avoid the complications of Roman censorship.

Most critics, accustomed to the mellifluous verses of Metastasio, found Alfieri harsh, obscure, and extravagant. The next six tragedies, appearing later that year and including *Saul*, Alfieri's most famous work, drew similar complaints. Only in Turin, where the dramatist enjoyed the special status of native son, were any of these works given public performance. Alfieri, visiting there in 1784 after an absence of seven years, found his *Virginia* planned for production and was urged by the director to give the actors some suggestions as he had done before for *Cleopatra*. Alfieri refused:

> for I knew only too well what our actors and pit were like at that time. I therefore had no wish to become in any way accessory to their incapacity, about which I was quite convinced before I even saw them. I knew that I should have to begin with an impossible task: to teach them to speak Italian and not the local dialect; to speak for themselves and not rely on the prompter; to understand (to say "feel" would be to expect too much) but to understand at least enough to get across the basic idea to the audience.(31)

Alfieri promised to attend the performance and did so, though with little pleasure. *Virginia* received the same polite approval *Cleopatra* had—nothing less and nothing more. Alfieri vowed that in the future he would write to satisfy himself and forget the dream of success in the theatre.

In 1785 Alfieri moved to France and there undertook the first collected edition of his works and his autobiography. The fall of the Bastille aroused his enthusiasm and inspired a celebrative ode, *Parigi sbastigliata*, but within a few months the road the revolution was taking filled him with misgivings. On a visit to London in 1791 he encountered by chance the young Walter Savage Landor and disagreed sharply with his enthusiasm for what was occuring across the channel. "Sir," he said, "you are a very young man. You are yet to learn that nothing good ever came out of France, or ever will. The ferocious monsters are about to devour one another; and they can do nothing better. They have always been the curse of Italy; yet we too have fools among us who trust them."(32) Scarcely a year later Alfieri was forced to flee France, leaving behind his house and possessions and narrowly escaping arrest and probable execution as an aristocrat.

Settled again in Florence, he was pleased to find his plays increasingly read and occasionaly performed. Once again he was drawn to the theatre, becoming fascinated with the process of acting.

He organized a group of amateurs which between 1793 and 1795 performed his *Saul, Bruto Primo* and *Filippo* in private houses. The playwright himself took the leading roles and even toyed with the idea of establishing a regular company. In three or four years, he felt, he could develop a passable group "quite different from those actors generally called tragic in Italy and firmly dedicated to the pursuit of what was best and truest." Then, on sober second thought, he decided he had "neither the time, the health, nor the money" for such an enenterprise.(33) He resigned himself to seeing no significant reform during his own lifetime. Against his better judgment he attended a production in Florence of his *Agamemnone*, to find that "the prompter spoke continuously and as loudly as the actors" who scarcely knew half of their lines. "Thus the art progresses rapidly toward its perfection and we can assume that by 1892 at the latest Italy will possess a theatre."(34)

The antagonism and fear Alfieri felt toward the French naturally increased after 1793 when first Piedmont, then all of Italy became involved in the French wars. In the spring of 1796 Napoleon invaded Italy. By the end of 1798 he had conquered Lucca, on the border of Tuscany, and it was clear to Alfieri, and to all of his countrymen, that French occupation was imminent. Under these conditions he completed his *Misgallo*, a bitterly anit-French drama and one of the first works since the sixteenth century to make a clear call for a free and united Italy. With this work the Risorgimento, at least so far as the Italian theatre was concerned, may be said to have begun.

The Musical Theatre

During the seventeenth century Venice, where the first public opera house opened in 1637, was universally acknowledged as the opera capital of Europe. The great operatic composers of the century regarded Venice as their base, wherever else they took their works, and in the later years of the century Venice, a city of 125,000, managed to support six opera troupes simultaneously. Venice retained its position as a theatre center during the following century largely because of the success of Goldoni, but the leadership in the musical drama, which remained Italy's most successful and best known theatre, passed during this period from Venice to Naples. The leading composers and librettists of the period for the most part lived and worked now at the southern capital and here the reforms of Zeno and Metastasio were first developed. These artists sought to purge the opera of many of the exaggerated elements used in the previous century—erratic plots resolved with supernatural appearances, comic episodes interrupting serious stories, machine spectacle and the like—replacing them with a smoother, more controlled and generally more rational action. The result was a rather predictable form of alternating recitative and aria representing, as it were, the dramatic and lyric parts of the work. Since the virtuoso singer dominated the music world then as the virtuoso pianist did in the nineteenth century and the virtuoso conductor in the twentieth, it is hardly surprising that audiences tended to pay attention to the arias and ignore the rest. This oddly divided attention struck most foreign visitors. De Brosses in 1739 reports essentially the same conditions which struck Richard thirty years later:

> As soon as the theatres open here, gatherings cease at the Princess Borghese's home, at the Casa Bolognetti, etc. Everyone goes to the opera, which is very long, lasting from eight or nine until midnight. The ladies hold *conversazione* in their boxes where spectators of their acquaintances pay them little visits... The taste of these folk for spectacle and music appears much more in their attendance than in the attention they pay. Once the first performances are over, where there is a modest silence even in the parterre, it is considered bad form to listen except to the interesting parts. The major boxes are well furnished and illuminated with candles. Sometimes there is gambling, more often simple conversation, seated in a circle around the box... Chess is a marvelous invention for filling the void of the long recitatifs and the arias for preventing too great a concentration on chess.(35)

The flowering of Neapolitan opera coincided with the granting of independence to Naples after a generation of Austrian domination and more than two centuries' rule by Spanish viceroys. By the treaties ending the War of the Polish Succession in 1736 the Austrian Emperor renounced all claim to the Two Sicilies (Sicily and Southern Italy) provided that these were never to be united with Spain. Thus Charles, though a Spanish Prince, became ruler of an independent kingdom created and protected, as has often happened in history, by the balanced ambitions of two powerful rivals. Some visionaries, not understanding this dynamic, began dreaming at once of a united Italy with Naples as its base, but they were soon disillusioned. The one thing all of Italy's powerful neighbors could agree upon was that none of them wanted a new political power, in the form of a united Italy, to further complicate European politics. More than a century would pass before the Italian people could triumph against this determination.

In any case few Neapolitans in 1736 looked far beyond the pleasure of their unaccustomed freedom from foreign domination.

Naples began at once to take on the appearance of a major European capital. King Charles surrounded himself with a luxury and system of royal decorum reminiscent of Louis XIV, turning his palace into a miniature Versailles. Music, Italy's predominant art form, was given special attention and encouragement and Naples' leadership in the world of music was soon almost universally acknowledged. "Music is the triumph of the Neapolitans," wrote a traveler in 1796. "It seems that in this country the fibers of the ear are more sensitive, more receptive to sound and harmony than in the rest of Europe; here everyone sings; everything expresses, exhales music—gestures, conversation, the inflection of the voice, the rhythm of the syllables. Naples is the fountainhead of music."(36) Rousseau advised any musician who wished to improve his art to betake himself at once to Naples.

When Charles came to the throne Naples possessed three theatres. The dominant one, in history and reputation, was the Fiorentini. Founded in 1618, it was for many years the home of spoken drama, especially that derived from the Spanish tradition, but in the eighteenth century, in large part because of the popularity of Scarlotti, music began to predominate, with only occasional spoken dramas offered by touring companies, among them that of the ubiquitous Medebac. In 1724 two smaller rivals opened, the Teatro della Pace and the Teatro Nuovo, both specializing in the popular new comic form, the opera buffa, developed in Naples at the opening of the century. Begun as comic interludes *(intermezzi)* between the acts of serious opera, these comedies gradually developed an independent tradition, aided by the efforts of Zeno and his followers to make a clear division between light and serious elements in opera. The short intermezzo with two or three characters gradually gave way to a more complicated and lengthy work, often with a large cast. Until about 1730, these works, though extremely popular, were created exclusively by artists of the second rank, but the stimulus of the new theatres and the ever-increasing public interest then began to attract both singers and composers of greater stature. Giovanni Pergolesi (1710-1736) added to his church work and serious operas the brilliant *La serva padrona* (1733), still popular today.

King Charles was not himself a lover of opera, but he knew well enough that the Conservatori of Naples provided singers, instrumentalists and composers for courts throughout Europe, and one of his first major projects was the building of a Neapolitan opera house worthy of his capital. The architect Giovanni Medrano and the court festival master Angelo Carasale planned the theatre, which was

begun in the spring of 1737 and ready to open by November 5, the
King's saint's day, for whom it was christened the San Carlo. The
theatre was of course one of the grandest in Italy, with 184 boxes in six
ranks, some 600 seats in the parterre and room for another one or two
hundred persons standing in the dress circle. "The King's Theatre,
upon the first view is, perhaps, almost as remarkable an object as any
man sees in his travels," wrote an English visitor. "The amazing extent of the stage, with the prodigious circumference of the boxes and
the height of the ceiling, produce a marvellous effect on the mind."(37)
The theatre's unusual seating arrangements were also considered worthy of remark:

> The seats have elbows, which circumstance, I believe, is peculiar to
> this theatre. The seat of each chair lifts up like the lid of a box, and
> has a lock to fasten it. There are in Naples gentlemen enough to hire
> by the year the first four rows next to the orchestra, who take the key
> of the chair home with them when the opera is finished, lifting up the
> seat and leaving it locked. By this contrivance they are always sure of
> the same place at whatever hour they please to go to the opera; nor do
> they disturb the audience, though it be in the middle of a scene, as the
> intervals between the rows are wide enough to admit a lusty man to
> walk to his chair, without obliging anybody to rise.(38)

The boxes of course also had individual keys and many were
permanently rented and furnished to the tastes of their owners according to the general practice throughout Italy. The number of candles
allowed in a box was, however, strictly regulated in Naples according
to the occupant's rank (giving rise to a Neapolitan expression: "He's
only a one-candle gentleman!"). Similar regulations applied to
all aspects of opera-going, again suggesting the influence on Charles of
Louis XIV. No audience member was allowed on stage, no one could
clap or light a candle during the performance, no one but the King
could call for an encore. The auditorium was generally darkened, but
was completely illuminated whenever the King was present.

For the opening night the opera selected was a new work by
Metastasio, now at the peak of his glory, *Achille in Sciro*. Though
Metastasio was actually Imperial Court Poet of Austria, his career
had begun in Naples and his popularity there still admitted no rivals.
A special prologue created for the occasion opened the evening.
Magnificence, Glory, and Speed (presumably commemorating the
construction of the building in 270 days) welcomed Royal Genius:

> Behold the new, sublime and spacious theatre,
> Vaster than which Europe hath not yet seen,

to which a Chorus responded: "Long live Charles." The scenery,
huge and elaborate, was the work Vincenzo Re (d. 1762), who

achieved his major success with this production. The opening scene was one of his most impressive—a baroque temple with two lofty flights of stairs surrounded by porticoes forming an open piazza. Through the colonnade a sacred wood could be glimpsed on one side, the court of Sciro on the other. The King, who much preferred visual spectacle to music, encouraged large battle scenes, which were directed by court fencing masters, and required at least two ballets for every act of an opera. Thus the intervals offered ballets of sailors and gypsies, the four seasons, and acrobatic butlers. The public apparently shared this taste, or felt it wise to support it, for a visitor reports that "notwithstanding the amazing noisiness of the audience during the whole performance of the opera, the moment the dancers begin there is a universal dead silence, which continues so long as the dances continue. Witty people, therefore, never fail to tell me, the Neapolitans go to *see* not to *hear* an opera."(39)

Carasale, the architect of San Carlo, was also its first director and between 1737 and 1741 mounted twenty spectacular operas there (twelve of them with libretti by Metastasio). He was followed by the Barone di Liveri who continued Carasale's tradition of spectacular production (his major innovation was apparently the first stage use of an elephant, a gift from the Sultan of Turkey, in *Alessandro nelle Indie* in 1749). At Charles' court Liveri provided entertainment of a much more significantly experimental nature. At almost the same time as Goldoni he also undertook to replace the commedia with literary comedies. Goldoni's alternative was simple comedies of everyday life, but Liveri created huge, complex, sprawling works, lasting up to seven hours and requiring enormous casts. King Charles began sponsoring them as early as 1735 and continued until 1757, with one produced almost every year during the 1740s. Surely the most striking feature of these now almost totally forgotten spectacles was their attention to realistic detail, for which Liveri, who served as director as well as playwright, showed a concern far in advance of his time. He rehearsed his actors a full year for each production, several hours a day, paying particular attention to mimic expression, which he felt was more critical than the words. Francesco Cerlone, another dramatist of the period, recalled:

> A sigh (and I speak as an eyewitness), a sign which a character had to exhale, as rehearsed by the late Marquis di Liveri of ever glorious memory, a sigh was rehearsed by him thirty-two times during an evening, and still the poor actor, his brow covered with cold sweat, was unable to please the famous director, who wished a hundred things to be expressed in that sigh.(40)

The same care, which we now assume to be an innovation of recent theatre directors, was to be observed in his crowd scenes:

> When shall we ever see again so great a gathering of knights as in the *Contessa* or a meeting of two mighty lords with such retinues as in *Solitario*, or a scene like that in *Errico* which revealed to us a royal court anticipating a great event? The characters were all appropriate and picturesque, yet natural, and whether silent or speaking they were equally successful in making clear the particular purpose of each group without the slightest confusion.(41)

The great years of the Neapolitan serious opera were over by 1740, though composers continued to produce works in this style for the rest of the century and though Naples itself remained a major city of musical training. By mid-century there was a distinct reaction to the old style, derived in part from the influence of the only serious competitor to Neapolitan opera, the French style, and in part from a general turn toward greater emotional expressiveness in all the culture of the period. The highly polished, artificial, singer-oriented works of the early eighteenth century gave way to works seeking greater simplicity and flexibility of style, a deeper emotional tone, and a better balance between singer and orchestra. The major representative of the new style was Christoph Willibald Gluck (1714-1787), whom the temperate Metastasio called a composer of "surprising fire, but... mad."(42) Even in Naples such composers as Davide Perez and Jommelli contributed importantly to the shift in taste. Perez' *Siroe re di Persia* was presented at San Carlo in 1740 and by the end of the decade he and Jommelli were providing half of the premieres at that theatre. The first offering from Gluck himself (with a libretto by Metastasio) was *La clemenza di Tito* in 1752.

The decline of the old Neapolitan serious opera was hastened even more by the growing popularity of the comic opera, which not only appealed to the new taste for simplicity and naturalness of style, but mounted a more direct attack on the old tradition by means of parody and satire. The opera buffa itself underwent a change around mid-century also, becoming in general more dignified, better structured, and more refined in action and language—a process strikingly similar to the reform Goldoni was just then working in the spoken comedy. It is therefore hardly surprising that the major composer of the new opera buffa, Baldassare Galuppi (1706-1785), used libretti by Goldoni as the basis of his reform. Beginning with *L'arcadia in Brenta* (offered at Venice's Teatro San Angelo in 1749) Galuppi produced over a twenty-year period more than twenty comic operas with Goldoni libretti. Most of these were premiered in Venice, but they were soon offered throughout Europe. Of course other composers soon followed Galuppi's lead; one of the most successful works of the period was Niccolò Piccinni's (1728-1800) *La cecchina* (premiered at Rome's Teatro della Dame in 1760), based on Goldoni's *La buona figliola.*

Piccinni was invited in 1766 to Paris where his arrival divided the French operatic world between his followers and those of Gluck. The year of his depature Naples heralded a brilliant new composer of comic opera, Giovanni Paisiello (1740-1816), whose *La vedova di bel genio* at the Teatro Nuovo established him at once as another major rival for Piccinni. A brilliant series of successes followed, although after 1772 Paisiello reluctantly and with considerable ill grace was forced to share his popularity with a new composer, Domenico Cimarosa (1749-1801). In 1776 Paisiello was invited by the Empress Catherine to St. Petersburg where he remained until 1784, exercising a continuing powerful influence on comic opera. Here he created some of his most popular works, including his masterpiece, *Il barbiere di Siviglia* (1782), which achieved so great a renown that Rossini thirty years after was widely condemned for presuming to create another work on the same subject. Back in Naples in the later 1780s, Paisiello produced perhaps the outstanding work in the genre of sentimental comic opera, *Nina*, presented first at the Royal Palace in 1789, then at the Fiorentini. His old rival Cimarosa, who had followed him as court composer in St. Petersburg in 1788, returned to Naples in 1793, where his *Il matrimonio segreto* and other works were welcomed with an enthusiasm which infuriated Paisiello.

Paisiello now enjoyed the privileged position of royal chapel master, but the days of this favor were numbered. In 1799 when Naples was occupied by French troops, the theatres and many of the leading artists, either from conviction or expediency, hastened to support the new order. The theatres remained open during the anarchic days of the battle of Naples, with the San Carlo offering Giuseppe Tritto's *Nicaboro in Jucatan* "in celebration of the birth of Ferdinando IV, our most beloved sovereign." After a three-day closing at the time of the occupation the San Carlo reopened, rechristened the Teatro Nazionale, with *Nicaboro* now billed as a work "to celebrate the expulsion of the tyrant, with an analogous hymn and ballet."(43) Artists underwent scarcely less rapid conversions. Cimarosa openly supported the liberal cause and Paisiello lobbied the new government for the position of national director of music. Unfortunately for these plans the new Parthenopean Republic lasted scarcely five months. With the aid of Nelson, the Bourbons regained their throne and at once instituted proceedings against all who had collaborated with the French. Prominent artists like Cimarosa and Paisiello were especially vulnerable. Cimarosa was condemned to death, but the intercession of many powerful friends changed this sentence to banishment. Paisiello by the most abject abasement won his way back into court favor and was thus, ironically, in a position to profit from the Neapolitan-French alliance which Napoleon imposed on Ferdinand in 1801. The First Consul had been interested in Paisiello since he had heard the composer's march in honor of General Hoche, composed in 1797, and in 1802 he asked the Neapolitan court if they would release the composer for a time to work in Paris. Ferdinand was at this point incapable of refusing any request from Napoleon and so Paisiello went to Paris in 1802, enjoying there a position which placed him above all his French contemporaries.

Notes to Chapter I

1. Carlo Goldoni, *Mémoires* (Paris, 1822), I, 3.
2. Goldoni, *Mémoires*, I, 8.
3. Goldoni, *Mémoires*, I, 152.
4. Charles de Brosses, *Lettres écrites d'Italie à quelques amis en 1739 et 1740* (Paris, 1836), II, 338-39.
5. Norbert Jonard, *La vita a Venezia nel XVIII secolo* (Milan, 1967), p. 174.
6. Jonard, *Vita*, p. 175.
7. Goldoni, *Mémoires*, I, 264-65.
8. Goldoni, *Mémoires*, I, 279-80.
9. Carlo Goldoni, "Prefatory Note" to *The Comic Theatre*, trans. John W. Miller (Lincoln, 1969), p. 3.
10. Goldoni, "Prefatory Note," p. 10.
11. Goldoni, "Prefatory Note," p. 31.
12. Abbé Richard, *Description historique et critique de l'Italie* (Paris, 1769), V, 182.
13. Goldoni, *Mémoires*, II, 105-106.
14. J.J. Lalande, *Voyage d'un français en Italie* (Paris, 1769), V, 187-88.
15. Richard, *Description*, V, 188.
16. Carlo Gozzi, *Mémoires*, trans. John Addington Symonds (New York, 1890), II, 111-14.
17. Gotthold Lessing, "Tagebuch der italiänischen Reise," *Lessings Werke* (Berlin, 1925), XXV, 184.
18. J.C.L. Sismonde de Sismondi, *Historical View of the Literature of the South of Europe*, trans. Thomas Roscoe (London, 1846), I, 539.
19. Richard, *Description*, III, 255.
20. Luigi Riccoboni, *Histoire du théâtre italien* (Paris, 1731), I, 16.
21. Riccoboni, *Histoire*, I, 83.
22. Quoted in Robert Freeman, *Opera without Drama*, unpublished diss., Princeton, 1967, pp. 21-22.

23. Voltaire, *Oeuvres complètes* (Paris, 1879), XXV, 191.
24. Antonio Conti, "Lettera," *Le quattro tragedie* (Florence, 1751), pp. 1-5.
25. Richard, *Description,* II, 34-35.
26. Sismondi, *Historical View,* I, 567n.
27. Vittorio Alfieri, *Opere* (Asti, 1951), I, 147n.
28. Alfieri, *Opere*, II, 288.
29. Alfieri, *Opere*, II, 141.
30. Richard, *Description*, I, 53-54.
31. Alfieri, *Opere*, I, 253-54.
32. John Foster, *Walter Savage Landor* (London, 1874), p. 34.
33. Alfieri, *Opere*, I, 301.
34. Vittorio Alfieri, *Lettere edite e inedite* (Turin, 1890), p. 248.
35. de Brosses, *Lettres*, II, 358-59.
36. Lalande, *Voyage*, VI, 345.
37. Samuel Sharp, *Letters from Italy in the Years 1765 and 1766* (London, n.d.), pp. 77-78.
38. Sharp, *Letters*, pp. 85-86.
39. Sharp, *Letters*, p. 82.
40. Francesco Cerlone, *Commedie* (Naples, 1778), XIV, ii.
41. Pietro Napoli-Signorelli, *Storia critica dei teatri* (Naples, 1813), X, 22.
42. Charles Burney, *Metastasio* (London, 1796), I, 402.
43. Carlo de Nicolà, *Diario napoletano,* 1798-1825 (Naples, 1912), quoted in Benedetto Croce, *I teatri di Napoli* (Bari, 1916), p. 265.

II

French Occupation

At the beginning of the nineteenth century, the Italian peninsula was in upheaval, torn by the often conflicting ambitions and political strategies of France, Austria, Spain, Russia, and England. The political unification of Italy was a vision with a long history—Dante and Petrarch had dreamed of it and Machiavelli had ended *The Prince* with a plea for unity under a national leader. More recently, in the eighteenth century, as we have seen, this ideal was again expressed in Naples and in the writings of Alfieri and others of his generation, but the great powers of Europe found it to their mutal advantage to keep Italy weak and divided. Thus little progress was made toward either freedom or unification during the final years of the eighteenth century or the opening ones of the nineteenth.

Somewhat ironically in Italy as in Germany it was French invasion and occupation which provided the catalyst for the eventual winning of these goals. Ideologically the French Revolution provided the inspiration for Italian liberals, despite the excesses of the Terror, and politically Napoleon not only weakened the power of royalty on the peninsula but during his occupation began the consolidation of small political units and the development of uniform political and legal systems which would provide a base for future unification. The French occupation of Italy came in two waves. The first was from 1792 to 1799, at the end of which time all mainland Italy except Venice was under French control. This occupation lasted only five months in Naples and by the end of 1799 the combined forces of the Austrians, Russians, and English had driven the French from the entire area except the vicinity of Genoa.

The political pendulum swung back the following year with Napoleon crossing the Alps in May and wresting a significant victory from the Allies at Marengo on June 14. Once again the French moved from victory to victory. In 1805, with most of northern Italy under his

33

control, Napoleon created there the kingdom of Italy with himself as monarch. His stepson, Eugène de Beauharnais, was appointed to be viceroy. Before the end of the year Napoleon forced Austria to cede Venice to the newly created kingdom.

Fedinand in Naples had given weak but faithful support to Austria during this struggle, for which Napoleon declared him deposed, dispatching his brother Joseph to Naples to assume the crown there. Ferdinand was able with British help to retain Sicily, but the mainland part of his kingdom was converted into the French-dominated Kingdom of Naples. Only Tuscany and the Papal States now remained independent of France, and this condition did not long endure. In 1808 French troops occupied both and made Pius VII virtually a French prisoner.

From 1808 until 1814 the peninsula was administered under a more or less uniform legal system, the Code Napoleon, and a political system which was also essentially uniform, in a small group of nominally separate but French-controlled states. The most important of these was the Kingdom of Italy with Eugène de Beauharnais as its viceroy. Included in this was much of northern Italy—Milan, Venice, Bologna, and the eastern coast of Italy to the river Tronto. Milan, the capital of the new Kingdom, became Italy's leading theatre city, especially after the viceroy established here Italy's first important state-supported troupe, the Compagnia Reale Italiana. The leading actors and leading dramatists of the time naturally gravitated to this new center. In opera, too, Milan now began to eclipse Venice, and La Scala assumed the preeminent position which it has held ever since.

After French occupation of the Papal States most of Italy south of the Kingdom of Italy was occupied by the Kingdom of Naples, ruled at first by Joseph Bonaparte and then, after 1808, by Napoleon's brother-in-law, Joachim Murat. In the spoken theatre, Naples contributed much less to this period than Milan; the traditional commedia was so popular as to discourage most other experimentation. In opera, the two cities were more evenly matched, particularly after 1809, when Domenico Barbaja, the great impresario of La Scala, moved to Naples.

Except for the little principality of Lucca, which accepted the rule of Napoleon's sister Elisa in 1805, all of mainland Italy outside the Kingdoms of Italy and Naples was assimilated directly into the French Empire under Napoleon's personal rule. This now included Turin, Genoa, Florence, and Rome. Protests in Tuscany subsequently caused Napoleon to modify this arrangement to the extent of creating there another principality for his sister Maria. The close relations of the new rulers and the dominance of Napoleon over all gave to Italy during this period a sense of unity which it had not experienced since the time of the Roman Empire. The disappearance of customs barriers and the building of new roads encouraged trade and a growing feeling of interdependence of the Italian states. Napoleon himself encouraged a vision of Italian independence, though a qualified and conservative one. In 1796 he wrote that three sorts of party existed south of the Alps: "First, the friends of the old government; second, the supporters of an independent but somewhat aristocratic constitution; third, the supporters of the French constitution or of pure democracy. I suppress the first, I support the second, and I moderate the third."(1) Despite some resistance from members of the third group, manifested in anti-French secret societies, the Emperor and his surrogate kings ruled over a fairly tranquil Italy until 1813 when, as the Empire began to collapse, Austria again invaded. In Italy, as elsewhere in Europe, 1815 brought a restoration of kings and political absolutism.

Milan and the Royal Company

One of the results of the French dominance of Italy was the development of Milan as a major cultural center. Milan was a capital of little theatrical interest when Goldoni took his new work to that city in the 1730s. Lombardy was a minor state, like Parma or Modena, with the obligatory theatre but with no permanent company and only minor governmental support. The region's political background contributed to this cultural indifference. Though a dialect of Italian was of course the native language, the aristocracy spoke French and tended to look to France as their cultural home. Since the beginning of the century, however, Austria had been in control of Milan, and thus the dominant political language and focus was German. In the theatre, orchestral works, oratorios, and cantatas were the favored offerings in the early eighteenth century, but opera gradually grew in importance, first with the appearance of touring companies, and at last with an occasional premiere of real importance. The young Gluck, studying music in Milan, began his operatic career with *Artaserse* (set to a libretto by Metastasio), offered at Milan's Teatro Ducale in 1741, and four other premieres of his early works were given here. The native Milanese composer Giovanni Lampugnani (1706-1784) offered a series of popular works during the same period, including another version of *Artaserse* in 1739 and several operas based on libretti by Goldoni. Appointed composer in residence and *maestro al cembalo* (harpsichord) at the Ducale, Lampugnani played in 1770 for the premiere of a new opera, **Mitridate, re di Ponto**, by Wolfgang Amadeus Mozart, then only fourteen. The following year the theatre premiered Mozart's *Ascanio in Alba* and a year later his *Lucio Silla*.

Then in 1776, with opera clearly assuming a position of importance in Milan, the old Teatro Ducale was destroyed by fire. The Milanese sought and obtained permission from Maria Theresa, Empress of Austria and Duchess of Milan, to replace it with two theatres, one to be built on the site of the Church of Santa Maria delle Scala and the other at the adjoining Scuola Cannobiana. The architect Giuseppi Piermarini completed the larger house, the Teatro alla Scala, in 1778, and the smaller Cannobiana the following year. Both houses were opened with operas by the Austrian court composer Antonio Salieri (1750-1825). The interior and general proportions of the magnificent larger theatre have changed little since its opening, though the stage and orchestra pit have been since enlarged. Except for this and for some redecoration, the house seen in Milan today is essentially that described with enthusiasm by an English traveler soon after its opening:

> Surely a receptacle so capacious to contain four thousand people, a place of entrance so commodious to receive them, a show so princely, so very magnificent to entertain them, must be sought in vain out of Italy. The centre front box, richly adorned with gilding, arms and trophies, is appropriated to the court, whose canopy is carried up to what we call the first gallery in England; the crescent of boxes ending with the stage consists of 19 on a side, small boudoirs—for such they seem—and are as such fitted up with silk hangings, girandoles, etc. and placed so judiciously as to catch every sound of the singers if they do but whisper. I will not say it is equally advantageous to the figure as to the voice, no performers looking adequate to the place they recite upon, so very stately is the building itself, being all of stone, with an immense portico, and stairs which for width you might without hyperbole drive your chariot up....(2)

During the **nineteenth** century, of course, La Scala became the best known operatic theatre in the world, but its reputation developed gradually, and despite its impressiveness as a theatre, its first twenty years were not particularly distinguished. Serious operatic works were offered only during the Carnival season, with opera buffa presented at other times, not infrequently varied by crude farces, marionette plays, and acrobatics.

Italy's political vicissitudes at the end of the century were reflected particularly strongly in Milan, which suffered from a vulnerable geographical position. In 1793 the theatre held festivities to mark the coronation of the Emperor Josef II, with free admittance to all, then in 1796 heralded the arrival of the French troops with the Marseillaise. Under the new regime the theatre became a temple of reason, liberty, and democracy. The royal box was divided into six smaller boxes for the people, and the repertoire devoted to such patriotic works as the ballets *Junius Brutus* or *Les Dances du pape*. The return of the Austrians was celebrated by a *Te Deum* in 1799, but within a year a French official was reading from the forestage a dispatch announcing the defeat of Austria at Marengo and the imminent return of the French to Milan. The short-lived French Cisalpine Republic was thus replaced by the somewhat more lasting Kingdom of Italy, with Milan as its capital.

With the establishment of this new state, Milan's importance as a cultural capital grew rapidly. The dramatist most closely associated with this period of expansion was Vincenzo Monti (1754-1828), generally regarded as the leading successor of Alfieri. As the new century opened, there was a clear sense of change in Italian letters, inspired in large part of course by the political upheavals, but also by the more natural passing of the highly influential leaders of the previous century. Goldoni died in Paris in 1793. His rival Gozzi and the great tragedian Alfieri were still alive, but contributed little to the new era. Gozzi's last new work was *Il montanaro don Giovanni Pasquale*, premiered in Trieste in 1800. Alfieri, though his works were eagerly embraced by the French and their supporters as heralds of the new age of liberty, found his hatred of the French confirmed by their occupation, and spend his final years discharging his anger in a series of unsuccessful political pieces and satiric comedies. He died in Florence in 1803.

Monti was much, perhaps too much, an author of his time, and his works are inseparable from the political events which inspired them. His first attempt at a tragedy was undertaken after he attended one of Alfieri's private readings of his *Virginia* at an aristocratic gathering in Rome. The result was *Aristodemo* (1786), which was submitted with success to the annual competition for new tragedies in Parma. Monti then followed Alfieri's example in giving recitations of the work in the homes of Roman aristocracy. Goethe, then visiting Rome, was invited to one such gathering and prevailed upon, as the author of *Werther*, to say a few words of praise about Monti's work. When the play was accepted for public performance at the Teatro Valle, Monti asked Goethe to join him in his box for moral support, though when the evening came Monti was unable to face the experience and Goethe went alone. The author, Goethe reported, need not have worried:

> The boxes were unsparing in their applause. The pit was won over from the outset by the beautiful language of the poet and the striking delivery of the actors, and it omitted no opportunity of expressing its pleasure. The bench of German artists distinguished itself not a little, and this time their feelings were appropriate, though they are as a rule too loud.... The acting was most praiseworthy, and the chief actor, who appears throughout the play, spoke and acted very well; we could almost fancy seeing one of the ancient Caesars before us. Costumes such as we find so impressive on statuary were translated very well to the stage, and it was clear that the actor had studied the antique.(3)

Encouraged by this success, Monti undertook a new tragedy in the Alfieri manner, this time with a subject drawn from fifteenth-century Italian history, *Galeotto Manfredi*. Presented at the Valle in 1788 with the same leading actor, Petronio Zanarini, whom Goethe had so admired, it was much more coolly received. Perhaps this was because Monti had introduced autobiographical references, or perhaps because, despite the more domestic subject of this work, he had followed the example of Alfieri in assiduously avoiding any local color. The disappointed author turned for a time away from the theatre to lyric poetry, with distinct political overtones. He bitterly attacked the French Revolution, especially its anti-clericalism — hardly surprisingly, since he was himself an abbot with relatives high in the papal court. Yet when Napoleon took Northern Italy, Monti began to view the French in a different light. He moved to Milan in 1797 and became a sort of unofficial poet laureate for the ephemeral Cisalpine Republic.

When the French left Italy in 1799 Monti left with them, and wrote his third and best drama, *Caio Gracco*, in Paris the next year. The play drew inspiration from a variety of sources. Its language and its appeal to Italian patriotism recalled Alfieri; the general subject matter and treatment suggested French Revolutionary political-patriotic drama, especially the works of Marie-Joseph Chenier (whose own *Caius Gracchus*, with its appeal for "laws and not blood" had been banned during the Terror). Perhaps the most strikingly significant influence, however, was Shakespeare, a dramatist at this time only faintly recognized in Italy. A minor follower of Alfieri, Alessandro Verri (1741-1816) had translated *Hamlet* and *Othello* during the 1770s and written an original work, *La congiura di Milano*, which took tentative liberties with neoclassic rules, but these efforts were little read and never presented. Monti's work, though still far from Shakespearean, was by its popularity a much more significant step. There are hints of

Othello in the plot of *Galeotto Manfredi*, and the evil courtier Zambino resembles Iago, but echoes of *Julius Caesar* and *Coriolanus* are far more pronounced in *Caio Gracco*. Still Monti, like the rest of his countrymen, first became aware of Shakespeare through French and German adaptations in which most of the more radical elements which so fascinated the later romantics were subdued or entirely suppressed. The Shakespeare Monti knew had been considerably "civilized" in accordance with neoclassic theory.

When the French returned to Italy, Monti also returned, this time official Poet Laureate of the new French Kingdom of Northern Italy. In addition to creating poems of fulsome praise to Napoleon, he supervised the production of *Caio Gracco* and *Aristodemo* at the Milan theatre most closely associated with the new order, the Teatro Patriottico.

This venture had been founded under French occupation in 1796 by a group of young supporters of the French, the Compagnia dei Giovani Repubblicani. Their goal, as they explained to the occupying general Despinoy, was "to present works spreading democratic ideals to the people," and their repertoire contained such pieces as Alfieri's *Virginia* and an adaptation of Schiller's *Wilhelm Tell*.(4) The Austrian occupation naturally halted such efforts, but with the return of the French the group was reorganized and housed in a new theatre. The stage was fairly impressive—with a proscenium eight meters wide and 15.5 deep, but the auditorium was a mere 10.3 meters wide and 11.6 deep. It was totally democratic, with four balconies but no boxes, and at least for the opening performances was open without admission prices for all. Even so, it was not particularly popular. Audiences preferred more music and spectacle, less preaching, and more skilled artists than the Patriottico could offer. In 1805 it was renamed the Filodrammatic and offered a more popular blend of prose drama and lyric opera.

Monti's new theatrical works at this time were quasi-dramatic cantatas, *Teseo* (1804) and *I pittagorici* (with music by Paisiello, 1808). The former was premiered at La Scala, which now offered a broad range of theatrical works—opera, ballet, cantatas, comedies, tragedies, and sentimental dramas. *Teseo* was an obvious political allegory, with Napoleon represented by Theseus who returns to restore order to feuding Athens and Trezene. Although Napoleon as a general rule had little taste for tributes of this sort, he thought highly enough of Monti to award him a post of considerable artistic authority. In 1809 the Direzione Generalle dell' Istruzione Pubblica nel Regno Italico founded a contest for serious and comic drama modeled on that established by Napoleon in Paris, and Monti was made head of the panel of judges. In Milan as in Paris this contest had little positive effect on the drama, since the most rigid precepts of neoclassicism were the basis of judgment. Arici's *Calliroe* was probably the best serious work considered the first year, but it was disqualified on the grounds that unity of place had not been observed in it (one act showed the interior of a temple, another the exterior), and worse, the first act ended with an arietta instead of a full chorus.

Such hairsplitting was satirized in Angelo Anelli's *Dalla beffa al disinganno*, with music by Pacini, at La Scala in 1815, but this work, though popular, touched the sensibilities of the officials too closely, and it was soon banned. Anelli (1761-1820) was little affected by this setback, since he was extremely prolific, supplying plays and libretti to most of the Milan theatres of the period. He provided the text for Rossini's *L'Italiana in Algeri* (1813) and Pavesi's *Ser Marcantonio* (1810), which in turn served as the basis for Donizetti's *Don Pasquale*.

A more positive result of the new Kingdom's determination to imitate Paris on all cultural matters was the establishment of an official state-subsidized theatre, the Compagnia Reale Italiana. It was given the extremely generous subsidy of 50,000 francs annually, the Minister of the Interior appointed the members of the company, and a royal commission, of which Monti was naturally a member, selected the plays. These were primarily by Alfieri, Goldoni, and Gozzi, with some foreign works and a few by contemporary Italians. The troupe was probably the best in Italy at this time, the heir of the great eighteenth-century companies of Medebac, Sacchi, and Battaglia. It was composed of eleven members with a machinist and a prompter. The leader of the company was the beloved comedian Salvatore Fabbrichesi (1760-1827), but its most highly acclaimed member was the actress Anna Fiorilli-Pellandri (1771-1840) who was considered equally outstanding in dialect comedy and stylized tragedy, drama and improvised commedia. Her father Antonio played Dottore roles in the renowned Sacchi company and Anna was introduced to the stage early, already beloved for her ability to recite and improvise at the age of nine. Her performance of Alfieri's *Mirra* in 1803 in Florence with the author present was one of the most memorable events of the Napoleonic years. The Viceroy Eugène de Beauharnais insisted upon the hiring of Fiorilli-Pellandri for this new company whatever the cost, and her salary was in fact more than twice that of Pellegrino Blanès, the next highest-paid member.

Blanès (Paolo Bello, 1770?-1823) achieved his first great success in 1799 in Alfieri's *Bruto Primo*, presented in Naples at the Teatro del Fondo (which became the Teatro Patriottico under French occupation). He became so closely associated with the French that like Monti he was forced to leave with them, returning, again like Monti, to settle in Milan in 1803. His preeminence in tragedy was established by performances at La Scala during the following year of Alfieri's *Oreste*, Monti's *Aristodemo*, and Giovanni Pindemonte's *Lucio Quinzio Cincinnato*, an early attempt at a tragedy of mixed genre in the Shakespearean style. In 1807, when the new royal company was formed, he was the inevitable choice for first tragic actor and he remained with the company until 1812, when he and Fiorilli-Pellandri formed their own company and toured with great success throughout Northern Italy until 1817. They achieved particular success in Florence in the premiere of *Polissena*, the first major work of Giovan Battista Niccolini, who defied the growing interest in a vaguely Shakespearean approach by creating a tragedy based directly on Greek structure. Like his French contemporary Talma, Blanès was a pioneer in realistic effects even though the tragedies in which he performed were predominantly neoclassic. He ran the risk of catching cold by having a pail of water poured over him in the wings before entering as a king escaped from a shipwreck; he once stabbed himself in earnest while playing Aristodemo; and he so frightened Pellandri on several occasions that she requested and obtained from the Milan government a law against actors' using real weapons on stage.

The royal company's leading actor in comedy and prose drama was Giuseppe De Marini (1772-1829), a native of Milan and considered with Blanès one of the strongest actors of the period. "In the eyes of Italian audiences (and more especially the feminine section thereof), none holds a higher place in the hierarchy than De Marini," Stendhal observed.

> In Italy, for a variety of reasons not wholly known to myself, natural simplicity is distinctly out of favor on the printed page; the average Italian must have his literature tricked out with all manner of high-flown and bombastic rhetoric.... Here you have the principle which explains and underlies the boundless reputation of De Marini. He fashions his art upon nature, yet distantly; indeed, nature may hardly be held to challenge the divine prerogative of *Rhetoric* within his heart. In days gone by, he was wont to steal away the very soul of Italy in his various *jeune premier* roles; nowadays, he has turned to *Noble Father* parts; and since such parts admit a fair degree of bombast, I have often found entertainment watching his performance.(5)

The alternate leading actor was Giovanni Bettini (1789?-1822?), whose wife Lucrezia became the company's second leading actress. Noble fathers were portrayed by Antonio Belloni (1759-1842), a stout partisan of republican ideals who had been forced to flee Naples when the Bourbons were restored in 1799. Somewhat ironically, one of his most favored roles was the aristocratic Milord Bonfil in Goldoni's *Pamela*. His greatest success in a new work with the Reale Italiana was as Ottavio Augusto, the father in Sografi's popular *Ortensia* (1809).

Simeone Antonio Sografi (1759-1818) served as a playwright in residence for the new company. He began his theatrical writing with libretti for the opera houses of Venice, then turned to brief farces and adaptations of German (*Verter*, 1794), French (*Il padre di famiglia*, 1795), and English works (*Tom Jones*, 1796), with growing success. The influence of Goldoni was strong on his most popular work of this period, *Le convenienze teatrali* (1794), a broad satire on the pretensions of theatre artists. He also contributed significantly to the popular genre of sentimental drama in such works as *La putta di sentimento* (1798). The arrival of the French inspired a series of Jacobin dramas, the most successful of which was *Il matrimonio democratico*, premiered at La Fenice (then renamed the Teatro Civico) in 1797 by the Battaglia company and offered later that same year at the Teatro Nuovo in Padua for Napoleon himself. In 1800 Sografi became playwright for the Venier company, whose leading actress was Anna Fiorilli-Pellandri, and they shared the success of several popular romantic comedies such as *Lucrezia Dondi Orologio-Obizzi* (1803). So successful were they as a team that Sografi naturally followed his leading actress to the new company in Milan, continuing to create vehicles for her as well as popular historical dramas and comedies in neoclassic style.

The royal company naturally underwent many changes during its first years, since Italian actors were unaccustomed to remaining in any group for long. The most important adjustments occurred in 1811 and 1812 when three leading actors departed to establish new companies—Belloni, Blanès, and Pellandri. To replace Blanès and Belloni, Fabbrichesi promoted two other actors, Giovanni Bettini and Alberto Tessari (1780-1845). A new actress had to be brought in to fill Pellandri's roles and Fabbrichesi was fortunate in his selection of the young Carolina Cavalletti (1794-1845), who became a favorite with La Scala audiences. She and Tessari eventually married.

Though **Blanès** and Pellandri left Milan with their new company, Belloni decided to remain in the capital and establish a rival troupe there. His base was the Teatro di Santa Radegonda, which had been founded in 1801 in a convent closed by the French army of occupation. The standard fare here was popular comedy played in commedia masks with Milanese dialect, such as Gustavo Piomarta's *L'avventure di Meneghia Peccenna* (1805). Belloni assembled a company composed partly of actors trained in the traditional masked comedy, such as Angelo Marchionni, a popular Brighella, and partly of those associated with the more realistic Goldoni style, such as his leading man, Ferdinando Meraviglia. A year before the new company was formed, Marchionni's daughter Carlotta (1796-1861) had made her debut. She soon became the outstanding artist of the new troupe.

Belloni's company achieved some success, but Fabbrichesi, playing sometimes at La Scala and sometimes at the smaller Cannobiana, had the advantages of better facilities, a generally superior company and a state subsidy, giving him a steady superiority over his rival. Sografi continued to provide him with new sentimental and historical dramas, but between 1808 and 1814 an important part of his success was due to the premieres of five comedies by Alberto Nota (1775-1847), the leading comic dramatist of the period. Nota, like most of his contemporaries, worked primarily in the tradition of Goldoni, though his work reflected some shift in comedic taste. In the late eighteenth century the leading Italian comic dramatists could be divided into three fairly distinct camps. Some, of course, sought simply to carry on Goldoni's tradition, like his friend Francesco Albergati (1728-1804). Others continued to champion the ancient but never very successfully realized ideal of neoclassic comedy, with strict observance of the unities, simple actions, an aim of social betterment, and purity of genre. Such was the inspiration behind the sixteen plays and prefatory *Ragionamento* (1790-1798) produced by Gherardo de Rossi (1754-1827). Most of his contemporaries, unfortunately, shared the opinion of Sismondi, who wrote, "The wit of Gherardo de Rossi is, indeed, too much the result of study, to meet with the success which more spontaneous effusions never fail to obtain."(6) A third group took almost the opposite approach, under the influence of French authors such as Diderot and Beaumarchais and the popular Germans Iffland and Kotzebue. In these works there was a free mixture of emotional tones and little regard for classic structure. The plays of the popular Camillo Federici (1749-1802) and his son Carlo (1778-1849) showed this tendency clearly.

The coming of the French gave some support to the cause of neoclassic comedy. Indeed citizens of Milan had frequent opportunity now to see French companies trained in the presentation of such works. French troupes alternated regularly with native ones at the Cannobiana, and in 1813 a branch of the Comédie Française itself, led by Mme Raucourt, offered the first prose works at the recently opened Teatro Carcano. Thus the taste for comedy in the early eighteenth century, in Milan at least, drew in some measure upon all of these sources. Nota produced highly successful works which were almost pure examples of each of the three styles, and a variety of equally successful blends. He had little interest in the opposing claims of literary schools, and it is hardly surprising that in the battle between classicists and romantics which developed around 1815 Nota remained neutral, utilizing some elements from each persuasion.

Despite the successes of Fabbrichesi's company, La Scala was from the beginning of the century preeminently the home of lyric drama, particularly as Milan began to replace Venice as the operatic capital of Italy. A key transitional figure, both geographically and musically, was Johann Simon Mayr (1763-1845). The attempted reforms of such mid-eighteenth-century composers as Perez and Jommelli had not accomplished the sort of revolution in Italian opera which Gluck and his followers had achieved elsewhere. It was Mayr who finally established a new direction in the Italian opera seria. It was still conservative by general European standards, but radical enough to Italian ears. Drawing inspiration from Mozart and the French as well as from Gluck, he expanded the role of the chorus and orchestra and introduced a generally greater flexibility in the structure of the opera, thus preparing the way for Donizetti, who was one of his pupils, for the serious operas of Rossini, and ultimately for Verdi. Mayr was born in Bavaria but studied music in Italy, arriving in Venice about 1789. In 1794 his *Saffo*, with libretto by Sografi, was successfully offered at La Fenice. His second work, *Lodoiska* (La Fenice, 1796), won him a European reputation, confirmed by the musical farce, *Che originali* (1798) and the opera seria *Adelaide di Guesclino* (1799). His first premiere at La Scala was in 1800 and during the next fifteen years, his most productive, he normally provided a new work almost yearly for La Scala as well as one for the Venetian theatres and often one or two others for Rome or elsewhere. He made Bergamo his home after 1802 and greatly improved the musical life of that town, founding a school of music in 1805 which counted Donizetti among its students.

Venice, Naples and Rome

The political and cultural rise of Milan was directly paralleled by a decline in Venice. The thousand-year republic fell to the French in 1797 but its situation in the years before its fall was so difficult that many of its citizens welcomed foreign occupation. The political system had become totally corrupt and near bankruptcy, the army powerless, the poor helpless and deprived of employment, the republic preserved only by a strong police presence and a lack of focus for the many malcontents. Venice attempted to remain neutral in the developing French-Austrian confrontation, and was thus left helpless in the face of the French advance. Among the citizens who welcomed the French army of occupation in the hopes of gaining a more even-handed and liberal regime was young Ugo Foscolo (1778-1827), whose first play, *Tieste*, was presented with great success at the Teatro San Angelo the year of the French invasion. The work was strongly influenced by Alfieri in poetic style, in structure, and in character (with a typical Alfierian conflict between tyranny and liberal thought, represented by Atreo and Tieste). The theme was perfectly suited to the time and doubtless the enormous enthusiasm which greeted the play owed more to political than artistic considerations. Foscolo and his supporters were soon disillusioned. In less than a year the French handed Venice over to the Austrians, who at once imposed a far more absolutist rule. Rigorous censorship and constant police supervision were imposed on the theatres. Aside from Goldoni, almost no authors saw their works presented intact. A number of theatres closed in protest, but they were soon forced not only to reopen but to present patriotic works celebrating Austria, such as A.M. Cuccetti's *Carlo in Sciaffusa* (1799). The theatres could be forced to perform such material, but the public could not be forced to attend, and the houses remained often almost empty.

Foscolo, selecting the lesser of two evils, departed with the French who had betrayed his hopes and even fought alongside them at the end of the century to drive the more hated Austrians from Northern Italy. When the Kingdom of Italy was established Foscolo, like Monti and Nota, settled in Milan, the new capital, but Foscolo did not share Monti's inclination to adjust his political views according to each new regime. His second tragedy, *Aiace*, presented at La Scala by Fabbrichesi's company in 1811, reflected essentially the same concerns as his first. Whether the general theme of liberty versus tyranny was offensive to the French censor or whether specific references to

Napoleon were suspected, the work was banned and Foscolo left Milan in protest. His third play, *Ricciarda* (offered at Bologna in 1813), Foscolo saw as a new experiment, a drama of romantic love, somewhat in the manner of *Romeo and Juliet*, set in medieval Italy. The usual Foscolo concerns dominated the love story, however. In the characters of the two feuding fathers, Guelfo and Averardo, Foscolo worked out his favorite opposition of tyrant and libertarian and the play is full of passages extolling freedom and Italy. The events of 1815 drove Foscolo from Italy altogether and he lived in London from 1815 to 1827. His political sympathies would have made him a natural ally of the young romantics but artistically he was in the opposite camp and from exile he fulminated against the new non-Alferian style.

The departure of Foscolo from Venice may be taken as representative of the dying of the major dramatic tradition of that city. The popular Federici kept the spirit of Goldoni alive and contributed significantly to the new genre of sentimental drama as well with two or three new works a year through the end of the century, but when he died in 1802 no new Venetian dramatist appeared to replace him. Cimarosa had died in Venice the year before, leaving another void. Giovanni Greppi (1751-1827), whose *Teresa* trilogy (San Luca, 1786), based on Richardson, was one of the great successes of the sentimental tradition, joined Foscolo in following the French out of Venice. The only dramatist of any importance to remain was Sografi, who created a series of patriotic pageants of interest only to the Austrian forces of occupation before he too left for Milan in 1807.

The eight theatres regularly open in Venice during the eighteenth century shrank to four by 1815 and only one of these, La Fenice, devoted primarily to opera, maintained a reputation and dignity equal to the major theatres in other leading Italian cities. The lesser Teatro di San Moisè enjoyed a final moment of glory before its closing in 1818 by premiering the first comic operas of young Gioacchino Rossini (1792-1868), four *farsas*, beginning with *La cambiale di matrimonio* (1810), based on a play by Federici. So great was the popularity of these new works that according to Stendhal a popular Venetian saying of the period was, "Cimarosa has come back among us."(7) The success of those works gained Rossini a commission in 1812 to compose an opera for La Scala, now Italy's leading theatre, and the triumph there of his *La pietra del paragone* established him as the leading young composer in Italy.

The rise of Milan in dramatic and particularly in musical prominence paralleled a decline in the importance of Naples but the proud Neapolitans refused to acknowledge this shift. Although they were from 1805 to 1815 assimilated into the Napoleonic empire, most Neapolitans continued to think of themselves as distinct not only from that empire but from the rest of the peninsula. Nowhere was the influence of Gluck and Mozart resisted more stoutly than here, and even Rossini, on his first appearance, was condemned as an interloper "from Italy" (that is, from the north) by conservative Neapolitan composers and public. Opera continued to be the major theatrical activity in Naples, though the Teatro San Carlo possessed an outstanding commedia troupe, headed by a beloved pulcinello, Vincenzo Commarano, and later by his son Filippo.

With the departure for France of Paisiello, the tradition of Neapolitan opera was carried on by Nicola Zingarelli, who provided works for La Scala, La Fenice, and a great number of other theatres in addition to Naples' San Carlo and Fondo. The arrival of the leading impresario Domenico Barbaja (1778-1841) in 1809 began a new era of brilliance in Naples' musical theatre, though it was also the era in which the old Neapolitan style would give way to the new forces from the north. It was under Barbaja that La Scala had ascended to its position of prominence, and in the process Barbaja had amassed a fortune, not only because of his brilliance in the selection of operas and artists but also because of his success as a gambler and as an entrepreneur in games of chance. The foyer of La Scala was the gambling center of Milan during his administration, and his license from the government in Naples allowed him not only to operate the San Carlo but to set up gaming tables there as he had in Milan. Under his administration the San Carlo audiences were introduced to Mayr, to Spontini, and even to Mozart. Barbaja was the first major impresario to seek out young Rossini, and in 1815 signed a contract with him—whereby Rossini was to become musical director of San Carlo and the Fondo (both now under Barbaja's control) and to provide Barbaja with two original operas per year. Barbaja suffered a temporary setback early in 1816 when fire destroyed the San Carlo, but the impresario promised to rebuild it, with even greater magnificence, in record time and indeed the new theatre opened January 13, 1817. It was designed by Antonio Niccolini (1772-1850), a noted architect who also served as the theatre's scenic designer and as director of a school of scenography for young designers which he founded in 1816.

The Papal States were the last power in Italy to be subsumed into the Napoleonic empire. Pius VII, like Ferdinand IV in Naples, was allowed to reign by the grace of Napoleon for a few years at the opening of the century, but in both cases the Emperor found reason to revoke his agreements and send these rulers into exile. The major Roman theatres of the period were the Valle, the Argentina, and the Apollo (built in the 1790s on the site of the old Teatro Tordinona, destroyed by fire in 1789). During the French occupation in 1798-1799 all three produced dramas and musicals suiting Jacobin taste — topical spectacles, revivals of Alfieri and translations of Chénier and Voltaire. Between 1800 and 1808 the theatres offered operas, prose works and ballet but had few premieres of any importance. The Apollo, despite its magnificent new building, declined steadily, passing from hand to hand, and by 1812 offered only such bills as acrobatic and equestrian exercises and Pulcinella shows.

The position of Rome's leading theatre was assumed by the Valle, which in the years just before the French returned enjoyed the services of Giovanni Giraud (1776-1834), one of the period's most successful writers of comedy. His *Ajo nell'imbarazzo* (1807) in particular had a long career on the stages of both Italy and France. Strongly influenced by both Goldoni and Molière, Giraud deplored the commedia influence still strong in comic theatre at the beginning of the century. In the Advice to the Actors which accompained his *La ciarliera indispettita* (1808) he admitted that his notary was "a sort of Harlequin," but urged the actors to remember that he did not want "caricatured comedy" and that he abhorred "pigtails to the loins, black painted faces and suchlike foolery."(8) After the French occupation of 1808 the Valle and Argentina placed more emphasis on opera, and works by Mayr, Zingarelli and Zingarelli's popular student Francesco Morlacchi (1784-1841) were premiered at both theatres between 1808 and 1815. Rossini's first opera seria, *Demetrio e Polibo*, was presented at the Valle in 1812, four months before his first work at La Scala.

Notes to Chapter II

1. *Correspondance* (Paris, 1859), II, 207.
2. Hester Piozzi, *Glimpses of Italian Society in the Eighteenth Century* (London, 1892), p. 69.
3. Johann Wolfgang von Goethe, "Italiänische Reise," *Goethes Werke* (Weimar, 1903), XXX, 213-14.
4. Domenico Manzella and Emilio Pozzi, *I teatri di Milano* (Milan, 1971), p. 66.
5. Stendhal, *Rome, Naples, and Florence*, trans. Richard Coe (London, 1959), p. 394.

6. J.C.L. Simonde de Sismondi, *Historical View of the Literature of the South of Europe*, trans. Thomas Roscoe (London, 1846), I, 553.
7. Stendhal, *Life of Rossini*, trans. Richard Coe (New York, 1970), p. 50.
8. Guido Mazzoni, *L'Ottocento* (Milan, 1953), p. 141.

III

Restoration and Romanticism

Napoleon's defeat in Russia in 1812 signalled the beginning of the collapse of his Italian empire. In many cities secret anti-French societies, the Adelfi, the Guelfs, the Carbonari, began working vigorously to undermine the occupation. The next year Austria invaded Eugène de Beauharnais' Kingdom of Italy, with the support of Joachim Murat, the King of Naples, who had decided the time had come to turn against his protector, Napoleon. The final defeat of the Emperor in 1815 left Austria essentially in control of the Italian peninsula, a situation confirmed by the Congress of Vienna. Once again the map of Italy was redrawn, though with fewer separate states than before the Napoleonic Wars. Milan, the major cultural center under the French, was assimilated with all of Lombardy and Venetia directly into the Austrian Empire. Genoa, Piedmont, and Savoy were taken from the French Empire and joined in a conservative monarchy under Vittorio Emmanuele I or Sardinia. Several minor duchies were established to the south of these states — Parma, Modena, Lucca and, most important, Tuscany — governed by various members of the Hapsburg and Bourbon families. Across the middle of the peninsula stretched the Papal States, restored to Pius VII, whom Napoleon had driven into exile. Finally, encompassing the entire southern half of the peninsula, came the Kingdom of the Two Sicilies, now the largest political unit in Italy. The opportunistic Murat had attempted after Napoleon's return to France in 1815 to march northward against the distracted Austrians and create his own Italian state, but Austrian troops defeated, deposed and eventually executed him. Ferdinand then returned Sicily to Naples as Ferdinand I of the new kingdom.

The restoration of the ruling houses of Italy had both positive and negative effects on the theatre. On the negative side, the political conservatism championed by Austria's powerful prime minister Metternich and protected by Austrian troops insured that regardless of who ruled any particular state, censorship would be rigorous and a police presence strongly felt. The occasional popular uprisings, such as that in Naples and Piedmont in 1820, served only to increase the governments' severity. After 1820 only in Tuscany was a degree of freedom of expression allowed and the European-wide unrest of the early 1830s, affecting most of Italy, resulted in Tuscany's finally joining its neighbors in the rigid policing of the theatre and press.

The new school of romanticism, closely related in Italy to liberal idealism and often with overtones of freedom and unity for the Italian state, was a natural target for the forces of repression, and the young writers in this movement inevitably faced censorship and perhaps imprisonment. Nevertheless Alfieri's search for a serious modern Italian theatre was continued by such writers as Silvio Pellico, who spent ten years in an Austrian prison for his beliefs; Alessandro Manzoni, who championed Shakespeare and sought a socially and morally relevant Italian theatre; and Giovan Battista Niccolini, whose patriotic works were denied public production but were widely and enthusiastically read. The serious drama created during this period was too dominated by contemporary concerns to endure. Typical was Niccolini's boast that if one of his plays was not "a great tragedy," it was nevertheless "a courageous act."

Besides these political problems, the development of serious drama was hampered by the lack of a common Italian theatrical language other than the traditional elevated style of neoclassicism. Manzoni devoted much of his career to this problem, and provided a partial solution, but it remained to some degree a difficulty for Italian dramatists for the rest of the century.

On the positive side, the restoration brought back to Italy a period of royal support for the theatres and with this support the opera and the dance in particular, both less politically suspect than the spoken drama, enjoyed great success. The works of Rossini delighted the audiences of Rome, Venice, Naples and especially Milan and when Rossini departed for Paris a whole new generation of composers, Mercadante, Bellini, Donizetti, were ready to replace him. In their works the spirit of romanticism entered the Italian opera, though natually with less specifically political emphasis than in the spoken theatre. The great designers Sanquirico of Milan and Bagnara of Venice provided the proper visual cadre for the new movement.

Troupes in the spoken drama also gained increased support during this period, though less than the opera. State-subsidized companies appeared in every major principality. Their repertoire was carefully watched, but the major companies of the time, given a more

stable existence, laid the foundations for the great tradition of
nineteenth-century Italian acting which would dazzle the world in such
artists as Ristori, Rossi, Salvini and Duse. Before 1815 only the troupe
of Fabbrichesi enjoyed a major reputation in Italy; during the next fifteen years a number of major rivals appeared. Most of them were state
supported like the companies of Tessari in Naples and Mascherpa in
Florence and, most important of all, Bazzi's Compagnia Reale Sarda
in Turin, which by 1830 had become the new leader on the peninsula.

The Revival of Naples

Although the Naples of Ferdinand I offered little political
freedom and censorship was strong, as it was elsewhere in Italy, Ferdinand, like his father, saw the theatre as an essential part of the
magnificence of his capital and gave it strong financial support. By an
odd coincidence he, again like his father, began his reign with the
building of San Carlo, for the old theatre burned down early in 1816.
A magnificent new house was completed in less than a year and Stendhal, present for the opening, saw that it had political as well as artistic and social significance: "This mighty edifice, rebuilt in the space
of three hundred days, is nothing less than a coup d'état: it binds the
people in fealty and homage to their sovereign far more effectively
than any *Constitution*." Stendhal returned again and again to the new
theatre, dazzled by its splendor, which he considered unequalled in
Europe:

> The auditorium is a symphony in silver and gold, while the boxes
> are blue as the deep sky. The ornamentation of the inner wall—which
> is cut away in front of each box to form a balcony—is moulded in
> high-relief. Indeed it is this above all which sets the stamp of such
> magnificence—these golden torches artfully grouped and interspersed
> with massive *fleurs-de-lis*. At intervals, this frieze of ornament, which
> is of unimaginable richness, is cut by bands of low relief in silver. Of
> these I counted, unlesss I am mistaken, in all some six-and-thirty.
>
> The boxes, which have no curtains, are unusually spacious. I could
> generally observe some five or six persons seated at each balcony.
>
> There is a wondrous chandelier, all shimmering with light which is
> mirrored and refracted on every hand as it falls upon the gold and
> silver of the reliefs—an effect which would be lost utterly if the or-
> naments were two-dimensional. I can conceive of nothing more
> majestic, nor more magnificent, than the sumptuous Royal Box,
> which is set astride the central doorway, raised aloft on two great
> golden palm-trees, each of natural size; the hangings are fashioned out
> of leaves of metal, tinted in the palest red; even the crown, that

superannuated emblem, seems scarcely too absurd. In startling contrast to the sumptuous grandeur of the Royal Box, I could picture
nothing daintier nor more elegant than the tiny incognito boxes of the
second tier, set hard against the proscenium of the stage.(1)

At later visits, Stendhal became more critical. The immense
central chandelier proved *too* dazzling, drawing attention from the
stage. At La Scala there was no chandelier and all illumination during
the performance came from the stage, an innovation Stendhal heartily
supported. The settings in Milan were superior too, more grandiose
and with a subtler and richer use of color. A particular irritation in
Naples was the physical arrangement of the flats, which were hung,
apparently for ease in scene shifting, so that eight or ten inches of
space was left between their bottom edge and the stage floor:

> with the result that there is a constant procession of feet to be ob-
> served moving about below the pediments of the columns or among the
> roots of the trees. It is hard to conceive the absurdity of this perpetual
> distraction: the spectator's attention is held in hypnotic fascination by
> this shifting frieze of legs, and his fancy is constrained to guess at the
> purpose of each move.(2)

The problems of mounting both opera and ballet in the same
space were also great, especially in view of the custom of separating
the first and last acts of an opera by a spectacular ballet lasting an hour
or more. The display required for the ballet required a cavernous
stage, which tended to swallow up the voices of the operatic performers. The ballet *La virtù premiata,* for example, devoted an entire act
to the evolutions of a cavalry of forty-eight and ended with a charge at
full gallop to the very brink of the footlights.(3) In all, Stendhal,
suggested, the San Carlo was "a masterpiece of operatic architecture,
provided that the curtain remains *down.*"(4)

On the other hand, it must be said that these harsh judgments
were not shared by Stendhal's Italian contemporaries, among whom
the designer of the San Carlo, Niccolini, enjoyed an outstanding
reputation. He remained architect of the royal theatre for forty years,
created a staggering number of settings (for 146 operas and 115 ballets
at San Carlo between 1807 and 1822 alone). Leading designers of the
next generation such as Pasquale Canna, Domenico Ferri and Vittorio
Fico studied in his famous school of scenography. As an architect he
remained strongly in the tradition of neoclassicism, but his stage
designs showed equally clearly the influence of the new romantic
ideas. This flexibility of style allowed him to give unusual visual
variety to his work, and he is one of the first Italian designers concerned with adjusting scenic backgrounds so as to suggest an artistic
whole with the specific work being presented.

The major composer for the new theatre was, of course, Rossini, whom Barbaja had invited to Naples and who arrived there only a month before the new sovereign. His first San Carlo premiere, *Elisabetta*, was presented that fall (1815) before the new Bourbon court. The title role was the first Rossini created for the great dramatic soprano Isabella Colbran (1785-1845), his frequent leading lady thereafter and eventually his wife as well. King Ferdinand reportedly liked the work so well that he ordered Zingarelli to lift the ban he had imposed on the reading of Rossini scores by students at the Royal Conservatory.

Despite his contract with Barbaja, Rossini spent the next several months in Rome, where the Teatro Valle and the Teatro Argentina, the city's major opera houses, both sought new works from him. For the latter he created *Il barbiere de Siviglia*, which suffered perhaps the most disastrous opening of any opera later to gain a major reputation. Many in the audience considered an attempt at a new setting of Paisiello's beloved opera the height of presumption and came prepared to scoff. Circumstances gave them every opportunity. The actor playing Basilio tripped over a trapdoor in the first scene and played throughout with a continual nosebleed, a roving cat destroyed the finale, and through it all the unsympathetic audience whistled and jeered. Rossini must have returned to Naples, to Colbran, and to Barbaja with considerable relief, but nevertheless before leaving Rome he signed a contract to provide an opera for the Valle the next year, an opera which would be his noted *La cenerentola*.

It was while Rossini was in Rome that the San Carlo was destroyed by fire, and during its rebuilding major operatic premieres were held at the Teatro del Fondo, a theatre which normally did operatic work of "mezzo carattere" or "semiserie," but at an artistic level of production rivalling that of the more prestigious operas at the San Carlo. Here Rossini's *Otello* was premiered, with Colbran and Andrea Nozzari (1775-1832) in the leading roles. In 1818 Rossini returned briefly to La Scala with a new opera, *La gazza ladra*, and both Rome and Venice enjoyed Rossini premieres during the next five years, but the San Carlo remained the center of his activities until the premiere of *Zelmira* in 1822. The following year he and Colbran, now his wife, created their last new work in Italy, *Semiramide*, at La Fenice in Venice, then departed for Paris and London. At the age of thirty-one, the composer had completed his remarkable career in Italy.

Although the first love of King Ferdinand and of his subjects remained the opera and their preferred theatre the San Carlo, especially during those years when Rossini gave to the musical world of Naples an added lustre, the spoken drama was not forgotten. Ferdinand apparently felt that a royal troupe of actors should also be part of the cultural life of his capital, and since the fall of the French-supported monarchy in Milan had left the Compagnia Reale Italiana there without patronage, he invited them to Naples. The troupe will still led by Fabbrichesi, with De Marini, Bettini and Carolina Cavalleti as his leading players. They settled at first in the Teatro Nuovo and then in 1818 in the Fiorentini, where they soon became as popular with the Neapolitan public as they had been with the Milanese. Comedies, farces and sentimental dramas made up most of the repertoire, but a number of serious works were provided by the prolific neoclassicist, Cesare Della Valle (1777-1860) who faithfully followed Euripides and Racine in such works as *Medea* (1814), *Ippolito* (1818), and *Ifigenia in Aulide* (1818). These helped fill the void left by the suppression of a number of standard works by Alfieri and Monti at the hands of the royal censor. Stendhal reported that in Naples only three of Alfieri's tragedies were now permitted on stage; in Rome, four; in Bologna, five; in Milan, seven; and in Turin, none at all.

The reactionary governments established throughout Italy in 1815 naturally stimulated resentment and the growth of opposing underground movements, some of which had already been formed as a reaction to the oppression of the Napoleonic years. Among the strongest of these organizations, especially in Naples, was the Carbonari, which sought a constitutional monarchy similar to that recently established in Spain. The first serious uprising of the post-Napoleonic period occured in Naples in July of 1820. Early that year news reached Italy of a revolution in Spain which had obliged the Bourbon monarch, Ferdinand VII, to agree to a constitution. His cousin, Ferdinand I of Naples, approved the change and subsequently acceded to pressure from his subjects, including his ministers and the army, to provide a similar constitution for his own kingdom. The conservative monarchies of Europe, led by Austria, summoned Ferdinand early in 1821 to explain this development; soon after, Austrian armies invaded his kingdom, occupying Naples and returning the king to rule with a more despotic hand than before. This setback naturally increased the bitterness and determination of the underground.

As a general rule, the actors of Naples, being much in the public eye, attempted to avoid involvement in the turbulent political situation, but a striking exception was Fabbrichesi's popular character actor Nicola Pertica (1769-1820) who, perhaps out of a sense of loyalty to his royal patron, made public denunciations of the plots of the

Carbonari. One night after a performance he was waylaid by four masked men with daggers who threatened his life if he did not thenceforth support the Carbonari cause. The incident so unnerved him that he was attacked by a violent illness which soon after led to his death.

To replace the unfortunate Pertica, Fabbrichesi enlisted Luigi Vestri (1781-1841), the leading actor of the new generation. Vestri had begun his theatre career in 1804, acting at first with minor companies. Then in 1812 he joined the new troupe being established by Blanès and Pellandri after their departure from the Compagnia Reale. Between 1812 and 1816 his reputation grew to rival that of Blanès himself. He then established his own company, with Carolina Internari (1793-1859) as his leading lady. She was another former member of the Blanès company who had replaced Pellandri upon her retirement from the stage in 1816. Their repertoire consisted of farces, sentimental dramas and Goldonian comedies. Stendhal said that Vestri

> for all his stoutness is the finest actor in Italy—indeed, in all the world; in *Il burbero benefico* as in *L'ajo nell'imbarrazzo*, not to mention that host of worthless rhapsodies to which he alone gives shape and meaning, his skill is equal to that of Molé and Iffland. His performance will bear watching twenty times in succession without the slightest fear of boredom.(5)

In 1818 Vestri's company was engaged for a three-year period at the Teatro Valle in Rome, and in 1822 he was hired by Fabbrichesi to fill Pertica's place in the Neapolitan company. He was at first poorly received after the popular Pertica, but gradually became one of the company's most admired actors. He was the leading player in the troupe by 1824 when Fabbrichesi began to tour through central Italy and to Venice and Trieste. His usual leading lady was Amalia Bettini (1809-1894), whose parents had been with Fabbrichesi from the founding of his company and who was by the age of fifteen playing leading roles with great success.

The company also included the romantic Francesco Lombardi (1792-1845), who did the first Shakespeare in Italy after Morrochesi's 1783 *Hamlet*. Unlike his contemporaries Vestri and Modena, actors with a rich and moving but highly controlled style, Lombardi was erratic and emotional, rather in the manner of Edmund Kean in England. Othello was his favorite role and he performed it for more than a decade in a violent, sensational manner wherein, apparently, his epileptic seizure was particularly impressive. He brought more control but equal passion to the great roles of Alfieri, in which many considered him the greatest actor of the period.

The departure of Fabbrichesi from Naples left the Teatro Fiorentini without a permanent company and the court invited the troupe of Alberto Tessari, then in Rome, to fill the vacancy. Tessari and his wife Carolina Cavalleti were, as we have seen, former members of the Fabbrichesi company, he playing noble fathers and tyrants (such as Alfieri's Filippo and Creon), she as prima donna in such roles as Mistress Herfort in Nota's *Atrabiliare*. When Frabbrichesi announced his plan to leave Naples for touring, they decided to remain behind, forming a new company which included Giovane Visetti (1780-1840), another actor from Fabbrichesi's troupe, and Giovan Prepiani (1808-1851), a tragic actor from Venice. Their first engagement was in Rome, where they followed Vestri at the Teatro Valle before they were invited back to become the official royal company in Naples. There they remained throughout the 1830s, becoming one of Italy's best-known companies.

The remainder of Fabbrichesi's company toured through northern Italy until his death in Verona in 1827. Its members then dispersed, but several of the best of them, headed by Vestri, found their way to the Compagnia Reale Sarda in Turin, which would hold a position of preeminence during the next generation similar to that held by Fabbrichesi in the early years of the Restoration.

Milan and the Romantics

Milan, Stendhal observed, still preserved after 1815 some remnants of its rapid cultural expansion at the opening of the century:

> Fourteen years under the rule of an inspired despot had made Milan, a city once renowned for nothing but over-eating, into the intellectual capital of Italy; and in 1817 it could still number among its citizens some four or five hundred individuals—the remnants of that army of administrators which Napoleon had recruited from every corner of Italy, from Bologna to Novara and from La Pontebba to Ancona, to hold high office in his kingdom of Italy—who stood head and shoulders above the general run of their contemporaries. These sometime civil servants, who remained in Milan, partly through fear of persecution elsewhere, but partly in answer to their own preference for the life of a capital city, were in no wise disposed to acknowledge the superior critical acumen of the Neapolitans in any field whatsoever.(6)

The major cultural bastion of these defenders of Milan's hegemony was of course La Scala. "All society in Milan," Bryon reported, "is carried on at the opera."(7) The Austrian occupation brought a stronger German influence to the theatre, most notably with the works of Mozart, but Cimarosa and Mayr were the dominant composers. French works were forbidden entirely and all works were rigorously censored. Stendhal, delighted by the music of Italian opera and disgusted by the libretti, asked a friend in Milan the reason, and was told "In Italy all thought is dangerous, and writing the epitome of indiscretion."(8) Of course many writers adjusted their convictions willingly enough to suit the new regime, most obviously Monti, the notorious political weathercock, whose cantata *Il ritorno di Astrea* was offered at La Scala to welcome the Austrian Emperor Francis I in 1816. All of Monti's income and privileges had of course been cancelled by the new order and he doubtless hoped to resume the role of Milan's leading poet with Austrian backing. His latest political reversal followed too many others, however. It gained him no favor with the Austrians and contributed significantly to his unpopularity with his countrymen. He then turned from public display to linguistic and literary studies, selecting another losing cause by attempting to defend classicism against the coming generation of romantics. He was still engaged in this unhappy struggle when he died in Milan in 1828.

During the decade after 1812, the area of real distinction at La Scala was the dance. Milan had long been particularly influential in this art, probably in large part due to its close ties with France, since ballet made little headway against the far more popular opera in southern Italy. Noverre had established his *ballets d'action* in Milan between 1771 and 1775, and a series of ballet masters had followed him, with moderate success, culminating in the triumphs of Salvatore Viganò, beginning in 1812. Viganò (1769-1821) brought the dance to new significance. He possessed a private fortune and was therefore not restricted as his predecessors had been by the incessant novelty demanded by the box-holders at La Scala. His interest in making the dance emotionally expressive led to placing new emphasis on mime as well as on the interplay of dancers. This required far more extensive rehearsal than dance had traditionally utilized. "He will stand on the stage at La Scala," reported Stendhal, "surrounded by eighty dancers, with a band of ten musicians in the orchestra-pit at his feet, there to spend a whole morning composing and implacably rehearsing, over and over again, ten bars of choreography which seem to him to fall short of final perfection."(9)   The results were dazzling. During Viganò's regime, from 1812 until 1821, Milan and St. Petersburg were the unchallenged leaders of the ballet world, with productions far beyond anything available in France or England.

Rossini, discovered by the theatres in Venice and nurtured in Naples and Rome, naturally encountered some resistance from the audiences of La Scala, who felt their standards were higher and more exacting. *La pietra del paragone* had received a most enthusiastic welcome at La Scala in 1812, but two subsequent offerings there were judged by the Milanese boring, sluggish and repetitive. Rossini therefore lavished extra care on *La gazza ladra* in 1817, knowing that his Milan audiences were difficult to please. His efforts were amply rewarded. The opera was constantly interrupted by enthusiastic "bravos" and "vivas," and the dazzled and exhausted composer was called forth for innumerable bows. Only the pro-German press, such as the Leipzig *Allgemeine musikalische Zeitung*, found fault with the work. The Italian papers and the Milan public hailed Rossini as the new master in the glorious tradition of Cimarosa and Paisiello.(10) For the next decade he was the composer most represented at La Scala.

The designer for *La gazza ladra,* and for most of the major operas and ballets at La Scala during this period, was Alessandro Sanquirico (1777-1849), chief designer from 1817 to 1832. He was trained in the neoclassic tradition and kept the most powerful features of that tradition, a profound sense of architectural space and the power of light, as he adjusted his art to the developing romantic spirit of the time. He continued to utilize the diagonal perspectives of the Bibienas and internal framing devices like modified prosceniums but he departed from his predecessors to seek more evocative blendings of natural and architectural elements and a more striking and powerful use of color. The ballets of Viganò, with distinctly romantic elements, provided him with excellent subjects for this development, as did the coming of romantic opera to La Scala. Rossini began clearly to turn in this direction with *La donna del lago*, premiered at San Carlo in 1819 and presented at La Scala in 1821. The same year Saverio Mercadante (1795-1870), whose works provided a sort of bridge between Rossini and Verdi, was first represented at La Scala with *Elisa e Claudio*. Mercadante, interested in increasing the emotional depth of his characters, turned to libretti drawn from those playwrights most dear to the Italian romantics — to Shakespeare (*Amleto*, premiered at La Scala in 1822), to Schiller (*I briganti*, premiered in Paris in 1835), and to Hugo (*Il giuramento*, premiered at La Scala in 1836). In 1822 La Scala offered its first work by the great French romantic composer, Meyerbeer.

During the early 1820s opera libretti began to be drawn from romantic texts. With Vincenzo Bellini (1801-1835) the spirit of romanticism entered the music itself. Bellini's first two works were offered in Naples, with such success that he attracted the attention of the ever-alert impresario Barbaja, now back to La Scala after five years at the San Carlo and another five at the Teater an der Wien in Vienna. Invited by Barbaja to create a work for Milan, Bellini sought out the most highly regarded librettist of the period, Felice Romani (1788-1865), and with him created the popular *Il pirata* (1827). Romani, an avid reader of Metastasio in his early years, and a friend of Monti in Milan, began his career strongly under the influence of these poets. His first important libretti were written for Mayr, *La rosa bianca e la rosa rossa* and *Medea in Corinto* (both 1813), and he contributed the text to Rossini's ill-fated *Turco in Italia* at La Scala in 1814. Many of his early libretti were based on French sources, and he was not surprisingly the adapter of the first Meyerbeer operas offered in Italy. In 1822 Donizetti collaborated with him for the first time in *Chiara e Serafina*. The great years of both Donizetti and Bellini lay just ahead and Romani would share in most of their triumphs. He attempted to remain neutral in the great struggle between classicists and romantics which divided the Italian literary world, claiming that he took beauty wherever he found it. Nevertheless he provided the libretti for most of the great romantic operas of the 1830s and drew his inspiration from the standard sources of romanticism—Shakespeare and Scott, Hugo and Byron, Soumet and Chateaubriand.

For these works Sanquirico, similarly basing a romantic creation on classic foundations, provided the designs. He was widely accepted as the outstanding designer in Italy in a period when Italian design was still generally considered superior even to the work of the great French romantic designers. An article in the *Revue de Théâtre* for 1837 reported that the Italians scorned the cardboard effects, the cluttered stage and the often ludicrous mechanical contrivances of the French:

> Their architecture is noble, *true* and historical, their colors exact and natural, their tones lively and the aspect of the places represented has always the appropriate character, unlike the work of our own painters, who transport us to the four corners of the world, but always keep the sky of Paris.(11)

Even the great French designer Ciceri was faulted on this score compared with Sanquirico. *La Muette de Portici*, much praised in Paris, especially for the Vesuvius effect in its final act, was dismissed with contempt by the *Revue*:

> The decorations of *La Muette* threw young ladies, children and many journalists into ecstasy; the verdure and the vegetation of the environs of Paris clustered around the foot of a tiny little Vesuvius placed twen-

ty-five feet from the spectators, they found sublime. This masterpiece cost the modest sum of one hundred forty thousand francs, including travelling expenses of V. Ciceri, who was talented enough to study and familiarize himself with Vesuvius by going no farther than Bologna.

In contrast to this "innocent and prosaic mountain in the suburbs of Paris," the article cited Sanquirico's design for an 1825 production at La Scala of *L'ultimo giorno di Pompei*, by Giovanni Pacini (1796-1867), a friend and follower of Rossini: "Sanquirico, a man of genius, represented Vesuvius with a frightful truth and a grandeur unthinkable in France. Ingenious machinery simulated naturally the flow of the lava and the explosions of the crater, and all combined to make this scene sublime."(12)

No other Italian designer of this period achieved the international reputation of Sanquirico, but he was by no means unique in such achievements. A designer of equal reputation within Italy was Francesco Bagnara (1784-1866), who was perhaps even more influential in establishing the romantic style. He designed at La Fenice for almost twenty-five years, beginning in 1812, but he was a frequent guest designer at a host of other theatres throughout northern Italy as well. Like Sanquirico he combined an architect's eye with a painter's sense of color, and was much praised both for his skill at realistic detail and for the enchanting, almost magical quality of his spectacle.

The "truth" of Italian design, often praised by French critics, was considerably aided by the Italian practice (unlike that of the French) of creating a new decor not only for every opera but every scene, an obvious aid to appropriateness. Stendhal noted in wonder: "No setting is ever used for two distinct spectacles; if the opera or ballet should prove a failure, the set, which may have been magnificent, is nevertheless ruthlessly painted out on the following day, even if it has been only seen at a single performance; for the same flats are used over and over again for new scenes."(13)

During the years between 1815 and 1830 the spirit of romanticism entered the spoken theatre as well, and despite the suspicion and occasional strong resistance of the Austrian authorities, the city of Milan played a central role in the development and diffusion of the new movement. Romanticism as a major literary force may be said to have begun in Italy in 1816. In January of that year Mme de Staël published an article in the recently founded *Biblioteca Italiana*, "On the Method and Value of Translations," in which she urged Italian writers to study foreign models as a means of freeing themselves from pedantic traditionalism. Since the *Biblioteca Italiana* was in general a reactionary journal, supported by the new Austrian rulers of Milan, the publication of this article was a bit surprising, but it was not at all surprising that the de Staël piece was immediately followed in the journal by a series of rebuttals from disgruntled neoclassicists. Other Italian critics, however, arose in Mme de Staël's defense with a series of pamphlets published in Milan before the end of the year. The most influential of these manifestos of Italian romanticism was the *Lettera semiseria di Crisòstomo* by Giovanni Berchet (1783-1851).

In his *Lettera* Berchet distinguished between the "poetry of the dead," which imitated classic models in form and subject, and the "poetry of the living," which was drawn directly from the life and culture of the artist, from accessible contemporary sources, from the experience of the common man. Not surprisingly, Berchet cited the ballad as a particularly successful and effective "living" artistic form. This emphasis, together with a strong interest in national independence and unity found in most Italian romantics and shared with the majority of the fellow citizens, gave the Italian romantic poet a rather different image than that of his English, French, or German counterparts. Elsewhere the romantic poet tended to be seen and to see himself as a rather isolated figure in revolt not only against a dead tradition but against his contemporary society. The Italian romantics saw themselves and were seen as the outstanding spokesmen for the highest common ideals in national life and politics.

The most significant voice of the new movement was the journal *Il Conciliatore*, founded in 1818. Its secretary was Silvio Pellico (1789-1854) who had achieved wide fame with his Alfierian tragedy *Francesca da Rimini* (1815). The passionate intensity of its language and its stirring patriotic passages made this play a major precursor of Italian romanticism and guaranteed Pellico a place of honor in the new movement. In *Il Conciliatore* he championed the study of foreign poets in the manner of Mme de Staël and argued for a theatre of reality in harmony with the times and free from the sterile conventions of neoclassic mythology. The journal urged no specific program, but its orientation was for the Austrian authorities suspicious if not actually threatening. In its pages Niccolini suggested the new movement "makes a principle of literary liberalism" and Pecchio defined "romantic" as the quality of being "Italian, independent, and modern."(14) The terms "progress," "patriotism," and "liberty" were sprinkled through its articles, whether they dealt with agriculture or Portuguese literature. By the time the sixth issue was out, the journal and its creators were being regularly and carefully watched by the authorities. Censorship became more and more severe and after thirteen months *Il Conciliatore* was forced to cease publication entirely.

The uprising in favor of a constitutional government in Naples in 1820, followed by another in Piedmont the following year, strengthened the Austrians in their determination to stamp out any possible constitutional sympathy in Milan. Pellico, suspected of ties with the underground Carboniera, was arrested, along with dozens of others, and when he could not be forced to reveal the names of his associates, was sent to the prison of Spielberg castle, where he was held until 1830. His book on this experience, *Le mie prigioni*, stirred sympathy for the Italian cause throughout the world. One actor from the Belloni company, Antonio Cavona, was arrested at the same time as Pellico. The rest of the company was spared, but after 1820 they found the cultural and intellectual life of Milan steadily declining under the new strictures. Their role as the city's only permanent company after Fabbrichesi's departure had been a profitable one, but it remained so no longer, and in 1823 they also left the suffering city.

"Alas," says Stendhal, speaking of the ballets of Viganò and the premiere of Rossini's *La gazza ladra* in Milan, "this glorious epoch was soon to crumble into dust, to disintegrate, around 1820, in a welter of arrests and *carbonarism*."(15) Indeed, many Milanese followed Pellico into prison during these years, and many more were driven into exile. The young romantic movement, at least in Milan, rapidly faded away. Yet the seeds had been planted, and the following years saw the steady spread of romantic ideas elsewhere, despite the continued opposition of conservative artists, critics and censors, and the eventual triumph of the *Conciliatore* ideals both in literature and in politics.

The leading Italian writer of the post-Napoleonic years, Alessandro Manzoni (1785-1873), called himself a classicist, but championed and carried out many of the ideals of Italian romanticism. In Milan at the opening of the century he was for several years a close friend of Foscolo and a follower of Monti. By 1816 he had moved to the position held by Berchet and other early romantics, ridiculing Monti's dependence on classic themes and championing subjects drawn from common life. This winter he began his first major romantic work, a verse tragedy called *Il conte di Carmagnola*, and on March 25 he wrote to Claude Fauriel, his close friend in Paris, that the drama would represent "Something new in Italy."

> The action begins with the declaration of war on the Duke of Milan by the Venetians, and ends with the death of Carmagnola.... It covers a period of six years; this will be a strong blow to the rule of the unity of time, but you are not a man to be shocked by that.
>
> After having read Shakespeare thoroughly and some of the things

recently written about the theatre, and after considering them, my ideas about certain reputations have changed. I do not dare say more, since all I want to do is to compose a tragedy, and nothing would be so ridiculous as to criticize those who have already done so and who pass for masters in the art. But how much pain has often been taken to produce bad work! to avoid those great and beautiful things which present themselves naturally and whose only drawback is that they do not conform to the narrow and artificial system of the author! How much effort to make men speak neither as they speak ordinarily nor as they might speak, to set aside both poetry and prose and to substitute a rhetorical language which is the coldest and the least adapted to produce any sympathetic reaction!(16)

Manzoni's enthusiasm for Shakespeare was unbounded and often expressed (in such phrases as "marvelous genius," "grand and almost unique poet" and "the greatest of poets") and in this he seems quite in accord with romantic authors elsewhere. Still, romanticism did not bring with it a surge of Shakespearean criticism, translation, and productions in Italy as it did in Germany and France. There was instead a slow and gradual building of interest in the English poet, led by the major writers of the period but only affecting the theatre indirectly and after the full tide of the movement had passed. As early as 1769 Alessandro Verri published a halting verse translation of *Hamlet* which the great interpreter of Alfieri, Antonio Morrocchesi, offered in Florence in 1783. Hobbled by this inadequate translation and cast in an unfamiliar style, the experiment was a total failure and was not repeated.

At the same time Verri was making his translation, Giuseppe Baretti (1719-1789), a member of Samuel Johnson's circle and a major literary link between Italy and England in the eighteenth century, anticipated in his writings many of the concerns of the later romantics, particularly in respect to Shakespeare. As early as 1747, in his *Prefazioni alle tragedie di Pier Cornello*, Baretti attacked the unities. In the eighth issue (January 15, 1764) of his journal of literary criticism, *La Frusta Letteraria*, he took issue with the neoclassic Piedmontese critic Carlo Denina, suggesting that if Denina were not blinded by his "profound veneration for the theatrical dogma promulgated by the tremendous French tribunals," he might realize "that Shakespeare is a poet both in comedy and tragedy that in himself is more than equal to all the Corneilles, all the Racines, and all the Molières in Gaul." The French rules, he continued, were irrelevant beyond the channel and beyond the Alps. "Shakespeare, like Ariosto, is one of those transcendental poets whose genius soars beyond the reach of art."(17)

Baretti's fullest development of these ideas came in 1778 when in a *Discours sur Shakespeare et sur Monsieur de Voltaire* he responded to Voltaire's famous attack on the English poet. He accused Voltaire of misunderstanding Shakespeare because his grasp of English was inadequate, then went on to anticipate many of the pro-Shakespearean arguments of romanticism. The unities of time and place he dismissed as artificial, since the theatre required in any case a suspension of disbelief. Whatever pleased an audience should be allowed. Similarly, though Aristotle argued for unity of action, the experience of Shakespeare and Lope de Vega proved him wrong and Baretti argued that had Aristotle known them he would have written differently. Finally, Baretti reversed Voltaire's charge that Shakespeare's style was "unnatural" arguing that the French classic stage itself dealt in highly artificial situations, character arrangement and language.

Few of these arguments were quickly picked up by Baretti's contemporaries, although his admiration for Shakespeare was shared by Alfieri, Monti and Foscolo. The influence of French practice during the Napoleonic years prevented any serious development of Baretti's concerns. On the few occasions when Shakespearean works were offered, they had been thoroughly domesticated by filtration through French neoclassic adaptation. Thus the *Amleto* offered in Venice and subsequently in a number of Italian cities in 1793 and 1794 was translated by Francesco Gritti not from the English but from the French of Ducis and the *Giulietta e Romeo* of Giuseppe Ramirez published at Venice in 1797 and widely performed was taken from the adaptation by Mercier. One of the specific suggestions of Berchet's *Lettera semiseria* had been for Italian translations of Shakespeare but only after 1816 was the path open. Between 1819 and 1822 Michele Leoni translated the tragedies in an edition of fourteen volumes, though by then most of the first generation of Italian romantics had already discovered Shakespeare on their own, largely through the French translations of Le Tourneur, who at least avoided the neoclassic excesses of writers like Ducis.

These were the sources of Manzoni's acquaintance with the English dramatist and Manzoni, the dominant literary figure of the period, was also the most influential spokesman for Shakespeare and for the freer style of dramatic composition which he represented. *Il conte di Carmagnola* appeared in Milan in January of 1820 with a preface in which Manzoni, like Baretti, condemned the unities of time and place as based on a false authority, in Aristotle, and a false assumption, that the spectator is unaware of illusion in the theatre. He also defended the chorus as a lyric commentary on the action of the drama. Unhappily, *Il conte di Carmagnola* suggests Shakespeare in little save its historical subject and its disregard of the unities. The plot is weak and diffuse, the characters thin, and the most effective element probably the chorus ending the second act, a lyric rather than dramatic creation. Its passionate plea for Italian unity struck a responsive note in the public, and it was widely repeated (here translated by W.D. Howells):

> They are all of one land and one nation,
> One speech; and the foreigner names them
> All brothers, of one generation;
> In each visage their kindred is seen;
> This land is the mother that claims them,
> This land, that their life blood is steeping....

Clearly *Carmagnola* had little strength as a theatre piece; it was presented only once, in Florence in 1828, with no success; but it was attacked less on those grounds than for the lack of poetry in its dialogue. Manzoni probably expected the scorn of the conservative *Biblioteca Italiana*, but he received little more support from such authors as Foscolo and Pellico, who presumably should have been more sympathetic to his aims. Foscolo, now in London, joined the English critics who generally praised the lyric chorus in the second act, but found the rest of the work feeble and the challenge to the unities uninteresting. Pellico made no public comments, positive or negative, about the play, but to his brother Luigi he wrote:

> The hero is left too close to life. Poetry is a world more beautiful than reality; the inhabitants of that world should be a rung above us in love, in feeling, in political virtue, etc. But keep my opinion private, since I wish at all costs to do nothing which would undercut Manzoni's merits.(18)

Even so, Manzoni found a powerful and unexpected advocate in Goethe, who in *Über Kunst und Altertum* wrote at some length and with warm praise about *Carmagnola*. Goethe expressed strong sympathy with Manzoni's stated aims:

> The author states at the beginning of his preface his desire to free himself from all alien criteria, wherein we are in complete agreement with him, for a noble work of art, just as a healthy product of nature, should be judged by its own rules.(19)

In each act Goethe found matter to praise; he concluded by calling for a careful and thoughtful German translation. In another article the following year he defended the play again, refuting point by point a negative review in a London journal, the *Quarterly Review*. After taking the London critics to task for indulging in only negative criticism Goethe quoted his famous three questions for the constructive critic: "What has the author attempted to do? Was his goal reasonable and intelligent? And to what extent has he achieved this goal?" Manzoni thanked Goethe in a letter of January 23, 1821, saying that the German critic's support had encouraged him

> to proceed in these studies more happily, confirmed in the idea that to produce a work of art, the best method is to consider the subject one wishes to treat through a contemplation which is both lively and relaxed, taking no notice of conventional rules and of the wishes, ephemeral for the most part, of the majority of readers.(20)

Nevertheless, Manzoni ultimately proved far more effective in the theatre as a critic than as a playwright. *Adelchi*, his only other play, took another historical subject, this time from the period of Charlemagne. In its general character it was nearer to Shakespeare than *Carmagnola* had been, though in neither work did Manzoni mix tragedy and comedy, plebeians with aristocrats in the Shakespearian manner. Though the language departed from the rhetorical tradition of neoclassicism, the tone remained solemn and elevated throughout. *Adelchi's* stage history has been more extensive than *Carmagnola's*, with occasional revivals on into the present century, though it did not first reach the stage until 1843.

On the other hand, Manzoni's critical writings on the theatre, his prefaces and especially his *Lettre à M. Chavret sur l'unité de temps et de lieu dans la tragédie* (1823) were widely read and extremely influential in developing romantic theory (even though Manzoni in the *Lettre* calls himself "a good and loyal partisam of classicism"). The *Lettre* was written in response to an article in the Lycée Française deploring the modern tendency to break classical rules. Manzoni based his refutation on an allegiance to reality and historical truth. The unities, he argued, were less important than an accurate portrayal of past events, to a dramatic system that was also a "système historique." No poetry, he stated, could equal the close study of and reporting of the thoughts, passions, and conflicts shown by history. Intensive research such as had gone into his own two dramas should serve as the foundations of theatre rather than allegiance to arbitrary rules not of history but of artistic custom. Unlike most of the romantics, Manzoni denied love's potential as a leading motive for tragedy. Social, political and moral themes he felt were more suitable, especially those with clear parallels to the present; so *Adelchi* expresses the hopes of native Italians under foreign domination in the Dark Ages. The moral tone of Manzoni's argument distinguished him from most other writers on the subject of romanticism, but most of his specific ideas and general lines of argument were picked up by Victor Hugo and utilized in the Preface to *Cromwell* (1827), the major manifesto for the French romantic theatre.

Florence and Niccolini

As political and artistic freedom lessened over much of Italy around 1820, a happy exception was the state of Tuscany, where Duke Leopold II refused to be panicked into repressive measures. Not surprisingly, Florence, his capital, now became a haven for political exiles from all over Italy. In 1821 Pietro Vieusseux, a Swiss who had settled in Florence, founded a journal, *L'Antologia,* which carried on the goals of the suppressed *Il Conciliatore.* Giacomo Leopardi, then living in Florence, wrote, "When I think that a paper like this is made and published in Italy at this time, I feel that I'm dreaming." (21)

Manzoni was far less involved than many others in the events of 1821 in Milan, but his sympathies were with the constitutionalists (he composed a patriotic ode on their behalf, *Marzo 1821,* which did not appear at this time but was widely quoted during the subsequent revolt of 1848). The crushing of the rebellion left him shaken and despondent and he planned a vacation to the more relaxed region of Tuscany. There were literary as well as political motives for this journey. Manzoni was now engaged in the composition of his masterpiece, *I promessi sposi,* and confronting the problem which would occupy him for years, the search for a simple, direct, contemporary Italian language. Written Italian at that time, as enshrined in the *Dizionario della Crusca,* was a pompous, elevated mode of expression, full of bombast and circumlocutions, admirably suited for neoclassic tragedy but totally unfit for the representation of common speech. Italian comic writers, most notably Goldoni, had turned to one of the twenty or thirty local dialects, many of them almost unintelligible in other regions. To make matters worse, official and court languages were foreign: French at the Bourbon courts of Naples and Parma, Spanish in Milan until the late eighteenth century, then French and under the Austrians, German. In Manzoni's home the Milanese dialect was spoken, and he was delighted with Goldoni's supple Venetian, but he wished in *I promessi sposi* to find a medium for a broader public and gradually came to the conclusion that it should be basically Tuscan, with a flavoring of Milanese.

There were strong historical reasons for this choice, of course. Dante had begun a tradition of emphasis on Tuscan as the literary language of the Italian people, a tradition carried on by Tasso and Machiavelli. Still, Manzoni seems to have been attracted to Tuscan more for the richness and quality of the dialect than for any historical reasons. In a letter of December 10, 1822, to Claude Fauriel, Manzoni proposed that they meet in Tuscany, and hinted delicately (Milan censors were keen) at the political and linguistic advantages of that state:

> The doctors have advised my Henriette to spend some time in a more active air than we breathe here, to strengthen her eyesight which has become quite troublesome to her; and we thought of Tuscany which has the advantage of good air and joins with that so many others, particularly that of being one of the few countries in Europe where there is less passion in movement and at rest, less irritation and pain: an advantage especially precious for me, as I feel an inexpressible desire not only to experience but to observe tranquility. In thinking over all the reasons this project would be pleasant for us, it occurred to us that these reasons would also be valid for you—that distraction, new objects, a lovely country, etc., even that language which you know so well and which you love just a bit for what, at least, it may become, might make you consider this little excursion with interest.(22)

In fact, Fauriel was unable to come to Italy and Manzoni himself did not make the often postponed journey to Florence until 1827, shortly after the publication of *I promessi sposi*. His delight in hearing spoken Tuscan was unbounded and confirmed him in his selection of that dialect as the basis of his work. He began rewriting *I promessi sposi* (a project which continued for the rest of his life) with the aid, among others, of Florence's leading playwright, Giovan Battista Niccolini (1782-1786), who became the best known serious Italian dramatist of this period.

Niccolini, professor of history and mythology at the Accademia di Belle Arte of Florence, began his playwriting career as a strict neoclassicist. His first tragedy, *Polissena*, was offered, with great success, in Florence by the traveling Blanès-Pellandri company, as we have seen, in 1813. He followed this with a series of similar works, adhering closely to Greek models: *Ino e Temisto* (1814, presented in 1824), *I sette a Tebe* (1816), *Edipo nel bosco delle Eumenidi* (presented in 1823) and *Medea* (presented in 1825). Around 1815 Niccolini, like most of his contemporaries, began to develop an interest in romanticism. He looked into Shakespeare, Schiller, and Byron and began to work with non-classical subjects. His first such experiment was *Matilde* (1815), a reworking of the *Douglas* of John Home, Scottish precursor of romanticism, and although Niccolini carefully corrected Home's mild tampering with the unities and changed the setting from medieval Scotland to feudal Sicily, he retained at least some hint of romantic themes and language. In the same year Niccolini wrote *Nabucco*, which indicated much more clearly the direction his later plays would take. Nabucco, a thinly disguised portrait of the recently fallen Napoleon, is shown returning from an expedition to Scythia and opposed by an assembly of kings. The play is clearly an attack on political despotism, a subject to which Niccolini would frequently return, but one which he probably could not have treated anywhere in Italy at this time except in Florence.

In 1823 he wrote to a friend "Mythological subject matter has become antipoetic for our time,"(23) and confirmed this by the publication of *Antonio Foscarini*, a clear step closer to romanticism. The play mixed political repression with thwarted love in the Venetian Republic of 1450, and aroused considerable protest. The eulogies on liberty caused authorities in Milan and elsewhere to ban the play outright, and the dark picture of the Venetian government aroused particular protest in that city. Luigi Carrer (1801-1850), a popular author of ballads and sometime playwright in Venice, published several scenes of what was announced as a dramatic refutation of Niccolini, *L'ultimo colloquio di Antonio Foscarini* (1827). Nevertheless, Niccolini's play was presented very successfully at Florence's Teatro Cocomero in 1827.

Florence, the center of Italian theatre under the Medici, provided little competition for such cities as Naples and Venice during the following centuries. It possessed five public theatres at the beginning of the nineteenth century but none were of any particular significance. The Abbé Richard in 1769 remarked that Florence had "several theatres, which have nothing remarkable about them, either in their construction or their ornamentation,"(24) and Stendhal, thirty-seven years later, observed: "Poverty is the bedevilling feature of the Florentine opera: costumes, décor, singers — nothing is exempt; the atmosphere reminds me of some third-rate French provincial town. Ballets are unheard-of, save during the Carnival. All in all, Florence, set in a narrow valley amid a wilderness of bare mountains, offers little to justify its reputation."(25)

The Florence opera house which so appalled Stendhal after the glories of Naples and Milan was the Pergola, founded in 1652. There was also a secondary lyric theatre, the Pallacorda, opened in 1794; the city's other theatres offered both lyric and spoken works. One, the Teatro Goldoni, opened in 1817, the year of Stendhal's visit, with

Goldoni's *Il burbero beneficio*, interpreted by the touring Vestri-Venier company. The other two theatres, both small, had gained a certain brief fame near the end of the eighteenth century thanks to one of Florence's best-known actors, Antonio Morrocchesi (1768-1838). At the Teatro Borgognissanti the young Morrocchesi had selected for his first benefit, in 1791, Shakespeare's *Hamlet*, the first performance of a Shakespearean play in Italy. Seen in retrospect, this was an experiment of enormous significance for the Italian stage, but Morrocchesi's audience was indifferent and with good reason. The translation by Allessandro Verri was in plodding verse and taken not directly from the English dramatist but from Ducis, his French neoclassic adaptor. Not surprisingly, it was several decades before Shakespeare would again be attempted on the Italian stage.

Morrocchesi's contribution to the Teatro Santa Maria was more quickly recognized and rewarded. In 1793 and 1794 he offered Alfieri's *Saul, Oreste,* and *Virginia,* with enormous success, so great that he was called back to repeat certain scenes, as operatic stars did with popular arias. A critic of the romantic period called him "the first actor to penetrate to the core of Alfieri's recondite thought" and "the first to reveal the hidden beauty of Alfierian tragedy."(26) Alfieri himself attended the fifth performance and sent a copy of *Saul* to the actor along with an expression of his pleasure at the interpretation. In commemoration of these famous productions, the Santa Maria was rechristened the Teatro Alfieri in 1828. Morrocchesi retired from the stage in 1811 to become professor of declamation at the Florence Accademia di Belle Arti, a post he held until his death twenty-seven years later.

Florence's major theatre, aside from the Pergola, was the Cocomero, founded in 1650, and here the major premieres of Niccolini took place. Under the impresarios Mariano Somigli and Cosimo Cajani the Cocomero became for the first time one of Italy's leading theatres. Critical for this new success was the establishment in 1825 of a permanent state-subsidized company at the theatre, the Compagnia Nazionale Toscana. The troupe was essentially the traveling company of Antonio Rafstopulo (1780?-1830?), given a home theatre and augmented with important new actors. Rafstopulo achieved his first great success in the early years of the Restoration with popular historical spectacles requiring hundreds of extras and dozens of horses, cannon, military bands and so forth—Marchionni's *Chiara di Rosenberg* and *Enrico IV alla presa di Parigi,* Avelloni's *Carlo XII di Svezia,* requiring three evenings to perform, and such "classic" subjects as *La fondazione di Roma* and *Il ratto delle Sabine.* His repertoire also included plays of more literary merit, by Goldoni, Alfieri and later Nota and Giraud and these were emphasized after his arrival in Florence.

The leading actor to the troupe in 1825 was the young Ercole Gallina (1800?-1840?) and the following year the leading female roles were assumed by a newcomer, Maddalena Pelzet (1801-1854), who had begun her acting career in Florence between 1818 and 1822, then left to develop her skills with various touring companies. She was considered by Niccolini the best of his interpretors and the part of Teresa Contarini in *Antonio Foscarini* was created with her in mind.

Niccolini's *Giovanni da Procida*, presented at the Cocomero in 1830, was warmly received, but aroused even more misgivings in official circles than *Antonio Foscarini*. The main plot deals with the unwittingly incestuous love of a brother and sister, but the historical subplot, the Sicilian Vespers, by raising the question of foreign occupation and oppression, naturally caused the most difficulty. Probably the best-known line in the play, indeed in all of Niccolini's drama, is "Let the French recross the Alps and they shall return as brothers." At the tumultuous first performance in Milan the French minister is said to have expressed his displeasure to his Austrian colleague, only to receive the reply: "Don't be upset. The envelope is addressed to you, but the contents are for me."(27) The story is probably apocryphal, but the French and Austrian governments did join in calling for and obtaining the suppression of the play. Nevertheless it continued to circulate clandestinely and contribute to the growing spirit of Italian nationalism.

In the debate between classicists and romantics Niccolini took a middle ground, clearly influenced by his patriotic interests. His *Della imitazione nell'arte drammatica* (1828) praised Shakespeare warmly but cautioned that his rhetoric was not adapted to the Italian mode of expression and the imitation of any foreign writers was dangerous for the development of native expression. In 1827 he remarked to Maddalena Pelzet, "I believe that the present century is seeking a tragic form different from that of the English or the French, but who shall be fortunate enough to find it and to conquer the habits of the public, who have seen nothing of this but the works of Alfieri?"(28)

Lodovico Sforza, published in 1834, nevertheless was strongly romantic both in plot and atmosphere. Particular emphasis was laid upon the Milanese tyrant's invitation to Charles VIII which brought the beginning of foreign domination to Italy. In the character of Isabella, Niccolini promised Pelzet "a rival to Teresa"(29) but his hopes for presentation were thwarted by events. In 1831 and 1832 a new series of constitutionalist uprisings occurred in Italy, inspired by the July uprisings of 1830 in Paris. The rulers of Parma and Modena fled and large portions of the Papal States came under the control of the revolutionaries. Once again Austrian troops put down the rebellion and reasserted the power of reaction. The government in Tuscany, ringed by the states in upheaval, was so frightened by these events that repression of the sort common in the rest of Italy was now instituted in Florence as well. Under Austrian pressure, *L'Antologia* was suppressed and political censorship became far more rigid. Under these circumstances, public performance of a play like *Lodovico Sforza* was unthinkable and Niccolini was forced to excise much of it even to get it published.

After this check, Niccolini wrote no further patriotic works for public performances. His next two plays, strongly influenced by contemporary English romantic writing, contained no political sentiments whatever. *Beatrice Cenci*, drawn from Shelley, was not presented, but *Rosmunda d'Inghilterra*, a simple love story, was offered to enthusiastic applause in 1838. The warm reception accorded this mediocre work could well have been in tribute to the author's corpus, which most of his public knew but were prevented from seeing. Niccolini's last two plays, *Filippo Strozzi* and *Arnaldo da Brescia*, returned to his earlier manner and themes but were written to be read rather than to be staged. *Arnoldo da Brescia* is the fullest development of Niccolini's political concerns as well as his richest lyric drama, dealing with a twelfth-century revolutionary who denies the temporal power of the church, represented by the English Pope Hadrian IV, and foreign domination, represented by the Emperor Frederich Barbarossa. The play could not even be printed in Italy—it appeared in Marseilles in 1843—but it was read in secret from one end of Italy to the other and its fiery patriotic passages were everywhere committed to memory by the workers for Italian freedom and unification. Niccolini was well aware of the effect of his work. "If I have not written a great tragedy," he remarked, "I believe I have nevertheless performed a courageous act."(30) As polemicist for the new Italy Niccolini was indeed enormously successful, as a lyric poet somewhat less so. As a creator of works theatrically effective in their own right, he failed almost completely. This is, unhappily, the story of serious drama in general during this period. Pindemonte, who should have known as well as anyone, wrote in his *Discorso sul teatro italiano* in 1827: "Among the other miseries of our Italy is that it has no theatre worthy of the name."(31)

Turin and the Compagnia Reale Sarda

Turin, like Florence, had enjoyed a period of theatrical brilliance in the late Renaissance, but subsequently faded to relative obscurity. The happy accident of being the home city of the Alfieri family resulted in the city's possessing, as we have seen, one of Italy's most attractive theatres, where were given several premieres of that leading tragedian of the late eighteenth century. Aside from this, however, Turin offered little to compete with the major theatre centers. It had only three theatres (the Regio for opera, the Carignano for opera and spoken drama, and the little Angennes for comic opera), few premieres and no permanent company. Still, the establishment of the new kingdom of Piedmont-Sardinia provided the basis for the development of a theatre in Turin which would become the most honored in Italy.

In 1820 King Vittorio Emmanuele I issued a patent for the formation of a permanent company in his capital, to be called the Compagnia Reale Sarda. Vittorio Emmanuele, a conservative and xenophobic monarch, was a rather unlikely patron for such a venture. According to all accounts, he was as little interested in theatre as he was in the political questions of liberty and Italian unification. Thus it is probable that the major impetus for the company actually came from his Queen, the intelligent and vivacious Maria Teresa of Austria, who sought to bring to the little Sardinian court the trappings and brilliance of an imperial capital.

For the leader of the proposed new royal company a local director, Gaetano Bazzi (1771-1843) was selected. Though a native of Turin, Bazzi had established a strong reputation in other parts of Italy as well. He was a leading comic actor in the popular Belloni company when that troupe was enjoying the talents of Carlotta Marchionni and gaining brilliant successes with the comedies of Giovanni Giraud, such as *L'ajo nell'imbarazzo* and *La cialiera indispettita*. With this company at Rome's Teatro Valle, Bazzi created some of Giraud's most popular characters. By 1820 Bazzi was leader of his own company and back in his native Turin, where he was offered the directorship of the new venture. He was given encouragement and urged to seek out the best actors in Italy. In 1820 the clear choices were Marchionni, Vestri and De Marini, but although two of the three were eventually won for the Reale Sarda, none was available at this time. Marchionni, whom Bazzi naturally knew best, was still under contract to the Belloni company, now in Milan. Vestri was involved in building what he hoped would be his own theatre empire in Rome and De Marini was in Naples with Fabbrichesi, in whose company he remained until its dissolution in 1827.

Though he could not obtain any of these leading stars, Bazzi assembled a company of fifteen men and eleven women which was still among the best in Italy. The only two players who came from his own earlier company were Giovan Borghi (d. 1870), who played comic lovers and elegant young men, and Bazzi's wife Anna Maria, who played young lovers and was considered by some a worthy rival to the beloved Pellandri. Her age was beginning to tell, however, and two years later she moved to the roles of noble mothers. Younger roles were then assumed by Vincenza Righetti, who had been previously associated with the Blanès troupe and earlier still with Fabbrichesi. Her husband Domenico (1786-1859) became one of Bazzi's leading actors. Another veteran of the Fabbrichesi troupe was the popular Giovanni Boccomini (1784-1836), who in the roles of noble fathers was widely considered the equal of the great De Marini and lauded for the majesty of his person and the richness of his delivery. Boccomini apparently viewed performing in the same company with De Marini a disadvantage and seemed delighted by the alternative Bazzi offered. After 1829, when he left the Reale Sarda, he became one of the leading interpreters in the flood of Scribe translations then inundating the Italian stage.

Fortunately for Bazzi, the leader of one of Italy's most respected companies, Gaetano Perotti, died in Milan in 1820 and his actors were thus available just as Bazzi was assembling his own new troupe. Perotti's leading actress, his wife Assunta, retired for a time from the stage, but the other key members of the company came to form the basis of the Reale Sarda. In this way Bazzi gained a second leading man, Luigi Romagnoli (1794-1855) to supplement Righetti; an actress brilliant in the playing of comic servants, Rosa Romagnoli (1806-1886); a popular character actor, Francesco Miutti (1780-1850); and a witty and elegant portrayer of young lovers as well as one of the period's most popular comic authors, Francesco Augusto Bon (1788-1858).

The new company settled at the Teatro Carignano, the location of some of the first Alfieri presentations, but more recently the home of comic opera, especially the French school of Favart and Grétry. Now, of course, it returned to the spoken drama, for which it was given exclusive rights in the city. Like theatres throughout Italy, the Carignano was closed during Lent, a period traditionally used for the preparation of the next season. After performing from Easter until summer, the company took another recess, then opened in Genoa where they performed until Christmas. Their home in Genoa was the Teatro San Agostino, a large, but not particularly attractive house which offered both opera and spoken drama. According to the provisions of the Treaty of Vienna, Genoa was now a part of the kingdom of Piedmont-Sardinia. Although the Genoese were not greatly pleased by this arrangement the association lasted and may thus be viewed as Piedomont's first step in the process of gathering to itself all the states of the peninsula to fulfill at last the dream of an Italian nation. Leaving Genoa at Christmas, the company returned to Turin, and during the Carnival season performed at the little wooden Teatro d'Angennes, erected in 1786 as a marionette theatre.

The Reale Sarda was scheduled to begin its performances at Easter of 1821, but the monarch who had established it was by then no longer in power. The betrayal of the Neapolitan revolution by its king under Austrian pressure sparked uprisings throughout Piedmont, beginning on March 10. A constitution on the Spanish model was demanded and because the example of Naples had shown that this would prove intolerable to Austria, immediate war on that state was called for. Vittorio Emmanuele, caught between the demands of his subjects and those of the Allied sovereigns, abdicated in favor of his brother Carlo Felice, then in Modena, appointing Prince Carlo Alberto regent. In the absence of the new king, Carlo Alberto granted the demanded constitution, which was promptly repudiated by Carlo Felice. Carlo Alberto was finally forced into exile, the flames of dissent again stamped out by Austrian troops and a military tribunal set up to find and condemn insurgents. It closed the universities and condemned more than five hundred persons before Carlo Felice, still in Modena, granted a general amnesty.

It was during the dark period of the military tribunal that the newly established Compagnia Reale Sarda began its career. The time was anything but propitious and yet the theatre prospered, perhaps largely because its generally light fare offered an escape from the oppressive political climate. The repertoire included scatterings of French and German plays, from Molière, Voltaire, Racine, Destouches, Picard, Kotzebue and Iffland, but the bulk of the repertoire was Italian and the author most represented was Goldoni. Alfieri's *Saul, Agamemnone* and *Oreste* were offered, and Maffei's *Merope,* but more recent authors were as a rule too politically engaged for presentation in Turin at this time. Nothing was offered from Foscolo, Niccolini, Monti or Manzoni for a number of years, though Pellico's earlier *Francesca da Rimini* was revived in 1826. Cesare Della Valle, and the success of his wife and the wise Doctor Lorenzo in thwarting who had begun his career as an author of neoclassic tragedies for Fabbrichesi in Naples, was now, in the spirit of the times, turning to more romantic subjects, but without distinct political overtones. He provided the Reale Sarda with several works, most notably *Giulietta e Romeo* in 1826. A native Piedmontese author of serious drama appeared in Carlo Marenco (1800-1846), whose *Buondelmonte e gli amidei* was premiered by the Reale Sarda in 1827.

Comedy was much more fully developed at this time and if no masterpieces were produced, the warm and witty studies of contemporary life by such authors as Nota, Giraud and Bon drew applause throughout Italy and in translation in France, Germany, even far-off Russia. The Roman dramatist Giraud was represented at the Sarda during their first season by his most popular play, *L'ajo nell'imbarazzo*, and two other works; Avelloni, by three works; and from the older generation of comic writers, Sografi, by two Goldonian comedies, and Federici, by two comedies of sentiment. The leading contemporary playwright was Alberto Nota, eight of whose comedies were given during the Sarda's first season, though none for the first time. Several, such as *L'atrabiliare* (1812) and *L'ammalato per immagionazione* (1813), had been first offered by Fabbrichesi's company, which in a sense the new company replaced.

Three comedies were given by Francesco Augusto Bon (1788-1858), who was also a member of the company. Christened Francesco Antonio Maria, he took the name Augusto at the suggestion of Maria Luisa of Parma, to whom he dedicated the first edition of his works. She referred to him thereafter as "Signor Augusto Bon," explaining that for one of such genius the only satisfactory name was that of the caesar Augustus. He left the Reale Sarda after a single season to join a touring company and two years later established a troupe of his own. His comedies nevertheless continued to be regularly offered by the Reale Sarda and many, led by the popular *Niente di male* (1830), were performed in northern Italy through the rest of the century. His best works were the Ludro trilogy, in the manner of Goldoni: *Ludro e la sua gran giornata* (1832), *Il matrimonio di Ludro* (1837), and *La vecchiaia di Ludro* (1837), which have been successfully revived in the twentieth century.

When Bon left, his roles were assumed by Borghi and in the same year Francesco Barlaffa joined the troupe as the company's first portrayer of tyrants. The major event of 1822 was the premiere of Nota's *Allessina ossia Constanza rara*, a kind of forbidden fruit, since it passed the censor only with the greatest difficulty (not because of any specific political references, but simply because it was suspected of them since its heroine was a Russian). Vincenza Righetti achieved her greatest success in the leading role. It was one of her last, for she was forced into a secondary position the following year when Bazzi at last succeeded in obtaining the great Carlotta Marchionni. Henceforth Marchionni was almost inevitably associated with the comedies of Nota as well as with the leading tragic roles in the repertoire. Fourteen of the remaining sixteen comedies created by the "Piedmont Terence" were given their premieres by Marchionni and the Sarda company. Of the thirty-six works the Sarda added to its repertoire during her first year, seventeen were selected to display Marchionni's talents. Five of these were tragedies: Pindemonte's *Ginevra di Scozia* and Alfieri's *Ottavia, Antigone, Rosmunda* and *Mirra*. The latter was her greatest serious role and many echoed the sentiments of Mme de Staël, who rose pale with emotion on first seeing it to comment "She possesses the genius of her art."(32)

The accession of Marchionni solidified the Reale Sarda's position as Italy's leading company. Several members were lost in 1824, most importantly the character actor Boccomini, who joined Fabbrichesi, but the gains far outweighed the losses. Boccomini was at once replaced by the popular Giovanni Ghirlanda (1790-1850) and since Boccomini himself returned the following year the theatre was able to alternate leading actors in the various character roles so important to the tragedies and sentimental works of the period. Certain plays allowed them to appear together, which audiences considered a particular treat—Della Valle's *Giulietta e Romeo*, in which they played old Capulet and Friar Lorenzo; Alfieri's *Polinice*, in which they were Eteocle and Creonte; and especially Alfieri's *Filippo*, telling the same story as Schiller's *Don Carlos* but with classic regularity, in which they appeared as Filippo and Gomez.

During the first five years of its career, the Reale Sarda, building a repertoire, began with sixty-nine Italian plays and added an average of over thirty native plays each year. By 1826 the repertoire had begun to catch up with the available supply, so that only seventeen Italian plays were added that season and an average of only twelve per season for the next five years. Among the 1827 works were some of the theatre's most popular, however: a revival of Pellico's *Francesca da Rimini* and premieres of two of Nota's most beloved works, *La fiera* and *La novella sposa*. The former was an attempt to rejuvenate classic comedy and there are some echoes of Beaumarchais in the campaign of the Count di Valdimora to seduce a country girl him. But here and even more in *La novella sposa* the dominant tone is sentimentality—so that the effect is far closer to Destouches than to Beaumarchais. This emotionality was by no means seen as a disadvantage by Nota's audiences; on the contrary he was much praised for his insights into the human heart.

A new dramatist presented this season was Carlo Marenco, a Turin lawyer who would become one of the favorite serious playwrights of his generation. His first produced work, *Buondelmonte e gli amidei*, followed rigid classical practice. The entire action was set in Florence and transpired within twenty-four hours, though it anticipated at least one aspect of later romantic historical drama in its multiplicity of brief scenes, so many that contemporary critic Carlo Albertini dismissed it as a "lanterna magica."(33) The general public, however, enjoyed the spectacle and was much moved by the sentimental story of thwarted love. Marenco shrewdly retained these features in his subsequent works. He saw himself as occupying middle ground between the patriotic classicism of Niccolini and the romanticism of Manzoni (an interesting distinction, since each of these authors also saw themselves as occupying a middle ground). In the preface to his *Tragedie* (published in Turin in 1837-44), Marenco announced that his intention had been "to conciliate the antique and modern modes, both to protect myself from the excesses of the two opposing schools and to find that unique point of greatest power."(34) His *Pia dei Tolomei* (1836) would become a standard revival piece for the great Italian actresses of the second half of the century.

Between 1827 and 1829 the Reale Sarda underwent several major changes in its company. The young leading man, Borghi, left and was replaced by Giovanni Ventura (1800-1869), who gained a considerable reputation in the interpretation of Alfierian tragedy and romantic drama. Though small of stature, he had a rich, well-controlled voice, and effectively blended emotion with an intelligent study of character. By his contemporaries he was considered "romantic" (as opposed to the "classic" style represented by Blanès or Colomberti), but reports of his acting suggest little of the passionate abandon of a Kean or a Lemaître. On the contrary, the critic Bonazzi called him "the most intelligent and correct of the actors of his generation."(35) In any case, he suited well the taste of the period and gained a wide and enthusiastic following. Just as the Sarda had found it useful to have both Boccomini and Ghirlanda in the same sort of roles, those of young lovers were now shared between Ventura and another newcomer, Camillo Ferri (1810-1870). Ferri was particularly admired for his melodic voice, which, joined to that of Marchionni in Pellico's *Francesca da Rimini*, created one of the Sarda's most memorable offerings.

When Brazzi founded the Real Sarda in 1820 he dreamed of eventually attracting to it the three great actors of the period — Marchionni, Vestri and De Marini. He succeeded, as we have seen, in gaining Marchionni in 1823 and in 1829 came a step nearer his dream by engaging Luigi Vestri. Now, ten years after Stendhal had judged him the greatest actor in Italy, Vestri was more powerful and popular then ever. Even Francesco Righetti (1770-1828), the character actor whose roles Vestri assumed at the Sarda, praised his potential rival without qualification: "No Italian actor aside from him can arouse so much delight in amusing roles and so captivate the public's heart."(36)

Like most great comic actors, Vestri had the ability to assume totally different characters by adjusting his gait, his posture, his expression and his voice without the external aids of makeup or wigs and without losing a natural tone which commanded belief in even the most extreme characterizations. His most ridiculous characters still had a human emotional base, a particularly engaging feature in a period where comedy was rarely untouched by sentimentality. Under his leadership and that of Marchionni, the Reale Sarda now entered into its greatest decade.

Parma and Paris

Stendhal, writing of the Italian opera during the Restoration, reported that there were only two theatres in Italy of any real importance, only two which conferred real status on singers or composers—La Scala and San Carlo. Venice's Fenice he considered next in importance, though "today it is slowly sinking into degradation, together with the rest of Venice."(37) The Roman public were immensely vain about their critical prestige, but their theatres, ugly, cramped and uncomfortable, presented work of "dire and unrelieved poverty." The theatre at Turin was held in higher regard, though Stendhal found its formality and deference to royalty rather oppressive. Every town in Italy by this time had its theatre as a matter of municipal pride and likewise most commissioned several new operas each year, an enormous stimulus for Italian composers. Most of the larger theatres were subsidized to some extent by the local sovereign, though by the 1820s this was done more out of respect for tradition than from regard for the art, and Stendhal felt that even this motivation was disappearing:

> Nowadays, when such doubtful monarchs are almost permanently occupied, along with an army of priests and a few remaining nobles, in herding the vast majority of their subjects in directions which seem curiously unfashionable, they live, not in the love of their peoples, but in abject fear of them; and music is the last thing on which they are ready to spend money—rather a nice public hanging any day, than a new opera!(38)

The spoken theatre was as usual in an even more precarious situation than the more fully developed and supported opera. Still, traveling troupes brought their offerings to every city in Italy, and the larger capitals, such as Naples and Turin, generally enjoyed permanent, state-supported companies during this period. Even some of the smaller courts, either from love of the art or from a desire to emulate their more prestigious neighbors, established royal companies. One of these, the Compagnia Reale di Parma, achieved a reputation rivalling that of Tessari in Naples or the Compagnia Toscana in Florence. Maria Luisa, Duchess of Parma, decided in 1825 to established a court company, probably under the inspiration of neighboring Piedmont with its Reale Sarda. She invited a new company, organized the previous year by Romualdo Mascherpa (1785-1849) to Parma and granted them an annual subsidy that continued until 1846. Like most company leaders of the time, Mascherpa took little responsibility for the shaping of individual productions; this was left to the individual actors. His own major contribution, aside from his acting (and he was one of the most popular comic actors of the period) was the financial organization of the company and the hiring of actors. He had a particular gift for recognizing new talents and many of the best actors of the next generation were at one time or another in his company. Maddalena Pelzet, later the leading actress of the Compagnia Toscana, was with him from 1825 to 1827 and again in 1829-1830. In the interim, youthful leading roles were taken by Isabella Belloni Colomberti (1802-1832) with such success that Niccolini, seeing her in his *Antonio Foscarini*, wrote "I thought I had written Teresa for Pelzet, but I was mistaken. I wrote it for Colomberti."(39)

Isabella was accompanied to the Mascherpa company by her husband Antonio (1806-1892), who also assumed youthful leading roles. More mature leads were played by Luigi Domeniconi (1786-1867), who had established himself as a leading actor playing opposite Carlotta Marchionni in the Belloni company at the beginning of the restoration. Pellico created for him the part of Paolo in *Francesca da Rimini* and he shared with Marchionni the honors of that triumph. He remained with Mascherpa from 1827 until 1831, when he left to play opposite Maddalena Pelzet in a new company formed by her husband Ferdinando (1791-1885).

Between 1827 and 1829 the more mature prima donna roles were taken by Carolina Internari, who later became the leading lady for Vestri. In 1824 she and her husband had established their own company and after his death in 1825 she directed it alone. After her two seasons with Mascherpa she acted briefly for Rafstopulo in the Toscana company, then established her own company once again. Many of its members were drawn from the Toscana and their departure put an end to the important years of this company. Rafstopulo died not long after and his wife continued the directorship, but without notable success.

The new Internari company did not depend on the customary tours through the Italian peninsula; they took the unusual, indeed in those days unique step of touring to Paris, in June of 1830. As the *Moniteur Universel* noted in an article announcng their arrival, Italian companies had been a major part of French theatrical life in the sixteenth and seventeenth centuries, but the tradition had died out as native theatre flourished. During the restoration a Théâtre Royal Italien had been re-established in Paris, but, not surprisingly, it was devoted exclusively to opera. The Italian spoken theatre was quite unknown in France except of course for the late works of Goldoni, who had spent his final years writing in Paris and in French. The way for Internari's experiment had been somewhat prepared however, not only by Goldoni and by Italian opera, but by other experiments in foreign drama which Paris experienced as part of the romantic movement. English and German plays were widely read and occasionally produced and companies from these countries had been enthusiastically welcomed in the capital by the literary and theatrical avant-garde if not by a wide section of the theatre-going public. Works such as Mme de Staël's *Corinne* (1807) and Stendhal's *Rome, Naples et Florence* (1817) had opened Italy too to romantic consideration.

Unfortunately, the repertoire brought by the Italians in 1830 was most ill-suited to appeal to this potential public. Three years after the revelation of romantic interpretations by visiting English actors and several months after the battle of *Hernani* at the Comédie, the neoclassic tragedies of Alfieri, even given in French, would have seemed to most a rather sterile reworking of an out-moded style. Francesco Paladini, Internari's leading man, attempted to anticipate difficulties in a letter to the editor of the *Moniteur* published July 6:

> In the course of the presentations which we propose to give for about three months there will be few spectacle plays; our masterpieces are rarely of that type. Three or four actors, the simplicity of the classic theatre, a style of emotion and pathos—those are the means which sufficed for Alfieri and the best of his imitators to achieve the profoundest effect on their public. The natural harmony of our language, our declamation, which differs from that of French verse— these are differences which we call to the attention of our French audiences; the more difficult our task is, the more we dare to hope that we shall not be judged too severely by an enlightened and hospitable audience.

The company opened the following evening at the Salle Favart with Alfieri's *Rosmunda* and Goldoni's *La casa disabitata*. The audience was not encouraging, either in size or in enthusiasm, and the critics had generally kind words for the actors and the short Goldoni piece but found Alfieri arid and dull. Later offerings repeated this pattern. The company in general and Internari in particular were warmly praised in comedy, but the serious works aroused little interest. On July 17 the company gave a command performance of Goldoni's *La locandiera* with the short farce *Osti non osti*. In later years Internari claimed that this mark of royal favor was the first step toward the reestablishment of a court-subsidized theatre for the production of Italian plays in Paris. The evidence to support this is weak, but in any case the march of historical events made such a development impossible. Nine days after the royal visit to the Salle Favart, Charles X had published in the *Moniteur* the Ordonnances which inspired the uprising that cost him his throne. Deprived thus of any hope of royal subsidy and unable to attract an audience with their available repertoire, the Italians had no choice but to return home. A final benefit on July 29 was given to provide them with the necessary money for the trip.

Italian sources later suggested that political considerations destroyed the Internari project, but this seems a simplification of the situation. Public reception of the pieces offered was not particularly enthusiastic and by July receipts were getting dangerously low in any case. Still, the Internari tour was of great significance if only as a hesitant beginning of what would later in the century become for a time the central feature of the Italian theatre—the international tour. The great stars of the latter nineteenth century—Ristori, Salvini, Rossi—all built upon the example set by Internari and all launched their fabulously successful international careers by fulfilling her goal of a triumphal tour to Paris.

Notes to Chapter III

1. Stendhal, *Rome, Naples and Florence,* trans. Richard Coe (London, 1959), pp. 354-55.
2. Stendhal, *Rome,* p. 357.
3. Stendhal, *Rome,* p. 383.
4. Stendhal, *Rome,* p. 393.
5. Stendhal, *Rome,* p. 394.
6. Stendhal, *Rome,* p. 267.
7. George Gordon, Lord Byron, *Letter and Journals,* ed. Leslie Marchal (London, 1976), V, 125.
8. Stendhal, *Rome,* p. 11.
9. Stendhal, *Rome,* p. 370.
10. Herbert Weinstock, *Rossini: A Biography* (New York, 1968), p. 76.
11. *Revue de théâtre,* XI (1837), 2.
12. *Revue de théâtre,* XI, 5-6.
13. Stendhal, *Life of Rossini,* trans. Richard Coe (New York, 1970), p. 447.
14. *Il conciliatore, figlio scientifico letterario,* ed. Vittore Branca (Florence, 1953-54), II, 285, 676.
15. Stendhal, *Rossini,* p. 268.
16. Alessandro Manzoni, *Lettere* (Verona, 1970), I, 157-58.
17. Giuseppe Baretti, *La frusta letteraria* (Milan, 1914), I, 244-45.
18. Ilario Rinieri, *Della vita e delle opere di Silvio Pellico* (Turin, 1868), p. 261.
19. Johann Wolfgang von Goethe, *Gedenkausgabe der Werke, Briefe, und Gespräche,* ed. E. Beutler (Zürich, 1949), XIV, 814.
20. Manzoni, *Lettere,* I, 223.
21. Giacomo Leopardi, *Opera* (Milan, 1937), II, 880.
22. Manzoni, *Lettere,* I, 293. Thanks largely to the enormous influence of Manzoni, the problem of a proper theatre language seemed for a time solved, but in fact the dialect theatre persisted, especially in comedy, and returned with new vigor before the end of the century. The speech of Manzoni and Niccolini came to seem as arbitrary and artificial on stage as that of Alfieri. The problem remians unsolved today. See the discussion "Gli scrittori e il teatro" in *Sipario* 229 (May, 1965), especially pp. 8-12.
23. Quoted in Guido Mazzoni, *L'ottocento* (Milan, 1934), p. 831.
24. Abbé Richard, *Description historique et critique de l'Italie* (Paris, 1769), III, 111.
25. Stendhal, *Rome,* p. 310.
26. Francesco Righetti, *Teatro italiano* (Turin, 1828), II, 126-27.
27. Arthur James Whyte, *The Evolution of Modern Italy* (Oxford, 1944), pp. 42-43.
28. Quoted in Mazzoni, *L'ottocento,* p. 830.
29. Teresa Borgomaneri, *Il romanticismo nel teatro di G.B. Niccolini* (Milan, n.d.), p. 191.

30. Mazzoni, *L'ottocento*, p. 935.
31. *Componimenti teatrali* II (Milan, 1827), 280.
32. Giuseppe Costetti, *Teatro italiano nel 1850* (Rome, 1901), p. 40.
33. Mazzoni, *L'ottocento*, p. 924.
34. Luigi Tonelli, *Il teatro italiano dalle origini ai giorni nostri* (Milan, 1924), p. 375.
35. Luigi Bonazzi, *Gustavo Modena e l'arte sua* (Perugia, 1865), p. 27.
36. Righetti, *Teatro,* p. 153.
37. Stendhal, *Rossini,* p. 441.
38. Stendhal, *Rossini,* p. 443.
39. Quoted in Luigi Rasi, *I comici italiani* (Florence, 1897), I, 328.

IV

The Risorgimento

Outwardly there appeared to be little political change in Italy between the uprisings of 1830-32 and the mid-1850s. Once again in 1848 there was a series of severe political protests, but once again these were put down by the forces of reaction and the rule of the conservative courts established by the Congress of Vienna seemed likely to extend for many years. Beneath the surface, however, the groundwork was being prepared for the sudden thrust for freedom and unity in 1859 and 1860 when, thanks to the extraordinary diplomatic triumphs of Cavour and the military triumphs of Garibaldi, the long-held dream of Italian unification was suddenly realized. This period of germination and fulfillment is known in Italian history as the Risorgimento.

The leading actor of this period and the mentor of the great international stars of the next generation was Gustavo Modena. The realistic approach which he developed and passed on to his students exerted an immeasurable influence, for as realism was developing throughout the European theatre during the next generation, actors in many countries found inspiration in the work of Modena's students. Despite his fame and brilliance as an artist and teacher, Modena devoted only a part of his life to theatre. He was even more deeply engaged in the struggle for a free and united Italy, serving as the faithful lieutenant of Giuseppe Mazzini, whose Young Italy movement between 1830 and 1848 eclipsed earlier revolutionary societies such as the Carbonari and for a brief period seemed destined to lead Italy at last to freedom and independence.

His dedication to the political struggle prevented Modena from ever establishing the permanent company he sometimes considered and thus he never developed a company to rival Turin's Reale Sarda. Despite steadily decreasing governmental support, the Reale Sarda remained Italy's leading troupe. Here was gathered the greatest concentration of acting talent in the peninsula and here occurred many of the major premieres, even though rigorous censorship was a continual problem. Comedy authors unable to portray their surroundings and tragedy authors fearful of possible political references were alike cowed. Revivals and foreign translations dominated the repertoire until the upheavals of 1848 resulted, at least in Turin, in somewhat greater freedom. The comedies of Gherardi del Testa and the dramas of Giacometti enjoyed great popular success and heralded a new and more productive generation of playwrights. These successes could not, unfortunately, save the Reale Sarda when its state subsidy was terminated. Still, before it disappeared, it had a final moment of glory in a triumphant tour to Paris, where the success of the troupe and its leading actress Ristori reawakened Europe to the power of Italian acting.

By mid-century most of the state-supported permanent companies of the restoration, like the Reale Sarda, lost their support and disappeared. Italy's prose theatre returned to the traveling troupes, led in the 1850s by that of Domeniconi, whose realistic productions of the plays of Paolo Ferrari pointed to the social realism later in the century. During the 1850s also Shakespeare began at last to be seen in major Italian productions, mounted by the leading young stars Rossi and Salvini.

Both of these stars would eventually gain international renown but at this period, despite the isolated success of the Reale Sarda in Paris, the Italian theatre for most people meant opera. After 1830 Rossini brought to Paris the best young singers and composers in Italy and although no major composer remained, the leading Italian singers of the era began a permanent series of international tours, becoming more associated with theatres elsewhere in Europe than in their homeland. As the fame of these operatic stars grew in the works of Bellini and Donizetti, an even greater contribution to the fame of Italian music appeared in the mature works of Giuseppe Verdi. Despite the frequently strong flavoring of contemporary Italian concerns in their libretti, Verdi's operas musically conquered all of Europe. By mid-century his works were being premiered not only in the major cities of Italy but in London and Paris as well.

Mazzini and Modena

Giuseppe Mazzini (1805-1872), whose life-long struggle for the freedom and unification of Italy was a critical part of the Risorgimento, was a native of Genoa. When he was only fifteen the brutal suppression of the liberal uprising of 1821 in Turin filled Genoa with sorrowing refugees and created in Mazzini a young revolutionary. During the 1820s, with censorship strongly enforced in the theatres and presses and with troops guarding the University of Genoa and other potential areas of revolt, few outlets were available for Mazzini, but like many of his generation he found in the battle between classicism and romanticism a safe sublimation for his radical political ideas. Even in his first article, on the seemingly politically harmless subject of Dante, Mazzini hailed the poet as a prophet of Italian unity, driven into a martyr's exile by his refusal to compromise with his petty fellow citizens. Such ideas were impossible to publish in Genoa, so Mazzini submitted the article to Niccolò Tommaseo in Florence, for the *Antologia*. Tommaseo rejected the article at this time, though he published it a decade later in another journal. In the meantime, he encouraged Mazzini to continue his writing and did accept for the *Antologia* two lengthy critical articles from him, *D'una letteratura Europea* and *Del dramma storico,* both championing the cause of romanticism.

In Genoa itself Mazzini and his friends took over a modest journal, the *Indicatore Genovese*, converting it into a romanticist journal as dedicated as if necessarily more circumspect than the *Antologia*. Here Mazzini published articles on Manzoni, Scott's *The Fair Maid of Perth*, Schlegel's *History of Literature*. The topics were calculatedly non-political, but references to freedom and patriotism occurred too often for the government's comfort and in 1828 the new journal was suppressed. Among the articles published before its disappearance were two on the writings of Francesco Guerrazzi (1804-1873), a prolific author of historical novels and two now forgotten plays, *Priamo* (1826), never presented, and *I bianchi e i neri* (1827), offered with little success in the author's native Leghorn. *I bianchi e i neri*, set in medieval Italy, had little to commend it aside from disguised political references, yet this was in the 1820s sufficient to attract the attention of critics like Mazzini, who wrote that "despite a certain strangeness of form and the absolute want of all harmony in the verses 'the work' yet reveals the sufferings of a powerful intellect, full of Italian pride." (1)

These articles inspired a correspondence between Guerrazzi and Mazzini and in 1828 when the *Indicatore Genovese* was halted Guerazzi invited Mazzini to Leghorn to continue his work in a new journal there. Leghorn, a Tuscan city, shared the comparative freedom of Florence, the capital, and here Mazzini continued his support of romantic ideals in the *Indicatore Livornese* with articles on

Goethe's *Faust*, on Foscolo and on recent European literature. The upheavals of 1830 having stirred even what Mazzini called "the slumbering Tuscan government" to action, the *Indicatore Livornese* was suppressed in its turn, not long before Florence's *Antologia*. Guerrazzi was arrested and Mazzini sent back to Genoa, but not to liberty. In 1827 he had become a member of the outlawed Carbonari and after the unsuccessful uprisings of that summer he was arrested and imprisoned. A few months later he was set free, but on condition he leave Genoa. Thus began his years of exile. As is so often the case, the authorities found the absent rebel far more effective than he had been when under their direct supervision.

After the revolts of 1830 the influence of the Carbonari in the struggle for freedom rapidly faded, to be replaced by new forces and new visions, among the most powerful of which was that of Mazzini. In Marseilles he gathered a group of young liberals about him to found a society, "Young Italy," which he had conceived during his imprisonment in Piedmont. Its members were pledged to overthrow, by force of arms, the eight monarchies of Italy and to establish a single united republic. There were a host of rival societies with similar aims at this time, and dedicated republicans might belong to three or four, but Young Italy was one of the most open in its activity and soon came in the eyes of the Austrians, other Europeans and many Italians to be regarded as the central representative of the new, post-1830 revolutionary spirit. Young Italy thus became for the period from 1830 to 1848 what the Carbonari had been for that between 1815 and 1830.

Mazzini's lieutenant in the founding of Young Italy was Gustavo Modena (1803-1861), who has gained a double claim on posterity as one of the great patriots of the Risorgimento and as the leading actor of the period and the spiritual father of many of the great Italian actors who came after him. Indeed, the historian Rasi called him "by common agreement the greatest and most complete actor of our century."(2) His father was Giacomo Modena (1773-1841), a much admired protrayer of fathers and tyrants who performed for a time with Blanès in Milan and later with Internari. Gustavo studied for the law but turned in 1824 to his father's profession, enrolling with Fabbrichesi in youthful roles. His first great success was achieved in Venice as David in Alfieri's *Saul*, with an interpretation so powerful and original that he was soon after invited to share leading roles with Ercole Gallina in Rafstopulo's recently established Compagnia Toscana.

He remained with Rafstopulo only one season, then for the first time joined his father in a company which had as its leading lady Carlotta Polvaro (1801-1851), another veteran from Rafstopulo's troupe. For three years they toured Italy, achieving great success in such works as Schiller's *Maria Stuart*, Pellico's *Francesca da Rimini*, Voltaire's *Zaïre* and Goldoni's *Pamela nubile*. A glowing description of Polvaro has been left by the young Antonio Colomberti, who witnessed her as Joan of Arc in Florence for the Carnival of 1822-23:

> Seeing her dressed in armor, as the martyr has come to be represented in her statue, with her long and beautiful blond hair spread over her shoulders, with the most charming features imaginable, with those large cerulean eyes, I was dazzled. Popular opinion called her the most beautiful actress of her time and it was surely not mistaken.(3)

The young Modena, a man of strong patriotic and republican sentiments, found himself in regular conflict with censors and the government and he sought every occasion to avoid their strictures. In Padua in 1829, thanks to the wife of the Austrian general quartered there, he got permission to present Pellico's *Francesca da Rimini* uncut. The result was that the phrase "for you my Italy, I will fight," never before allowed on stage, "caused a delirium of applause lasting a full ten minutes, while Modena remained standing downstage, his head bowed, as if uncertain whether the acclamation was for the interpreter or the poet."(4) Not long after, in Bologna, Modena caused a similar demonstration by inserting, without permission, a speech calling for rebellion into Kotzebue's *Graf Benjowsky*.

Bologna was ripe for occasions of this sort, for even in the face of bitter persecution, secret societies were more active and determined here at this period than anywhere else in Italy, with the possible exception of Naples. Romagna, the farthest outpost of the Papal States and separated from Rome by the mountainous and almost equally rebellious provinces of Umbria and the Marches, had long been a center for the activities of Freemasons and Carbonari. In February of 1831 Papal authority was completely overthrown in Bologna and a provisional republican government established. Within a few weeks, and without a struggle, twenty cities in Romagna, Umbria and the Marches had joined the new state. Modena joined the forces of the liberals and participated in the freeing of Ancona and Rimini. The provisional government at Bologna expressed the hope that the neighboring powers would respect the principle of nonintervention, but such hopes were soon dashed by Austria, which within a month had sent troops to restore the rebellious provinces to Papal rule. Modena and others were forced to flee Bologna. In January of 1832 he participated in a last, hopeless attempt to reverse the Austrian victory in an uprising at Cesena, but when this too was brutally suppressed, he left Italy to join Mazzini in exile. From this time on Mazzini's writings, circulated in secret, became standard reading for the liberal underground remaining in Romagna.

Modena stayed in exile for the next decade. His father and Carlotta Polvaro continued acting, avoiding political commentary, but their company declined steadily and disbanded in 1840. The elder Modena then retired and Polvaro joined the company of Domeniconi, with whom she passed her final years. During these years the influence of Mazzini gradually spread, but for Mazzini himself it was a period of constant danger and frustration, both shared by his faithful companion Modena. Scarcely had Modena joined Mazzini in Marseilles than the French government ordered the leaders of Young Italy to depart. Soon after, with Mazzini and Modena in Switzerland, Piedmont took severe measures against their followers. Many were arrested, some executed and Mazzini was sentenced to death in absentia for sedition. Early in 1834 Mazzini's followers attempted a liberating invasion into French-held Savoy which was an unqualified disaster, gaining Young Italy the hatred of authorities in both France and Switzerland.

Forced for a time out of active conspiracy, Mazzini returned to literature. He collaborated on translations of Werner's *Der vierundzwanzigste Februar* and Vigny's *Chatterton,* published in Genoa, and planned to edit a Library of Drama which would introduce Italy to the entire range of European romantic theatre, but the spectre of censorship prevented this project from developing. He founded a new journal, *La Jeune Suisse*, and wrote for it some sixty articles outlining his visions of nationality and democracy. He also wrote two striking essays on music and drama, prophetically suggesting that the renaissance of both would soon take place in northern Europe. He condemned contemporary music and drama as pandering to mere effect and sensation without any over-riding belief to give them direction and value: "Nowadays we have no drama because we have no Heaven." Still he felt that in a dramatist like Schiller could be found the germ of a new synthesis, not the Fate or Necessity of Shakespeare or the Greeks, but a modern idea of Providence, which worked through men and nations to some significant ultimate goal:

> In Schiller man is free; free and possessed of power of which neither Shakespeare nor the Greeks had any conception. "In his breast," as he says, "burns the star of his destiny." But you feel at the same time that though he might prove false and close his eyes to that star, he

cannot extinguish nor inter its beams; you feel that if he becomes great and consecrates his life to the mission of spreading a sacred idea, he may succumb in the struggle but death for him is then not the death of the body; the living soul of the idea survives—and if his fate is unhappy and he sinks into the mire of individual passions with a sign on his forehead of an ego in rebellion against both society and the laws of the universe, again he may die but the idea will not. Providence, watching from on high over the fulfillment of its law, will cause even his striving against it, his ephemeral victory and the power he abused to bring forth some element of communal progress and to aid in the fulfillment of God's plan for his creation.(5)

Such a theory of drama clearly owes much to Risorgimento idealism, but critics who have been concerned with the social function of art in more modern times have often sought a basis for serious drama closely in line with that developed by Mazzini in this prophetic essay. Shaw's vision of such a drama, developed in the preface to *Back to Methuselah*, is essentially that of Mazzini, expressed in strikingly similar terms.

Although Mazzini had much popular support in Switerland, the Swiss central government, under pressure from Austria and France, repeatedly urged the cantons to expel him and eventually put a price on his head. Harrassed, in hiding, in constant danger, Mazzini in 1837 arranged for safe-conduct through France and sought refuge in England. Here he was joined again by his faithful lieutenant Modena, who had come by way of France and Belgium. Naturally Mazzini and his colleagues set to work at once arousing pro-Italian feeling in England. Articles appealing to English liberalism and Protestantism flowed from his pen, along with essays on Italian politics and literature, emphasizing the growth of a new national consciousness. Dante was often cited as a sort of patron saint of the new Italy, for his vision of an Italian state centered at Rome. Modena contributed to the cause in 1839 with a highly successful series of readings from Dante at the Queen's Theatre.

So great was Mazzini's notoriety throughout Europe by the 1840s that he was suspected, not always without reason, of helping to inspire every political disturbance that took place on the continent. Clearly only if the revolution for which he ceaselessly worked arrived, could Mazzini ever hope to return to Italy. Somewhat surprisingly, the Austrian Emperor proved willing to forgive and forget in the case of Modena, who in 1840 was granted amnesty to return to Milan. There he offered highly popular readings of Dante, closely watched by the police, at the Teatro Re and Teatro Lentasio. Obviously political activity, except for the most secret and subtle kind, was now impossible for Modena and he turned his efforts entirely toward the theatre, organizing and training his own company, which became the most famous of its time. The company was established by 1843, though Modena was unable to gain for it the state subsidy he had desired. He began at once a training program in a new style which stressed "verità" and "spontaneità" even in tragedy and drama, so long dominated by traditional grandiose and bombastic delivery. The careful and detailed rehearsals which De Marini early in the century had applied to contemporary works Modena now gave to historical dramas, setting a standard for rehearsals rarely matched elsewhere in Europe. According to Dall'Ongaro:

> Modena did not instruct his pupils. He read the part, he explained the personality of the character that he believed most appropriate to the actor's means, then left him free to follow the dictates of his heart. After having heard the students try one means or another, only if it did not appear to him that they were heading in a profitable direction would he say, do this. But his advice was never imposed nor given as absolute; never did he say: Do this, because you ought to do this, it is always done thus. Nature is varied and multiple. Grief and pleasure, anger and supplication can take and will take as many tones and colors as reflect the variety of characters which make up the human species. There is nothing absolute on earth. The beautiful is as varied as the aspects of nature; the truth of art does not lie in an inescapable line, but in the correspondence of the idea with the external image that must express it and render it accessible to all.(6)

According to Tommaso Salvini, Modena's new company was made up almost entirely of players under twenty years of age, but it was nevertheless a troupe of considerable talent and many of the leading actors of the next thirty years in Italy were among its members. Tommaso and his brother Alessandro were then only fourteen and sixteen and Tommaso himself admitted that Modena's interest was rather in the boys' father, Giuseppe (d. 1844), who assumed leading roles, while Tommaso "figured as the bone that is thrown in for good measure."(7) The leading actress of the troupe was Fanny Sadowsky (1826-1906), whom Modena discovered in Padua and who at the age of eighteen established herself as a major actress in the premiere of Dall'Ongaro's *Fornaretto* and in Vigny's *Maréchal d'Ancre*. Adelia Arrivabene (1818-1847), daughter of an aristocratic family in Mantua, was another Modena discovery and an instant success. In 1847 the *Mondo Illustrato*, reviewing her triumph in Scribe's *Verre d'Eau*, called her "the hope of the Italian stage." This sentiment, shared by many, went sadly unfulfilled, for the much-loved actress died after a brief illness later that same year.

Modena launched two sons of the great Luigi Vestri in theatrical careers, Angelo (1828-1889) and Gaetano (1825-1862). Of his four sons, Luigi encouraged only Angelo to follow him onto the stage. Gaetano was trained for a career in law, but after his father's death in 1841, he too turned to the theatre. The company's young leading man was the heir of another acting family. Carlo Romagnoli's (1820-1882) parents had occupied leading positions in the popular Bazzi company in Turin during the 1820s. Romagnoli, Angelo Vestri, and Tommaso Salvini had all left Modena before the beginning of his third season, Salvini to join the Fiorentini in Naples, Romagnoli to join the Dondini company, and Vestri to establish a troup of his own. Still, Modena managed to replace them with other youthful actors of equal promise: Alamanno Morelli (1812-1893), who had made his stage debut with Modena in 1829; Luigi Bellotti-Bon (1820-1883), adopted son of the popular dramatist and a young comic actor of great skill; and Luigi Bonazzi (1811-1879), a polished young romantic leading actor who assumed such roles as Lusignan in Voltaire's *Zaïre*. The company toured widely in northern Italy, but were most warmly received in Venice and Milan. In Venice they performed at the Teatro Apollo, recently remodeled by Bagnara. It was a large and elegant hall, the first in Italy to install gas lighting (in 1826), horseshoe shaped, with five ranks of thirty-two boxes each, seating approximately 1250 persons. In Milan they performed at the Teatro Re, where Modena had frequently appeared in the 1830s with the Reale Sarda.

The repertoire of Modena's company was a varied one, but like most Italian troupes of the period they relied heavily on the recent dramas of France—Hugo, Dumas, Scribe, Bayard and Dumanoir. They were the first company in Italy to offer Hugo's *Hernani* and Vigny's *Maréchal d'Ancre* and the leading female roles in the comedies of Scribe were the specialty of Sadowsky and Arrivabene. During the 1830s and 1840s, largely under the influence of translations of Hugo and Dumas, a generation of Italian playwrights, the "basso romantico," began producing declamatory dramas that emphasized striking effects, pathos, complex and marvelous plots. The major form of this drama was the historic drama, "dramma storica," which in Italy, as in France, relied heavily on melodramatic spectacle. Many of these Italian works sought an extra "artistic" merit by taking such figures as Raphael or Michelangelo as their subject, by adopting famous novels (such as *I promessi sposi*) or by simply converting the proven poetic dramas of Italian romanticism into prose.

Two companies, Turin's Reale Sarda and that of Modena, were the leaders in Italy both in the production of recent French works and in the premiering of the closely related Italian dramma storica. Giacinto Battaglia (1803-1861), who took over the Modena company in 1846, created a series of such works for the Sarda, from *Vittorina ossia la conseguenza di una scommesa* (1837) to *La famiglia Foscari* (1844). A favored author of the dramma storica during Modena's directorate was Francesco Dall'Ongaro (1808-1873), a journalist, politician and poet in the Mazzini tradition. Modena offered his first two plays, *I dalmati* (1845) and *Danae* (1846), but refused, apparently for fear of censorship, his *Guglielmo Tell*, and, with Sadowsky in the leading role, achieved a major success for *Il fornaretto* (1846), which had failed at its earlier premiere at the Reale Sarda. This story of a poor Venetian tradesman executed for a nobleman's wrongdoing inspired countless retellings—dramatic, musical and cinematographic.

After 1846, the political situation once more summoned Modena from the theatre. He turned his company over to Battaglia and except for occasional readings again abandoned the stage. Events were now moving rapidly toward the culmination of the Risorgimento. Far-reaching effects were set in motion in 1846 by the election of a new Pope, Pius IX, known before his election as a liberal, who electrified the peninsula by immediately granting a general political amnesty. During the 1840s there had developed in Italy a strong nationalist party moderate in tone, which opposed Mazzini's call to arms and dreamed of the bloodless creation of a new nation, secular in the vision of some, with Carlo Alberto, the king of Piedmont, as its leader, religious in the vision of others, under the leadership of the Pope. The events of 1846 strengthened both visions, for under the inspiration of the Pope, Carlo Alberto also took a liberal turn and began to emerge as a possible challenger to Austria. In Milan and in Venice prominent citizens, acting within their legal rights but with a new boldness, petitioned the Austrian government to correct a variety of abuses. In Milan the authorities delayed, in Venice they responded by imprisoning Daniele Manin, leader of the opposition. Modena, who was in Venice supporting Manin, left for Milan where in March of 1848 news of an insurrection in Vienna itself inspired the city to rise in a revolt for independence. In five days of bitter street fighting the city was free and was soon joined by cities throughout Lombardy, then Venetia and finally by Venice itself. Carlo Alberto, under extreme pressure from his own citizens, declared war on Austria and marched to occupy Milan. Rome, Naples and Tuscany also sent troops. The hated Duke of Modena was driven from his state and the

Duke of Parma only saved himself by granting a liberal constitution.

So rapid a rush of events proved disturbing for many. Almost at once the first troubling evidence of reaction appeared. The Pope announced in April that he would not support Piedmont's war against Austria. Ferdinand of Naples recalled his troops. Carlo Alberto announced to Europe at large that he was occupying Milan only to save it from the excesses of republicanism; then, refusing to employ troops of sympathetic republican volunteers, he fought a weak and dilatory battle against Austria on the Lombard plains. Mazzini, convinced that Carlo Alberto was betraying the Italian cause, urged the Milanese to renounce their would-be protector, but the city voted to fuse Lombardy with Piedmont under his rule. All too soon Mazzini's fears were realized. By the end of the summer Milan was stunned by the news Carlo Alberto had entered negotiations with the enemy. Once more the barricades went up, but too late. Austria once again occupied all of Lombardy and Venetia except for Venice itself, which resisted the enemy forces until the following August.

The hopes of Mazzini and his followers now shifted to the south. In October the armistice between Austria and Piedmont fanned the sparks of liberal revolt in Tuscany and in the Papal States. A radical ministry seized power in Tuscany, headed by Mazzini's old friend, the playwright and editor Guerrazzi. The Grand Duke fled, leaving the authority to a new Constituent Assembly. Rome also rose in rebellion and in November the Pope joined Tuscany's Grand Duke in exile in the Kingdom of Naples. Modena and Mazzini arrived in Tuscany early in 1849 and Modena remained to become a member of the new Constituent Assembly and to found a republican journal, *La Constituente Italiana*. Mazzini went on to Rome, where he was made a citizen of the new republic and elected to its assembly. These were the days of his greatest triumph, but they were brief. The situation in the north continued to shift. Carlo Alberto was pressed to renew the war by reports of Austrian brutality in Lombardy, but his forces were crushed within days by the Austrians. The disgraced monarch abdicated leaving the crown to his son Vittorio Emmanuele II. Immediately after this, the Grand Duke of Tuscany, with Austrian backing returned to his state, dissolved the new assembly and revoked its rulings. Modena took refuge to Rome, now with Venice the last citadel of Italian liberty. The Roman Assembly, threatened by both French and Austrian forces, elected a Triumvirate to lead the government, with Mazzini receiving the largest number of votes.

The fate of the Roman Republic, with Europe's greatest powers arrayed against it, was clear. Soon the only question facing

Rome was whether to fight the besieging forces in the streets or to surrender the city to them and carry on the struggle by guerrilla warfare in the countryside. Garibaldi led some four thousand followers into the hills. Mazzini remained in Rome, but resigned as Triumvir rather than agree to the inevitable capitulation. French troops occupied the city July 3, 1849. The day of the occupation Margaret Fuller, whom Mazzini had met during his London exile, sought him out:

> In the upper chamber of a poor house, with his lifelong friends, the Modenas,—I found him. Modena, who abandoned not only what other men hold dear,—home, fortune, peace,—but also endured, without the power of using the prime of his great artist-talent, a ten year's exile in a foreign land.... Mazzini had suffered millions more than I could; he had borne his fearful responsibility; he had let his dearest friends perish; he had passed all these nights without sleep; in two short months he had grown old...yet he had never flinched, never quailed; had protested in the last hour against surrender; sweet and calm, but full of a more fiery purpose than ever.(8)

The years 1848 and 1849 were the high-water mark of Mazzini's influence and success. The goal of his life, Italian unification, was near at hand, but it would come in a manner so alien to his vision that he henceforth would struggle against the new Italy as determinedly as he had hitherto struggled for it. After 1849 most Italian nationalists fixed their hopes on Piedmont, the most liberal state left in Italy, since the young King Vittorio Emmanuele II defied the power of Austria by refusing to give up the constitution. Piedmont's prime minister, Cavour, one of the greatest statesmen of the century, solidified the European position of his state and made it the basis for uniting all of Italy. Mazzini, who saw Cavour's accomplishments as a strategem for prolonging foreign influence and royal power in Italy, continued to struggle for a republic born of revolution. An abortive attempt in Milan in 1853, which the citizens this time refused to support, proved to most Italians that Mazzini's time was past. He continued to publish manifestos and launch raid after raid, with ever-decreasing liberal support, while Cavour's power and that of Piedmont steadily grew. Lombardy was annexed to Piedmont in July of 1859 and within fifteen months, with the aid of Garibaldi's army of liberation in the south, all of Italy except Venetia and a narrow costal strip subject to the Pope was united under Vittorio Emmanuele.

Gustavo Modena during the political reaction of 1849 was forbidden to enter any Italian state but Piedmont, so he took up residence in Turin, in comparative solitude, giving occasional recitations and publishing a series of political satires containing discreet criticism of the new order. In the late 1850s leading actors and troupes offered to arrange for his appearance in other cities in Italy and elsewhere. Ristori asked him to join her in Paris and Rossi invited him to Milan, but Modena refused to appear in areas still under the control of those powers that had destroyed the roman Republic. After Milan joined the new Kingdom of Italy in 1859 he consented to give some recitations there and was triumphantly received. As Modena, Bologna, Florence and Naples also joined the new state he appeared in these cities also. He died in Turin in February of 1861, one month before the new Kingdom of Italy was officially proclaimed. Its architect, Cavour, died three months later, Mazzini died in Pisa in 1872. He was there in disguise, under the threat of arrest, still plotting for the republican uprising which would never come.

The Reale Sarda

The Reale Sarda of Turin retained its position as a leading theatre during this period, but the growing political importance of Piedmont did not result in easier times for the state theatre. On the contrary Carlo Alberto clearly supported the troupe more from a sense of tradition than interest. A shrinking subsidy and growing censorship both political and religious made life more and more difficult for the Reale Sarda during his reign. A new contract in 1832 diminished the funds for salaries, scenery and costumes but allowed the company no opportunity to compensate by reducing their production schedule. The length of the season was unchanged, but at least one new play was required each week and no performances were allowed to last less than two and one half hours. The result was not the production of more new Italian plays; the majority of new offerings, as before, were translations from the French. Only fourteen original Italian plays were offered for the first time this season and in 1834 only six, the lowest number in the thirty-four year history of the company.

The major event at the theatre in 1832 was the premiere of a new work by Pellico, *Ester d'Engaddi*, written while the author was a prisoner in the Spiegelberg. One of the most famous of the political prisoners of 1820, Pellico was at last released after ten years and spent the remainder of his life in Turin. In 1832 he made his re-entry into public life with the premiere of his new play, heavily censored of course, and with the publication of *Le mie prigioni,* the chronicle of his life in captivity which gained him an international reputation and rivalled even Manzoni's *I promessi sposi* in popularity. A witness to the premiere of Pellico's play reported:

> The throngs were extraordinary, the effect marvelous, and the applause given to both play and author universal and prolonged at each intermission to such an extent that each time the author was forced to rise from his place and again acknowledge his public. The representations continued for three evenings to universal acclaim and would have surely continued with ever increasing enthusiasm if the theatre censors had permitted it. But they indignantly assumed that the spectators found in the character of Leite a sort of tragic Tartuffe, and might be too easily led thereby to make slighting associations with the Jesuits.... The result was that before the tragedy could return to the stage it had to undergo a new castration more scrupulous than the first.(9)

Two further Pellico premieres followed—*Tommaso Moro* in 1833 and *Corradino* in 1835—but despite the best efforts of Marchionni and Ferri, so successful in Pellico's earlier works, the public greeted these new offerings with indifference. In a despairing letter to a friend Pellico confessed: "I have written nothing further for the stage; it is too difficult to create good tragedies in times of political upheaval like ours. Allusions are seen everywhere, severe revisions are required, the public loses patience, the author offends one party or another and finds in his audience always angry people ready to hiss, as I found with my *Corradino*."(10) Pellico held to his decision and produced no more dramatic works.

With the departure of Pellico from the theatre, Carlo Marenco was generally acknowledged as the leading serious dramatist of the period. As if in demonstration of this position, he created no less than three works to be premiered by the Reale Sarda in 1836—*Manfredi, Adelisa* and *Pia dei Tolomei*. The latter, one of the great successes of the period, a triumph for its author and for Marchionni, succeeded in precisely suiting contemporary theatrical taste. The structure was loosely classic in the manner of Manzoni, with five acts and lyric choruses. The influence of romanticism could be seen in the Hugoesque characters, the superabundant lyricism and the *coups de théâtre,* there were hints of patriotic passion, though subtle enough to pass the censors, and a subject from Dante, now much in fashion. Finally, and perhaps most tellingly, there was a pervasive melancholy sentimentality, recalling Pellico's popular *Francesca da Rimini*. Opposite Marchionni appeared a new leading man, Giovan Gotthardi (d. 1849), who proved extremely serviceable in comedy, tragedy and drama alike.

In 1837 the Sarda welcomed the actress who was to become the most famous member of this outstanding company, Adelaide Ristori (1822-1906). From the beginning of Ristori's life she was to be an actress, as were both her parents. The newest family member was pressed onto the stage at the earliest opportunity. Her first appearance was at the age of three months as an infant in a basket in Giraud's farce *Regalie per Capo d'Anno*. At three years she appeared in Avelloni's *Bianca e Fernando* and by age four was performing regularly.

At twelve she was booked with the actor-manager Giuseppe Moncalvo (1781-1859), who within a year was assigning her roles as second lady. By fifteen she had gained enough experience to enjoy a great success in the leading role of Francesca da Rimini, which led to offers from several companies of positions as leading lady, surely a heady experience for a girl of fifteen. Ristori's father, however, felt that her career would be better served in the long run by placing her as an ingenue with the Sarda troupe and so in 1837 the girl who would become the most famous player of her time joined Italy's leading company. Carlotta Marchionni assumed her tutelage but the company provided many models for the young actress' study. Few troupes ever boasted so outstanding an assembly of talents. It was led by the great Marchionni and by Anna Bazzi in tragic mother roles, Vincenza Righetti in character parts, Rosa Romagnoli playing servants, and in the roles of young lovers, the recently arrived Antonietta Robotti (1817-1864), who had achieved a memorable success as the country girl in *Pia dei Tolomei*. The men were no less distinguished, headed by Vestri, Gotthardi and Righetti. Even the lesser actors of this brilliant company would have stood out in one of Italy's many minor companies.

During the late 1830s the major premieres at the Sarda were the two latter plays of Bon's popular Ludro trilogy; Bon works dominated the repertoire. In many of these, such as *Dietro le scene* and *S'io fossi ricco* (both 1839), Bon's comedy began to take on a sharply cynical edge; indeed, their author remarked that he had "given up comedy." The Sarda was one of the few companies that managed to strike the right note in these dark comedies. In the hands of others they generally seemed merely ugly or grotesque. The tone surely owed something to the theatrical conditions of the time. Many dramatists, like Pellico, gave up the theatre entirely, and the number of new works steadily declined. Others, like Bon, continued to write, but with a growing frustration and contempt for the conditions under which they were forced to work. Censorship was heavy, ubiquitous, yet capricious. Every drama was caught between the millstones of governmental censorship by the Austrian authorities and moral censorship by the Pontificate. In her memoires Ristori observes that plays "were mutilated to a mass of contradictions, being at times rendered completely silly and bereft of any interest." She continues with a series of examples, both ludicrous and depressing. All possibly religious references were banned, including all mention of God, angels, or devils. The line "While she with angelic utterance" in Verdi's *Luisa Miller* thus became "While she with harmonic utterance," arousing much laughter in the gallery and inspiring one wag in Rome to write under the name of the street Via Porta Angelica, near St. Peter's, "Via Porta Armonica." The names Gregory and John, borne by present and recent Popes, were also forbidden and even possible allegorical references to the Papacy. Thus one of the witches' lines in Macbeth, "Here I have a pilot's thumb/ Wrecked as homeward he did come," was cut in Rome because a censor considered the line a possible allusion to the boat of St. Peter! Possible patriotic references were handled with equal severity. Italy, like God, was not to be mentioned on stage, and so in Verona an Austrian censor changed the line "Beautiful sky of Italy" to "Beautiful sky of the world." "Fatherland" was another word never allowed, and so sensitive was the censor that on one occasion a play ran into difficulty when its principle character, a deaf-mute, returning home from a long exile was given the stage direction: "Here the actor must express the joy which he experiences in beholding his fatherland." The censor expunged the word "fatherland" and wrote in "native land," fearful of the banned word being expressed, even in pantomime!(11)

In 1840 the great Marchionni retired, still at the height of her power but unwilling to risk going into a decline. Her final appearance was in *La fiera* by Nota, the dramatist whose repertoire she had made her particular specialty. So close was their collaboration that after her retirement Nota also stopped writing for the stage, although the Sarda in later years premiered several of his hitherto unproduced works.

The company now had the difficult task of selecting someone to assume the roles of the most popular actress of her time. A few years later Ristori would have been the obvious choice, but in 1840 she was still too young at eighteen and the choice fell instead on Amalia Bettini (1809-1894). Bettini had an unusually fortunate start in her career since her parents were members of the famous Fabbrichesi troupe in Naples. Thus at thirteen she was allowed small ingenue roles with this company and the opportunity to work with such actors as De Marini and Vestri, playing leading roles opposite the latter within two years. Her mother Lucrezia left the company to act for a time in Verona, then to establish a minor troupe of her own which Amalia joined when the Fabbrichesi company dissolved in 1827. Verona remained the home of this company and here in 1831 another troupe was formed by Gaetano Nardelli (1786-1855), with Amalia as the leading lady and Ghirlanda from the Reale Sarda as her partner.

During the previous century actors tended to remain with a single company through most of their careers, but in the early nineteenth century this practice almost entirely disappeared. The troupe of Fabbrichesi and later the Reale Sarda were unusual in their longevity and stability, though even these experienced frequent and significant shifts in their membership. Certain courts established permanent theatres, but the touring company was still the most common acting experience and throughout the peninsula companies constantly formed and dissolved, with actors working their way up in the profession by moving to more prestigious companies or possibly to less prestigious ones which could offer them better roles and a chance for exposure that might stimulate other offers. The usual contract was for three seasons, but actors frequently terminated earlier if a better opportunity appeared, and to add to the complexity of the situation the dozens of managers, engaged in competitive bidding, would often attempt to make an offer more attractive by trying to put together a package—that is by appealing to one actor or actress with the promise that if they accepted, the manager would gain certain other performers with whom they might like to appear from still other companies.

Bettini's reputation gained with Nardelli earned her an offer from Romualdo Mascherpa in 1835 to replace Internari, who had just left for her tour to Paris. With Mascherpa, Bettini toured widely, to Bologna, Rome, Venice, Trieste, Milan and Genoa, always to great acclaim. In 1837 she returned to Nardelli and brought such prosperity to his company that Nardelli was able to retire in 1840. Her fame was now such that she received bids from dozens of directors. Mascherpa, now in Bergamo, expressed his strong desire to have her rejoin him and offers came from Rome, Ravenna, Bologna and Lucca as well. Package offers came too. Pietro Monti, director of the Fiorentini in Naples, offered her the opportunity to work with the leading actors Alberti and Prepiani. Camillo Ferri in Milan suggested that if she came he might be able to obtain Domeniconi for her leading man.

None of these companies could at this period compete with the prestige of the Reale Sarda, however, and Bettini probably had little difficulty deciding to accept the offer from Gaetano Bazzi to succeed

Marchionni in Turin. Still, her position as the Sarda's leading actress was not an easy one. On the one hand she had to endure inevitable comparisons with her beloved predecessor and on the other she faced the challenge of the rising star Ristori. Significantly, Ristori's memoires, warm in their praise for Marchionni, make no mention of Bettini. On the contrary, Ristori claims, incorrectly, that it was she who became the first leading lady of the company in 1840.(12) Nevertheless, Bettini met the double challenge successfully, partially by means of a memorable production in 1841 of *Iginia d'Asti*, one of the works created by Pellico during his imprisonment. Not long after this triumph by her rival, Ristori resigned from the company to become the leading actress with Mascherpa.

As is often the case with great actors, Bettini was said to speak while others merely recited. Her rich and natural delivery was universally praised. One critic observed: "She enters the stage and moves about, weeps, expresses joy and jealousy, happiness and sadness with the same naturalness as if she were truly jealous, offended, loved and betrayed." Her features were "not precisely handsome, but of the sort which could be dazzling on stage."(13) Her pathos and spirit were said to equal those of Fanny Kemble in England and her delicacy and polish those of the French star Mlle Mars.(14) Unhappily for the Sarda, this much-praised actress did not long grace its stage, for in 1842 she retired to marry a doctor in Bologna. She was often begged by various directors to return to the theatre, but though she was only thirty-three, her dazzling career was essentially over. Except for an occasional recital for a benefit, the theatre public saw her no more.

Although the Sarda was to endure more than a decade after 1842, there was at this time very much the feeling that the company had come to the end of an era. Within a period of three years Marchionni and Ristori had left and Bettini, like a passing comet, had come and gone. In 1841 Vestri retired, dying the following year. Anna Maria Bazzi retired the same year and a year later her husband Gaetano, director of the troupe during its greatest years, gave up the administration. One of his last important successes was Bon's *Addio alla scene*, in which that popular actor and playwright also bade farewell to the theatre.

Bazzi's actor Righetti succeeded him as director and guided the theatre through its difficult final years, as political events more and more overshadowed his concerns. Luigi Taddei, who had accompanied Internari to Paris, was hired to replace Vesti, but remained only two seasons. He was in turn replaced by the popular Luigi Domeniconi from the Mascherpa company, but Domeniconi also left after two years and the roles he created attracted less attention than political manifestations at the theatre. The more liberal and nationalistic atmosphere which appeared in Italy between 1846 and 1848 resulted in a relaxation of censorship and therefore in a series of dramas on hitherto unacceptable subjects. Achille Montaignani's *Adalberto all'assedio della Roccella* (1846) was a direct call to the King to challenge Austria to war. Briano's *Pietro Micca* (1847) openly discussed independance and Rotondi's *Guttemberg* (1847) championed freedom of the press. The plays of the revolutionary year 1848 were almost exclusively political and were universally cheered by patriotic audiences. Works appeared that were previously banned — Alfieri's *Bruto Secondo* and *Virginia,* Pindemonte's *Baccanali* — along with liberal new works — Giotti's *La lega lombarda* and Giacometti's *Siamo tutti fratelli*! Still, freedom had its price for the Reale Sarda for among the reforms of 1848 was an abolishment of the old privilege which gave this company exclusive rights to present prose drama in Turin.

A worse blow soon followed. The defeat and abdication of the King in 1849 deprived the Reale Sarda of a sovereign who had given it continual if sometimes rather indifferent support for almost twenty years. The new king, Vittorio Emmanuele, whatever his political promise, showed little interest in the arts and funding became more uncertain than ever. Nevertheless, the Reale Sarda began the new decade with renewed vigor and promise. The leading actor Giovan Gottardi died in 1849, but was soon replaced by a young actor, Ernesto Rossi (1827-1896), who would achieve a world-wide reputation. Rossi began acting while a student of law in Pisa and in 1846 entered the famous company of young actors organized by Gustavo Modena. Modena's example and teaching inspired him to develop characterizations of richer detail and more complex psychology, which became one of his greatest strengths both in comedy and tragedy. Among the roles he played at this time were David in Alfieri's *Saul* and Orestes (with Modena as Pylades). The influence of Modena can be clearly seen in Rossi's comments on the latter role. "Orestes is not a myth," he said, "Orestes is a man," elaborating as follows:

> I wanted blood to run in his veins, his muscles to be covered with flesh, a heart to beat beneath his breast, that in his face be reflected the various feelings of his soul, and that his words be given delicate shadings to correspond precisely to these feelings, that his gestures be subject and complementary to the words, so as to appear natural and nothing more than the unconscious accompaniment of the words and feelings.(15)

When Modena dissolved the company in 1848 Rossi organized

his own troupe with Giovanni Leigheb (1812-1866), a popular
Venetian actor much praised in the dialect comedies of F.A. Bon. In
such roles as Paolo in Pellico's *Francesca da Rimini* and Bonfil in
Goldoni's *Pamela nubile*, Rossi attracted such critical and popular attention that he was invited to assume leading roles at the Sarda. Here
his success expanded further still, covering the entire range of French
and Italian comedies, tragedies and sentimental works offered, from
Alfieri to Marenco and from Dumas to Scribe. His rising star easily
compensated for the loss of Gaetano Vestri in 1853. Vestri's wife, Antoinetta Robbotti, left with him, but Ristori returned.

The relaxation of censorship at the end of the 1840s brought to
an end the long drought in Italian comic writing. Between the last
triumphs of Nota in the 1820s and his death in 1847, new Italian
comedies were few and generally quite undistinguished. Then, as conditions for comic writing improved, a group of authors appeared
whose works have not survived the test of time but who enjoyed
during this period enormous success. The major contributor of
comedies to the Sarda at this time was Tommaso Gherardi del Testa
(1814-1881). Gherardi created his first play, *Una folle ambizione*
(1844) for the young Ristori, who offered it with such success in
Florence that Gherardi renounced his career in law to devote himself
to writing. By 1848 he had seen eleven of his plays produced by such
artists as Ristori, Robotti and Domeniconi, primarily at Florence's
Teatro Cocomero, where the major works of Niccolini had been given
their premieres. Indeed, his *Ludovico Sforza*, long banned from the
stage, was finally first offered there at this same time, in 1847.

Gherardi also contributed anonymous political satires to the
cause of liberation and in the uprisings of 1848 joined a body of
Tuscan volunteers who went to support Carlo Alberto's unhappy
struggle against Austria. Captured at the battle of Curtatone—the
"Tuscan Thermopylae"—Gherardi endured several months in a
Bohemian prison. Back in Florence, he created the first of his works
to gain success throughout Italy, *Il sistema di Giorgio* (1851), a
domestic comedy in which Carolina holds up her first husband,
Giorgio, as a model of all virtues to her second husband, Rodolfo.
This popular work gained its author a regular commission from the
Reale Sarda, for which he composed three new comedies in the next
year alone. During the following decade, Gherardi wrote for the Sarda
and elsewhere some thirty plays, all considerable successes except for
three or four dramas. His works were naturally tuned to the taste of the
times, with a trace of the comic spirit of Goldoni as filtered through
Nota and Giraud, with an emotional coloring showing the influence of

romanticism. Some were pure farces, such as *Il berretto bianco da notte* (Sarda, 1854); some were vehicles for Ristori, such as *Il regno d'Adelaide* (Cocomero, 1853), but the richest were traditional gay and witty comedies of manners such as *Le scimmie* (Sarda, 1854).

The serious drama achieved an even greater success in the works of the most popular and prolific Italian dramatist of his generation, Paolo Giacometti (1816-1882). Giacometti's range from the beginning of his career was wide, including historical comedies in the manner of Scribe *(Carlo II, re d'Inghilterra,* 1847*)*, sentimental dramas *(La benefattrice,* 1846), and Goldonian comedies *(Quattro donne in una casa,* 1842), but his particular specialty was the historical drama, the dominant genre of the "basso romantico," of which he was the outstanding dramatist. Among his early works *Isabella de Fiesco* (1843), *Fieschi e Fregosi* (1843) and *Camilla Faà da Casale* (1847) are clear examples of this type. Like most successful dramatists of his time Giacometti salted his dramas with touches of revolutionary sentiment, but first and foremost he was an entertainer, adept at utilizing the power of romantic, indeed melodramatic action and spectacle. In the preface to his collected works he observes, "I have written not for the learned but for the people and my motto has been 'Let us cultivate pure effect and pile effects upon effects.' "(16) In his early comedy, *Il poeta e la ballerina* (1841) the poet, though clearly speaking ironically, describes accurately enough the trends of contemporary "basso romantico" theatre and of his creator's own work:

> In our theatre's present critical situation, I asked myself: "The public has had enough of man in everyday circumstances; now we must call forth their passions. Is the reign of beauty past? Very well. Let us then turn to the creation of another dramatic world, based on the ugly."
> Having thus concluded, I began to read Victor Hugo, Ducange, Dumas, and I saw quickly that one could become a dramatic author by utilizing seduced ladies, illegitimate children, deceived husbands ... poisons, daggers, assassinations, stranglings, ghosts, butchers and gravediggers—provided that one scattered a few original ideas here and there.

Il poeta e la ballerina was itself a happy exception to this description, a clever comedy of manners with some serious social criticism. It was Giacometti's first important success and was soon offered throughout Italy.

Most of Giacometti's works of the 1840s were premiered by the traveling company headed by Gaetano Woller, but as early as 1844 a Giacometti historical drama, *La gioventù di Carlo II*, was premiered by the Reale Sarda. Woller himself joined the Sarda company in 1847 and the following year Righetti invited Giacometti to become the company poet, the position formerly held by the recently deceased Nota. For the Sarda, Giacometti was contracted to produce at least four works per year. The most popular of these was *La donna*, presented in 1850.

A lesser but popular author of social comedies for the Sarda in its final years was Vincenzo Martini (1803-1862), who served somewhat in the manner of Scribe of France as a bridge between the sensational drama of romanticism and the more realistic bourgeois drama of the next generation. His first great success was *Una donna di quarant'anni*, followed by *Il misantropo in società,* both with leading roles created especially for Ristori and both premiered by the Sarda in 1853.

Thus in terms of actors and authors the new decade opened with great promise for the Sarda, but the finanical outlook was far less bright. When royal patronage was withdrawn, the theatre was forced to appeal to Parliament for support and the deputies were disinclined to use money from the provinces to support a venture which they felt was a toy for the city of Turin alone. When the question came up for debate in 1853, the theatre was passionately defended by the deputy Angelo Brofferio (1802-1866), a follower of Mazzini who had for many years been involved in the struggle against Austria and provided the Reale Sarda with the number of dramas salted with discreet political references. His pleas, both artistic and political, went unheeded. Neither King nor Parliament saw the usefulness of a national theatre, and all support was terminated in 1854. Righetti struggled along without subsidy for a year and then, in a desperate gamble, the company undertook a repetition of Iternari's experiment a quarter-century before—a tour to Paris. This time, largely because of the triumph of Ristori, the tour was a great success, but the Parisian profits were soon exhausted. Only seven more works were mounted after the company's return to Italy and scarcely a year after its Parisian tour had made the Reale Sarda the first Italian company since the Renaissance to gain an international reputation, Righetti was forced to disband. Henceforth Turin's Teatro Carignano sheltered only traveling companies.

Verdi and Milan

Giuseppi Verdi (1813-1901) was born in a small town in the Duchy of Parma, which at the time of his birth was part of the French

Empire. During his youth it was an independent state under the relatively easy-going Maria Luisa, who was, within her means, a dedicated person of the arts. When Verdi's first compositions were winning him a local fame, the next step up might have been instruction at the musical conservatory in Parma or production at the Ducal Theatre there, but Parma was at this time more dedicated to spoken than to musical theatre. Mascherpa headed the ducal company, which was joined by Antonio Colomberti after his unsuccessful tour to Paris. During the 1830s and 1840s the fame of this troupe approached that of the Reale Sarda. Domeniconi joined the company from 1829 to 1831 and for a season in 1835 and Ristori was here for five years in the early 1840s. During the early part of this period the company was best known for its interpretations of Italian comedy—Goldoni, Nota and Giraud—but later French romantic drama and Italian tragedy became dominant.

Neighboring Milan was much weaker in the spoken drama, which had still not recovered from the political agonies of the early 1820s. The musical theatre on the other hand was thriving to such an extent that by 1830 Milan had clearly taken the lead in this genre from Naples and Venice. Accordingly, Verdi's local patron, Antonio Barezzi, decided the young artist must be sent to the Milan Conservatory. When Verdi arrived in 1832 La Scala was firmly established as the dominant theatre, but most of the city's theatres were devoted primarily to opera. Even the Teatro Re, with notoriously poor acoustics, presented occasional musical works. The Teatro Carcano had seen the premieres of Donizetti's *Anna Bolena* in 1830 and Bellini's *La sonnambula* in 1831 and in 1832, only a month before Verdi's arrival, the Teatro della Cannobiana had premiered Donizetti's *L'elisir d'amore*. Verdi was not accepted by the Conservatory, but he studied music in the city and absorbed its rich operatic life at one of its greatest periods before returning home to complete his own first opera, *Oberto*.

The rest of the decade was one of continuing musical brilliance in Milan, but the opening years of the 1830s were the most spectacular. A major shift now began to take place in the world of musical theatre, heralded by the departure of Rossini for Paris. The old centrifugal force of the Italian artistic world, observable since the Renaissance, again asserted itself, so that between the mid-1830s and 1860 the great Italian operatic singers were found not at La Scala, or indeed in Italy, but in Paris, London and St. Petersburg.

Rossini played a major role in this shift through his close association with the Théâtre Italien in Paris. He brought the leading younger composers here—Bellini with *I puritani e i cavalieri* (1835), Mercadante with *I briganti* (1836), Donizetti with *Marin Faliero* (1835), though none elected to remain, as he had, in the north. His more permanent acquisitions were major singers and thanks to his efforts, Paris and not Milan now became the city with the acknowledged greatest Italian operatic voices of the period. To the discriminating opera-goer of this era, the height of vocal excellence was symbolized by the "great quartet"—four artists brought by Rossini to Paris who subsequently became frequent visitors to London as well. These were Giulia Grisi (1811 1869), Giovan Rubini (1795-1854), Antonio Tamburini (1800-1869) and Luigi Lablache (1794-1858). Grisi was born in Milan and first seen by Rossini at the Pergola in Florence in 1829, where he recognized her promise at once. She appeared at La Scala in 1831 and was invited the following year to Paris, where she remained until she began a series of international tours in 1854. The tenor Rubini was discovered and encouraged by Barbaja, for whom he interpreted forty-four operas, primarily in Naples and Vienna. He sang with the bass Lablache in Vienna in 1823 and in Naples during the next several seasons. Rubini departed for La Scala in 1827 but in 1831 the two singers were united again by Rossini at the Théâtre Italien. The bass Tamburini, who had appeared during the 1820s in most of the major houses in Italy and shared the honors with Rubini of the premiere of Bellini's *Il pirata* at La Scala in 1827, joined the company of the Théâtre Italien in 1832.

The work which gave the great quartet international fame was Bellini's *I puritani* and until Rubini was replaced by Giovanni Mario (1810-1883) in 1839, the group was often called the "*Puritani* quartet." Mario, born Giovanni de Candia, became involved, despite his aristocratic background, in Mazzini's Young Italy movement. This led to a bitter break with his conservative father and young Giovanni left Italy for France, where he pursued his musical career under the name Mario. He was encouraged by Meyerbeer and established a reputation in French at the Opera before joining the Italien. The "great quartet," though they dominated the singing world of the period, did not frequently appear in the same work, since operas written for soprano, tenor and two basses were few and generally expressly written for them (the major example was Donizetti's *Don Pasquale* in 1843), but Grisi and Mario normally sang together and either Lablache or Tamburini would appear with them. Their tours made Italian opera an essential part of the international theatre scene and the way was prepared for the tours of the great artists of spoken drama which followed in the next generation.

It was fortunate for La Scala that just as this major competition was developing elsewhere in Europe, the theatre was blessed with a new operatic genius in Giuseppe Verdi, though it was several years before the significance of his contribution began to be felt. The process of getting *Oberto* presented at all was a difficult one, and two years passed between its completion and its premiere at La Scala in 1839. It was not a major success, but it was successful enough for Bartolomeo Merelli, director of La Scala, to contract Verdi for three more works. The first work completed, an opera buffa, *Un giorno di regno* (1840) was a disastrous failure, so crushing that Verdi renounced his contract and swore never to compose again. Happily, Merelli continued to encourage him and pressed upon him a new libretto based on the Biblical story of Nebuchadnezzar by Temistocle Solera (1815-1878), the young poet who had set the script of *Oberto* into verse for Verdi. Verdi took the libretto, determined not to consider it, but in later years recalled that a single phrase in the script caught his eye and began the process which led him back into composition. The phrase "Va, pensiero, sull'ali dorate" (Go, thought, on golden wings) Verdi made into a great chorus which became the most beloved and familiar of his early compositions. At the tumultuous opening performance, the audience, despite a special police prohibition against encores, demanded that the chorus be repeated and it was soon sung throughout the streets of Milan. The police were not concerned in vain, for the entire story of *Nabucco*, dealing with the Babylonian captivity of the Jewish people, had a clear allegorical meaning for its audience. In addition to its musical power, the work offered its public simple and moving statements of patriotism such as the oft-quoted and sung, "Oh mia patria sì bella e perduta" (Oh my country, so beautiful and lost), which were in these days the only safe way for Italians to express publicly nationalistic feelings. The success of *Nabucco* was unprecedented for Milan. In its first full season it set a record for number of performances and one of Verdi's biographies has calculated that the total attendance this first season was 20,000 more than the total population of the city.(17) As if to emphasize the arrival of a new musical lion in Milan the reigning composer, Donizetti, left the city just at this time to accept the post of Imperial Composer in Vienna. He remained in Milan a few extra days just to attend the premiere of *Nabucco* and according to an often-repeated anecdote talked incessantly of the brilliance of its score all the way to Bologna.

I Lombardi, Verdi's next work for La Scala, was an epic of the first Crusade and aroused the protests of Milan's Archbishop, who objected to certain religious references in the play and particularly to a scene of baptism. Verdi was by now so popular that the police feared riots were as likely to result from rumors of major cuts in the work as from offensive passages left in and at last, after much debate, the work was approved essentially intact. Musically, it was somewhat inferior to *Nabucco*, but politically it was even more stirring. The religious matter passed unnoticed, but the audience obviously saw themselves as the Lombards and the Austrians as the Saracens occupying the Holy Land. Encore followed encore, in defiance of the police, culminating in a frenzied demonstration when the tenor sang "La Santa Terra oggi nostra sarà" (The Holy Land shall be ours today) and the Chorus responded "Sì! ... Guerra! Guerra! (Yes! ... War! War!). Following this, the censors clearly resolved that whatever the cost, Verdi's works must be carefully edited.

Still it would be wrong on the basis of these events to regard the young Verdi as a patriot first and artist second, in the style of Mazzini or even of Modena. Clearly he shared the liberal, partiotic sentiments of the majority of his countrymen. Among his earliest extant works are musical settings for Manzoni's patriotic ode *Il cinque maggio* and several choruses for the tragedies. Certainly Verdi sympathized with his liberal librettist Solera, whose father, like Foscolo, had been confined in the hated Spielberg by the Austrians. But he joined no secret societies and seems to have generally cast himself with those who felt that a more tolerant political climate could evolve in the process of gradual moral pressure. Despite the revolutionary overtones of *Nabucco* and *I Lombardi,* Verdi saw nothing improper in dedicating the first to the Austrian Archduchess Adelaide (who that same year married the young Vittorio Emmanuele) and the second to Duchess Maria Luisa of Parma.

The major successes naturally brought offers to Verdi from the impresarios of Italy's other leading opera theatres and then from elsewhere in Europe as well. It was not customary for operatic composers, as it was for dramatic poets, to seek long-term contracts with a single impresario or theatre, so Verdi would probably soon have left Milan in any case. Still, Merelli did little to encourage his faithfulness, producing Verdi's works with less preparation than the composer desired, with occasionally inadequate casts and even at times in reworked form unacceptable to the composer. The final indignity seems to have been the decision in 1845 to present *I due Foscari* (actually premiered in Rome) with the third and last act preceding the second. Verdi broke off all relations with La Scala, and though his works remained a mainstay of the theatre, not another Verdi premiere was held there until 1869.

With the departure of Verdi the opera did not lose its preeminence in Milan, but dance and the spoken drama became for a time more significant competitors. These were the years of the great stars of ballet at La Scala, first Fanny Cerrito of Naples (1817-1909), who was prima ballerina at La Scala from 1838 to 1841, then Maria Taglioni (1804-1884), who divided the musical world of Milan as she had divided that of Europe into opposing camps of her own supporters and those of Cerrito. The Milanese police were powerless to stop the demonstrations of support whenever either of these popular stars appeared. Then, to challenge both Italian dancers and to add to the problems of policing La Scala, there appeared the Austrian Fanny Elssler (1810-1884), whose arrival in Milan created a third group of partisans and inevitably introduced the element of patriotism as well. She was warmly applauded at La Scala in *Giselle* in 1844 and again in 1847, but when she returned in February of 1848 Milan was on the brink of revolt and many considered her appearance a reminder of Austrian rule. A boycott virtually emptied La Scala and Elssler was appalled to find her corps de ballet preparing to go on stage all wearing medals showing the Pope blessing a united Italy. She refused to dance unless they were removed, but her victory was a hollow one, since whistles and obscene shouts accompanied the rest of her performance despite the presence of the police. She soon left Milan, never to return.

The tide which in 1848 was running against Elssler in Milan was running in favor of an actor in the spoken drama, the Milanese Giuseppe Moncalvo (1781-1859), who reached this year the peak of his popularity and influence. Between 1820 and 1857 Moncalvo was a central figure in Milan's theatre life, an indefatigable entrepreneur, director at one time of five theatres, a discoverer and encourager of young talent (Ristori, Rossi and Sadowsky were among those whose first steps he guided), a playwright and adapter, and above all the popularizer of the beloved Milanese dialect character Meneghino. Meneghino was a traditional commedia character, portrayed by many actors before Moncalvo, but Moncalvo enriched, deepened and established the character rather in the way his contemporary Debureau enriched and immortalized the previously minor Pierrot at this same time in Paris.

Meneghino, like the French Pierrot, showed the influence of the romantic era in which he came to maturity, but in France this resulted in a suffering, sentimental lover, while Meneghino, the native of Milan, was a very different type—a cynical, cold-hearted revolutionary. A critic of the period wrote that "Moncalvo identified himself with Meneghino, taking on his heart, his quick and shrewd perception, the biting wit, the rebellious spirit, the inclination toward satire, the taste for the erotic and the unconquerable hatred for all restraint in general and for Austrian rule in particular."(18)

Moncalvo's dream was the establishment of a theatre devoted to works in the Milanese dialect, but the Austrians, foreseeing clearly enough the patriotic potential of such an establishment refused to consider it. The public was nevertheless not at all deprived of opportunity to see their beloved Meneghino, for the indefatigable Moncalvo produced at the Carcano and Lentasio a host of original plays such as *Meneghino, medico per forze* (1844) and *Meneghino schiavo in Turchia* (1845) and moreover introduced his character into countless plays by Goldoni, Molière and more recent French and Italian authors. Meneghino's improvised jokes were the despair of Austrian censors, but even so Moncalvo naturally had to exercise a certain restraint. Meneghino's apotheosis came in 1848 in common with that of his native city, in the glorious "Five Days" of popular uprising. One of the citizens' barricades was thrown up in the streets at the very steps of the Carcano and when the city was liberated, Milanese flocked to the theatre to see Meneghino at last confront the enemy directly and without restraint in *Il dialogo fra Radetzki e Metternich con Meneghino locandiere.* The return of the Austrians put an end to such activity, but Moncalvo made his peace with the authorities and continued to mock them behind their backs, for the most part in a dialect incomprehensible to them. He suffered serious financial reverses in his theatre enterprises during his last years but before his death in 1859 he had the joy of seeing his beloved city at last freed from Austrian domination. He left, he said, "my body to the earth, my soul to God, my mind to Italy and my heart to my dear Milan."

During these years Milan also possessed an important prose company presenting works in the standard Italian *lingua.* This was the Lombarda, which was built upon the foundations laid here by Gustavo Modena in the early 1840s. When Modena returned to politics in 1846, the troupe of young actors he had developed in Milan was taken over by F.A. Bon from the Reale Sarda and the Milanese journalist and dramatist Giacinto Battaglia, who gave it the name Compagnia Drammatica Lombarda. Bon remained as director until 1852, offering many of his own plays including his final comedy *Pietro Paolo Rubens* (1852). He then retired to Padua to direct the Instituto Filarmonico-Drammatico there and to write his observations on theatrical art. His position as director was assumed by the company's leading actor, Alamanno Morelli (1812-1893), who had the distinction of offering *Hamlet* (at Venice's La Fenice in 1850) for the first time in Italy since Morrocchesi's attempt in 1793.

As director, Morelli followed his predecessor's practice of concentrating on translations from the French—works by romantics Hugo, Dumas, and Vigny, and the more realistic comedies and dramas of Scribe and his school. The Lombarda's leading lady, Sadowsky, achieved particular success in Scribe's *Adrienne Lecouvreur*, which remained permanently in her repertoire. She also commissioned a new comedy from the journalist and author Leone Fortis (1824-1898) with a leading part to be "a bit bizarre and unlike others." The result, *Cuore e arte* (1852) was a major success and was ever afterward associated with Sadowsky's name. Morelli remained with the theatre for only a year, then left to lead the Accadamia dei Filodrammatici of Milan. During the 1860s he returned to theatre directing and was a leader in presenting the new school of realist drama. Two other actor-directors followed him at the Lombarda, Carlo Zamarini (d. 1886) and Luigi Aliprandi (1817-1901), but despite these frequent changes of leadership the theatre, housed primarily at the Teatro Re, maintained high standards of production and the reputation of one of the leading prose theatres in Italy.

Verdi, Naples and Rome

When Verdi broke with La Scala, his reputation was so firmly established that he could have his subsequent works premiered at almost any opera house in Italy. The leading impresarios vied with each other in offering him conductors, singers and contracts which might gain them a Verdi premiere, and the seven works he completed after *Giovanna d'Arco* at La Scala were each premiered at a different theatre, covering the spectrum of the major houses to which Italian operatic composers then aspired. *Alzira* (1845) was given at the San Carlo of Naples, *Attila* (1846) at La Fenice in Venice, *Macbeth* (1847) at La Pergola in Florence, *I masnadieri* (1847) at Her Majesty's in London, *Jerusalem* (1847, a revision of *I Lombardi*) at the Opera in Paris, *Il corsaro* (1848) at the Grande in Trieste, and *La battaglia di Legnano* (1849) at Rome's Argentina. The two most successful of the works premiered in Italy were *Attila* and *Il battaglia di Legnano,* surely in part because these were also the two with the most direct political relevance. *Macbeth*, though well received in Florence, did indifferently elsewhere and only with the passing of time was recognized as one of Verdi's best works of this period. *Attila*, on the other hand, despite some musical value, was surely more prized by its contemporary audiences for its subject, the invasion of Italy by the Huns, and for such lines as the widely quoted "Avrai tu l'universo; resti l'Italia a me." (You take the universe, leave Italy to me.)

La battaglia di Legnano was even more thoroughly a political creation. Verdi had come to Milan in the spring of 1848, reveling in the city's freedom and probably anticipating a position of honor in the new republic, but like Mazzini he was discouraged by the city's willingness to throw itself into the arms of another king and within a month he left, disillusioned. One of his first reactions was to accept an offer from the librettist Salvatore Cammarano in Naples for an opera dealing with a united Italy, the Lombard League, defeating a German invader, Friedrich Barbarossa. The decisive battle took place in 1176 at Legnano, which in 1848 was an Austrian stronghold. The theatre selected for the premiere was the Teatro Argentina in Rome, which with a generally liberal government and a censor concerned primarily with religious questions and not answerable to Austria, seemed the most likely place for a tolerant reception. Events made this choice even more ideal. In November the Pope fled the city, a republican government was established, and political exiles like Mazzini flocked to Rome in hopes of seeing it become the center of the new Italy. Under these conditions *La battaglia di Legnano* was premiered and its success was almost inevitable. Perhaps under the circumstances, the most surprising thing about the work is that with all its leading characters' (and its audience's) obsession with "la patria," it has any musical validity at all. Verdi was, of course, hailed as one of the guiding spirits of the new age and "viva Verdi" could be heard almost as frequently as "viva Italia" in those buoyant days in Rome.

Still, the period of triumph was short, and with the fall of Rome the Mazzinian vision of an Italy united by spontaneous republican uprisings faded forever. After the events of 1848-1849, neither the Italian people nor Verdi saw their future in quite the same way as before. The shift in emphasis between Verdi's *La battaglia di Legnano* and *Luisa Miller* is a striking example of this change. Cammarano was bold enough to suggest a new opera based on Guerazzi's *Assedio di Firenze*, published in Paris in 1836 and never presented in Italy, but the censors put a stop to this project at once. Cammarano then bowed to the inevitable and created the libretto for *Luisa Miller*, based on Schiller's *Kabale und Liebe*, essentially a story of thwarted love from which the librettist removed all social and political references. The opera was premiered at San Carlo late in 1849 and was a substantial success, rather more striking in that it was Verdi's first work in some time which clearly owed its popularity to its qualities as an opera, not to any external concerns. The shift in emphasis from politics to love, with a resultingly more tender score, has led many critics to suggest that *Luisa Miller* began a new period in Verdi's development, his "middle period," occupying the next ten years. This period included four of his best known works: *Rigoletto* and *La traviata* (premiered at La Fenice in 1851 and 1853) and *Il trovatore* and *Un ballo in maschera* (premiered at Rome's Teatro Apollo in 1853 and 1859). It was a period of dazzling achievement for Verdi, but also one of constant stress, since there was always the danger that a work to which he had committed much time and thought would be halted by the censor. Both *Rigoletto* and *Un ballo in maschera* required extensive negotiations, legal action and significant rewriting before they could be presented. The official communication from the Austrian censors submitted to Verdi three months before the scheduled premiere of *Rigoletto* is a striking example of the attitude with which he had to contend:

> His Excellency the Military Governor Chevalier de Gorkowski in his respected dispatch of the 26th instant directs me to communicate to you his profound regret that the poet Piave and the celebrated Maestro Verdi have not chosen some other field to display their talents than the revolting immorality and obscene triviality forming the story of the libretto *La maledizione*, submitted to us for eventual performance at La Fenice.
>
> His Excellency has decided that the performance must be absolutely forbidden and wishes me at the same time to request you not to make further inquiries in this matter.(19)

If anything could be more ludicrous than the censor's preliminary judgment on such questions, it was the adjustments required to win eventual approval. Apparently, despite years of evidence to the contrary, censors in Italy believed that audiences would see no political or moral relevance in plays or operas if the names or locations were adjusted. So the French King in *La maledizione (Rigoletto)* became the Duke of Mantua, to protect the royal image. The Papal censor refused to pass *Un ballo in maschera*, dealing with a regicide in eighteenth-century Sweden, unless the action were set outside of Europe. Verdi considered both North and South America and even the Caucasus before finally giving the story its incongruous setting in colonial Boston.

But if the censors were fooled, or willing to close their eyes, the Italian people were not. Whatever the surface references in the operas, Verdi was generally considered an artist deeply involved with the dream of a free Italy. In 1859, when *Un ballo in maschera* appeared, Vittorio Emmanuele in Piedmont opened Parliament with a speech raising hopes that this dream would soon be fulfilled. It was observed that Verdi's name was an acrostic for Vittorio Emmanuele Re d'Italia, and the cry "Viva Verdi!" took on new meaning for Italian patriots. It was shouted on all occasions, but especially when Austrians were present. The aspriations of the Risorgimento were at last on the brink of fulfillment. The successes in political strategy of Cavour in the north and the military miracles of Garibaldi in the south carried all before them. When *Un ballo in maschera* was premiered, Italy was still essentially divided into the same system of states Napoleon had left. Less than two years later Verdi was on his way to Turin as an elected deputy from his home district to the first Parliament convened by the united Kingdom of Italy.

The prose theatre during the years of Verdi's greatest triumphs naturally received much less attention than the opera, but its tradition was continued by some forty to fifty major traveling companies and a much smaller number of troupes regularly settled into theatres in particular cities. Even Venice, where the opera at La Fenice far surpassed any other theatrical concern, there was still a permanent prose theatre, the Goldoni, which, while it had no resident troupe, was regularly visited by Italy's leading actors and companies, such as Marchionni, Mascherpa, Bon, Modena and Ristori. It even, from time to time, witnessed an important premiere, such as Giacometti's *Elisabetta regina d'Inghilterra*, created by Fanny Sadowsky in 1853. That same year a company headed by Cesare Dondini (1807-1875), a veteran of Mascherpa's company and of the Reale Sarda, presented at the Teatro San Benedetto the play which would prove the most significant of the decade, Paolo Ferrari's *Goldoni e le sue sedici commedie nuove*.

Paolo Ferrari (1822-1889) was the first important playwright to emerge as the new Italian state was being formed and was a leader in indicating the direction the major prose drama of the new nation would take. By the end of the century he was generally accepted as "the inaugurator of the modern theatre." Ferrari began his writing career in the late 1840s with a series of comedies in which he sought to shake off the influence of French and German theatre and return to the beloved "father of comic poets," Goldoni. The Goldonian influence extended even to the writing of plays in dialect, for despite the efforts of Manzoni and others the standard Italian *lingua* was still a rather stiff and artificial language, not very well suited to comedies attempting to capture the rhythms of everyday life. Ferrari's first work, *Baltromèo calzolaro*, was written about 1847 in the dialect of the Tuscan province of Massa and later reworked in standard Italian as *Il codicillo dello zir venanzio* for presentation in Turin and into Venetian dialect as *El libreto de la cassa di risparmio*. Ferrari's works in the years just after 1848 were primarily in the dialect of Modena.

Clearly, such works were not likely to move beyond local success without rewriting and during the 1850s Ferrari turned more and more to work in standard Italian. His first major attempt of this sort was *Goldoni e le sue sedici commedie nuove*, based on Goldoni's famous self-imposed labor of creating sixteen new comedies in a single season. The young author sent the work first to Gustavo Modena in Turin, hoping its national subject might appeal to him, but Modena, almost a recluse after the disasters of 1849, answered in the most discouraging terms: "Dear sir, I might have the time to present your play, but I do not have the patience. My spirit is exhausted. Art, justice, liberty and other beauties, I have bid them farewell long since and watched their trails disappear over the moon."(20)

Fortunately, Ferrari found a more sympathetic response to his work closer to home. Filippo Berti (1801-1872), a minor dramatist whose *Gli amanti sessagenari* was a popular offering at the Reale Sarda in 1832, had founded in Florence in 1845 a private school for recitation. In 1852 he began an annual competition for new plays to be represented at his Ginnasio Drammatica and Ferrari's *Goldoni* was selected as the first winner. It achieved a modest success there, but its real test came in Venice the following year, where it was presented by a professional company. Since Venice considered Goldoni its own property and moreover had its own traditional dialect for comedy, either the language or the subject of Ferrari's play could have caused its failure, but in fact it was a triumphant success, and this success guaranteed its production in other Italian cities. In Bologna it was given during carnival season, again with some risk, since for the Bolognese, comedies were traditionally either French or written in the local dialect. This audience too was totally won over and the curtain fell amid cries which heralded a new tradition and a new pride: "Viva la commedia italiana!"(21) A lesser, but significant success, was achieved by *Il Tartufo moderno* (1852) a play written in simple, straightforward language but not in dialect concerning a young French writer with an Italian mother and a romantic attachment to Italy. It was reworked in 1858 as *Prosa* and premiered at Milan's Teatro Re.

Both versions were first offered by the Domeniconi company, which during the decade after 1848 was probably the best in Italy. Domeniconi spent the years 1840 to 1843 at the Fiorentini in Naples, then left to establish two companies of his own, the first under his own direction, the second headed by Gaetano Cottellini (d. 1883). The companies were neither particularly distinguished nor successful and in 1845 they were collapsed into one, directed by Cottellini, while Domeniconi departed for the Reale Sarda. In 1848 he returned, however, and succeeded in winning for the troupe a number of outstanding players: the actresses Maddalena Pelzet, Adelaide Ristori and Anna Job; and the actors Gaspare Pieri and the young Tommaso Salvini. As first young lover Salvini joined Ristori in a number of notable romantic pairings—Paolo and Francesca, Pia dei Tolomei and Rinaldo, Romeo and Giulietta, Mortimer and Maria Stuarda. In 1847 Salvini achieved his first great success as a tragic actor, in Alfieri's *Oreste*. The Roman public still remembered the fiery Lombardi in this role and even Modena had been unable to compete with that memory. Salvini's triumph (supported by Ristori as Elettra, Job as Clitennestra, and Domeniconi as Egisto) established him at the age of nineteen as a major new serious actor.

The Domeniconi company was touring in Sicily when the revolution of 1848 broke out. They returned to Rome, where Salvini and other younger members of the troupe enlisted in the new republic's national guard. When the city fell, Salvini left, but was arrested and imprisoned in Florence until Domeniconi obtained permission from the Roman authorities to reassemble his company. At the Teatro Valle, renamed the Roma, they resumed their work with great success, but under constant surveillance by the authorities for any politically or morally suspicious material. All religious references were banned and the Italian colors, red, white and green could not be seen together. "If it chanced that one actress had white and green in her dress, another who wore a red ribbon must not come near her," Salvini reported. "I remember well that one night when I played the Captain in Goldoni's *Sposa sagace*, I was fined ten scudi for wearing a blue uniform with red facings and white ornaments, for the excellent reason that the blue looked green by artificial light."(22)

The departure of Rachel to join the Reale Sarda in 1851 was of course a major loss for Domeniconi. She was replaced by a distinctly lesser actress, Amalia Fumagalli (1824-1875), who had been trained under Augusto Bon and Carolina Internari and who according to Salvini was gifted with a "sweet voice, a most moving rendering of emotion, a dexterity that was beyond belief and a most uncommon degree of artistic intuition." As a romantic leading lady, however, she could never entirely overcome her "comic face" and "inelegant figure."(23) It was Salvini and Fumagalli who premiered Ferrari's *Il Tartufo moderna* in Modena in 1852. The following year Salvini's contract expired and he found himself at a crossroads in his career. He had established some goals for himself, but now realized they were incompatible with the Italian stage as it then existed:

> It was my aim to form a repertory of special parts so minutely studied and rounded that I might be able through them to attain a reputation. The conditions of the Italian stage at that time were not such as to offer me the means of attaining my end. Constrained as I was to busy myself with a new part every week, which, though often I did not know the text perfectly I had to play without reflection and without having a thorough grasp of it, how was it possible for me to prosecute a serious study of the philosophy and psychology of my art?(24)

Accordingly, he decided to retire from the stage for a year and devote himself to a study in depth of three parts: Orosmane in Voltaire's *Zaïre,* Alfieri's *Saul* and Shakespeare's *Othello.*

Domeniconi replaced Salvini with the popular Antonio Colomberti and continued to tour Italy with considerable success during the 1850s, presenting works by such French authors as Scribe, Bayard and Dennery, and by Alfieri, Monti, Pellico, Niccolini and Ferrari. In the early 1860s his company steadily declined, and Domeniconi retired from the stage in 1863. His sometime leading actor Colomberti wrote: "A good part of his misfortunes as a company leader resulted from the immense passion he felt for his art, neglecting nothing which would increase its dignity, dedicating to it continual study, vigilance and sacrifices of all sorts. He was the first to give a luxuriousness to the setting such that only Fabbrichesi might be compared with him."(25) For these services to the art, Domeniconi was decorated in 1863 with the order of St. Maurice, the first actor to be so honored.

After his season to study in 1853, Salvini returned to the theatre by joining a new company being formed by Giuseppe Astolfi (1795-1855) to perform primarily at the Teatro Re in Milan. Astolfi had acted for Mascherpa in the 1820s and Domeniconi in the 1830s, but his more recent and more successful work had been done in collaboration with Fanny Sadowsky in Milan. Sadowsky left for Naples the same year Salvini joined Astolfi, but this company, at the Teatro Re, still included many of the most promising actors of the new generation, among them Gaspare Pieri, Clementina Cazzola, Ernesto

Rossi and Luigi Belloti-Bon. The life of this brilliant company was distressingly brief. After two seasons in Milan they undertook an engagement in Bologna, arriving there not long before the city was attacked by an epidemic of cholera. The company decided to remain and indeed flight would probably have been useless, for the causes of the disease were still unknown and it swept unchecked across Italy and Europe in the 1850s as it had already done in 1831 and 1848. Astolfi himself fell a victim to the disease and his excellent company was disbanded.

A few of them remained together under the leadership of Gaspare Pieri, who found the new plays of Ferrari especially suited for his skills. They premiered *La satira e parini* in Turin in 1856 and for Pieri's benefits usually presented *Goldoni e le sue sedici commedie nuove.* For one such benefit, in Venice in 1854, Pieri reported:

> The most lovely articles were written about me in the *Gazzetta Of-ficiale*, as well as in all the other papers of Venice. They pronounced me superior to many and inferior to none of the leading actors who have represented *Goldoni.* Paolo Ferrari himself directed me and paid the most flattering compliments. He insisted upon fourteen days of study and rehearsal, by which you may be assured that one's memory is secure; in fact the first part of the third act was presented without prompting, which created a most beautiful effect.(26)

Pieri's troupe did not include Salvini and Cazzola, who departed to join another patron of Ferrari, Cesare Dondini. Dondini encouraged them to undertake penetrating and realistic character portrayals; Salvini called him next to Luigi Vestri "the most faithful follower of the school of truth." With the encouragement, both actors developed rapidly. Cazzola's interpretations, said Salvini, were "faithful and exquisitely subtle and the most minute analysis of every profound emotion was rendered by her with exactness and truth."(27) She dazzled audiences in *La signora dalle camelie* and *Pia dei Tolomei* and provided Salvini with what he considered to be the perfect Desdemona for his famous interpretation of *Otello,* first offered in Vicenza in 1856. This was followed a few days later by *Amleto.*

By a striking coincidence Ernesto Rossi presented these same two Shakespearean tragedies only a few weeks before Salvini did at the Teatro Re in Milan. It was, like Salvini's productions, a project he had dreamed of for years. After his trip to Paris with Ristori in 1855, Rossi had gone to London and there witnessed the Hamlets of Charles Kean and Alice Marriott, which provided him with further inspiration and impetus for his own productions. Both Salvini and Rossi eventually became known throughout Europe for their brilliant Shakespearean interpretations, but the Italian public in 1856, still accustomed to the neoclassic structures of Voltaire and Alfieri despite the experiments of the romantics, found Shakespeare's looser structure and broader scope confusing. The more subtle and personal style which Salvini particularly gave to the works was also difficult to appreciate after the broad and conventionalized strokes of the traditional tragic style. It was several months before any of these plays achieved much success and several years before they were recognized in Italy as important productions. Indeed, both actors were hailed for their Shakespearean work in Paris (Salvini in 1857, Rossi in 1866) before they achieved any such acclaim in their homeland. Nevertheless 1856 may be taken as the year Shakespeare truly became a presence in the Italian theatre, with two major tragedies presented by each of the two leading young actors of the period. Moreover, both actors persevered in the face of public preference for more familiar works in the classic manner and eventually carried the day for Shakespeare. Not only did they continue to revive *Amleto* and *Otello,* but they steadily added other works to the repertoire. Rossi offered *Romeo e Giulietta,* which was more quickly accepted, in Milan in 1857 and the following year presented *Re Lear* in Turin, *Mercante de Venezia* in Milan, and *Macbeth* in Venice. He gave *Giulio Cesare* in Venice in 1860, then *Coriolano* in Milan in 1861, and *Antonio e Cleopatra* in Milan in 1865. Salvini's Shakespearean repertoire was smaller, but he also offered *Macbeth, Re Lear,* and later *Coriolano.*

Notes to Chapter IV

1. Giuseppe Mazzini, "Note autobiografiche," *Scritti,* LXXVII (Imola, 1938), p. 13.
2. Luigi Rasi, *I comici italiani* (Florence, 1905), II, 132.
3. Quoted in Rasi, *I comici,* II, 303.
4. Bruno Brunelli, *I teatri di Padova* (Padua, 1921), p. 408.
5. Giuseppe Mazzini, "Della fatalità considerata com'elemento drammatico," *Scritti,* VIII (Imola, 1910), p. 198.
6. Luigi Bonazzi, *Gustavo Modena e l'arta sua* (Perugia, 1865), pp. 63-64.
7. Tommaso Salvini, *Autobiography* (New York, 1893), p. 10.
8. Margaret Fuller Ossoli, *Memoires* (Boston, 1852), II, 268.
9. *Ricordi biograf,* I, 145, quoted in Illario Rinieri, *Della vita e delle opere di Silvio Pellico* (Turin, 1898-1901), II, 252.
10. Rinieri, *Pellico,* II, 357.
11. Adelaide Ristori, *Memoires and Artistic Studies,* trans. G. Mantellini (New York, 1907), pp. 17-18.
12. Ristori, *Memoires,* p. 7.
13. Lamberto Sanguinetti, *La Compagnia Reale Sarda* (Bologna, 1963), p. 88.

14. *Revue de Paris,* Nov. 15, 1836.

15. Ernesto Rossi, *Quarant'anni di vita* (Florence, 1887-89), I, 31.

16. Paolo Giacometti, *Teatro scelto* (Mantua, 1857), I, iii.

17. George Martin, *Verdi: His Music, Life and Times* (New York, 1963), p. 107.

18. *Cronachie Bizantine,* vol. VII, quoted in Severnio Pagani, *Il teatro milanese* (Milan, 1944), p. 86.

19. Quoted in Martin, *Verdi,* p. 271.

20. Quoted in Jean Dormis, *Le Théâtre italien contemporain* (Paris, n.d.), p. 106.

21. Guido Mazzoni, *L'ottocento* (Milan, 1934), II, 988.

22. Salvini, *Autobiography,* p. 67.

23. Salvini, *Autobiography,* p. 72.

24. Salvini, *Autobiography,* pp. 76-77.

25. Quoted in Rasi, *I comici,* I, 775.

26. Quoted in Rasi, *I comici,* II, 280.

27. Salvini, *Autobiography,* p. 89.

V

The International Era

There was inevitably a sense of high drama, even of glorious victory, in the sudden unification of Italy after so many years of frustrated hopes and dashed dreams, but the years immediately following unification had little glory in them. No amount of high hopes could make Vittorio Emmanuele into a great sovereign and he proved barely capable of keeping the new state together during the stormy 1860s and 1870s. Ministers came and went with dizzying rapidity. The old Kingdom of Naples seethed with Bourbon supporters, brigands and a populace generally suspicious and jealous of the increasingly richer and more industrialized north. Austria remained in possession of Venice and other cities in the north and therefore was a constant military threat.

Rome too remained an unresolved problem during the 1860s, and Garibaldi, whose relations to the new government remained highly ambiguous, complicated matters by leading a series of revolts in an attempt to capture the city. These Vittorio Emmanuele was forced to resist and to repudiate, however much he may have agreed with Garibaldi's basic goal. One of the major diplomatic concerns of the new government was the removal of the French troops from the Papal States and the establishment of some accommodation with the Pope which would allow that area to join the new federation. The French were reluctant to leave Rome unless Italy could guarantee its protection, since the Austrians might take advantage of any weakness in the central part of the peninsula. For this reason Vittorio Emmanuele moved his capital in 1864 from Turin to Florence, both as a symbolic step toward Rome and as a more strategic location near the border of the Papal States.

The Austrian-Prussian War of 1866, in which Italy participated on the side of victorious Prussia, gained for Italy the long-desired province of Venetia. The main body of French troops left Rome soon afterward, but a small Papal army remained, the threat of French support for which, if Italy attempted to assimilate Rome, prevented the King from moving further at this time. Once again external events gave Italy her opportunity—this time the Franco-Prussian War of 1870. The defeat of France removed any serious obstacle to Italy's absorbing the Papal States, a move desired by the overwhelming majority of Romans as well as by their prospective countrymen throughout the peninsula. Over the protests of Pius IX the city was occupied and in 1871 it was proclaimed at last the capital of the new nation.

Despite these victories, the times were difficult and unsettled; the main concern of the politicians seemed to be jockeying for power and that of the central government the raising of troops to hold together the new and fragile state and to meet the continuing threat of the neighboring great powers. It is thus hardly surprising that the arts, which had enjoyed a certain regular financial and social support in the courts and capitals of divided Italy, found themselves given little attention by the new order. Salvini appealed personally to Vittorio Emmanuele in Florence in 1864 for state support of the theatre, but in vain. In 1872, after unification of the peninsula was complete, Verdi urged that the state subsidize at least three theatres, in Rome, Milan and Naples, but with no more success. It now became the general practice for a municipality, far from subsidizing its theatres, to put them up for auction each season to the highest bidder, who would then assemble a company and book in whatever traveling stars or companies he could as special attractions.

Naturally this created a highly unstable system in terms of both personnel and finances. A great star—a Ristori, Salvini or Rossi—could be and was hired for brief engagements or a management might similarly indulge in the enormous expense of mounting a grand opera in some faint approximation of the Paris style, but such indulgence was possible only on rare occasions and could be managed only with great sacrifice for a long time before and after. As a result, the new state, which had already begun to lose the major artists from its musical stage, now began to lose the leading actors from the prose theatre as well, as they discovered that other nations could offer them both higher wages and far better support for physical production. Ironically, as Italy brought home its political expatriots, it replaced them by a generation of artistic expatriots.

Ristori was the first major Italian performer in the spoken drama to establish an international reputation and her many tours set the pattern for the whole generation of international stars, Italians

and others, who followed her. She began in 1855 by redeeming Iternari's lack of success in Paris, then went on to other European capitals
and eventually to the New World and to Asia and Africa. Rossi, who
accompanied her to Paris, and Salvini, who came there the following
year, did not immediately follow her example in international touring
but attempted during the next decade to pursue careers in the new
Italy. Then, discouraged by lack of support and the generally
depressed conditions of the Italian stage, first Rossi, then Salvini
began international touring. After 1870 their countrymen saw the
greatest stars of the period only rarely, but in exchange audiences
around the world, for whom the Italian theatre had hitherto meant
only opera, were exposed for the first time to a quite different
manifestation of achievement in the theatre.

Ristori

The 1855 departure for Paris of the Reale Sarda company,
headed by Ristori and Rossi, clearly inaugurated a new era in the
Italian theatre. The attitude of Europe's cultured society toward Italy
had at this time a paradoxical quality. The time of the grand tour had
not passed and young aristocrats regularly visited Italy as part of their
education. For those who could not make the trip, journals of Italian
tours were the most popular and plentiful of all writings on travel.
Still, the focus of books and of tours was almost inevitably on the
Italy of the past. Aside perhaps from its music, contemporary Italy
was almost invisible, both culturally and politically, to the rest of
Europe. In Lamartine's famous phrase, it was the Land of the Dead.

A critical part of Cavour's policy was to demonstrate to the
great powers that Sardinia must be taken seriously as a political power
and with that aim in mind he dispatched a well-publicized force to participate in the Crimean War. Sardinia had little real interest in this
conflict, but Cavour's action not only demonstrated an independence
from Austria, which tried to reverse his decision, but forced France
and Britain to treat Sardinia as an ally of some significance. The tour
of the Royal Sardinian Company to the International Exposition of
1855 in Paris served on the cultural level the same purpose as the
Crimean expedition did on the political (indeed the two initiatives
were almost simultaneous; the soldiers left Turin in April, the actors
in May). Ristori observed: "My object was to vindicate abroad the
true artistic genius of the Italian stage and to show that Italy is not

only 'The Land of the Dead.' "(1) Two foreign companies were to appear at the Exposition but an English troupe failed immediately and returned home, leaving the Salle Ventadour to the exclusive use of the Italians.

Of course a more modest version of this project had been attempted in 1830 by Carolina Internari, with the most discouraging results, but Ristori and her company were more fortunate. While Internari encountered the revolutionary upheavals of 1830, Ristori had the advantage of the large public attracted by the Exposition. Moreover, the unsettled political conditions in Italy had spawned a significant expatriot Italian community in Paris which provided a highly sympathetic basic audience for the opening performances. Clearly the company directed its first offering more to this audience than to the French. It was Pellico's *Francesca da Rimini,* preceded by one of the author's patriotic odes.

Probably this audience would have remained essentially the same and the Reale Sarda company would have enjoyed a profitable but not particularly influential stay in Paris had they not been "discovered" and championed by the dean of the French critics of the period, Jules Janin. In a lengthy and highly enthusiastic review in the *Journal des Debats* he praised Ristori to the skies and compared her, always to her favor, with the reigning French tragic actress Rachel. Other major figures on the French literary scene rapidly followed his lead — Alexandre Dumas, Ernest Legouvé, Eugène Scribe, August Vacquerie, Théophile Gautier, Alphonse de Lamartine. The general public also flocked to the Salle Ventadour to see the new sensation, and the Italian tour became a triumph.

So much of this event was colored by the Rachel-Ristori conflict (Dumas even proposed that they should have a kind of artistic duel at the Opéra, performing alternate acts of two different tragedies) that it is nearly impossible to sort out the purely artistic merits of Ristori and her company in the eyes of the French public. Rachel was certainly past her prime and in declining health. She had moreover antagonized most of the critics and authors who supported Ristori by her unwillingness to accept without question their plays or their advice and she irritated many others in Paris by her frequent absences from the Comédie and her recent decision to undertake a tour to America. Ristori unwittingly provided a means for all these grievances to be expressed at just the proper moment. It is easy to see why Rachel's biographers have been tempted to explain Ristori's success essentially on these grounds. Still, Paris (whatever its cultural leaders thought) was not the world and Ristori had sufficient talent to win her world wide success for the next twenty years. In a sense, comparing her to Rachel was unfair to both, for as actresses their styles were so different that Ristori may be said to have brought to Paris a totally new approach. Rachel was herself a kind of throwback, perhaps the most brilliant classic actress France has ever produced, arriving after the full tide of romanticism. She was majestic and graceful, but always statuesque, even in tragic outbursts. In her, all was dignified and elegant. Ristori was far closer to realism, heir of the Italian tradition of Modena, and her more violent and emotional style was a revelation to Paris, even for those who did not entirely approve. Delacroix, for example, commented that in *Pia* she "rendered the agony of man in a very true but very repulsive manner."(2)

The first offering after Janin's enthusiastic review was Alfieri's *Mirra*, a drama whose classic subject and similarity of plot to *Phèdre* emphasized the Ristori-Rachel contrast. Ristori herself remarked on how *Mirra* provided an ideal showcase for her approach:

> This tragedy, revealing the pure and severe Italian style, with distinct Greek form, gave me an opportunity to demonstrate my artistic ability and the profound psychological study I had made of the part. It also proved that our Italian school knows how to ally the Greek plasticism with the natural spontaneity in reading the lines, while being entirely freed from academic conventionalities. It must be granted that academic teaching does not lack praiseworthy qualities, but we argue that in its portrayal of passion, one should not bear in mind the extent and the rules for raising an arm or a finger. Provided that the gestures are noble and not discordant with the expressed sentiment, one can allow the actor all his spontaneity.(3)

The performance was an enormous success. The audience seemed to Ristori to be in delirium and during the fifth act confrontation between Mirra and Cimpras (played by Rossi), shouting and applause were continuous. In the foyer afterwards, the literary world surrounded Ristori to express their admiration—Janin, Legouvé, Scribe, Gautier were there, with Dumas kissing her mantle and hands. Lamartine was inspired to write one of his last odes to her, calling her poetry itself. Ristori became the unchallenged queen of the Exposition, talked about and written about by everyone, her portraits sold everywhere. The theatre was filled to overflowing until the season ended in July.

At the beginning of August the Sarda troupe was invited to give *Maria Stuarda* at the Comédie itself for a benefit for a retired Comédie actress. Again their triumph was uncontested and Ristori was even invited to remain in Paris a year at the expense of the state to learn French and then to replace the departed Rachel at the Comédie. Ristori prudently refused, but arranged to return to the Ventadour for the next three years with Italian plays. The company then departed on a tour of France, then through Belgium to Dresden and Berlin before retuning to Italy in November. Ristori as received, as would be the case whenever she returned from touring, with the greatest enthusiasm. The French public resented Rachel's departures from France and at last rejected her because of them, but the Italians treated Ristori in just the opposite manner, agreeing with Cavour that her tours were making a significant contribution to the national cause. Naturally this enthusiasm was heightened when from time to time Ristori, despite her fame, ran afoul of the Austrian authorities. A suspected political allusion in *Donna del popolo* by the minor Sarda dramatist David Chiossoni (1822-1873) caused her expulsion from Leghorn in 1856 and two years later Giacometti's *Giuditta,* a version of the Judith and Holofernes story, was seen as a political parable by Venetian audiences and aroused such a demonstration that she was required to leave that city also. Such actions, of course, only made the actress even more welcome elsewhere.

The high point of Ristori's return to Paris in the spring of 1856 was the premiere of Legouvé's tragedy *Médée,* created originally for Rachel and subsequently rejected by her. Ristori had already presented two Italian Medeas — by Niccolini and Della Valle — but it was a character she did not like and she agreed with great reluctance to read Legouvé's version. It captivated her at once, however, and she arranged before leaving Paris in 1855 to have one of the political refugees there translate the work into Italian for her return. Her success was enormous, though somewhat qualified by the transparent desire of critics like Janin to use the occasion to mock Rachel. Marenco's *Pia dei Tolomei* and Pellico's *Francesca da Rimini* were less successful but *Mirra* and *Maria Stuarda* were as well received as before. Twenty years later Victorien Sardou wrote that like many of his acquaintances he had not missed a single representation by Ristori: "I have never seen anything so beautiful in the theatre as the playing of this marvelous woman, and the evenings of Pia, of Medea, of Judith and of Mary Stuart have remained the loveliest of my entire dramatic life."(4)

From Paris the company continued to London, where Ristori opened in *Médée* at the Lyceum. The English critics were united in their scorn for Legouvé's drama and in sympathy with Rachel for rejecting it, but they were equally united in calling Ristori an artist of unsurpassed genius who triumphed over this material. The *Spectator* called her "distinctly an *Italian* actress" and went on to explain by graphic example:

> There is a sort of realism mixed with the ideality of Italian acting that with natural disadvantages would almost become ridiculous. Thus when Medea describes the infuriated action of a leopard destroying its victim, she goes through all the process of rending limb from limb; when she calls to mind the horrible picture of her dying brother collecting in his hand the blood flowing from his wound and flinging it in the face of his murderers she seems to be actually collecting clotted gore and actually flinging it. But her figure is made for this picture-acting; and though the general principle on which it is based is most questionable, there is no question about the matter so far as Madame Ristori is concerned. She has a right to make such pictures, because she makes them so well.(5)

The public, at first made somewhat uneasy by the new style and the unfamiliar language, soon warmed to Ristori and enthusiastic crowds began to fill the Lyceum. Medea even achieved that sure indication of a London success—a whole series of burlesques and travesties. Ristori herself attended one such burlesque at the Olympic at the the close of her London season and was honored by the unveiling of a bust of herself at the end of the performance. Little notice was given during the whole of this or subsequent tours to her supporting actors. The Reale Sarda was no more and Ristori after her first tour to Paris selected no one of the stature of Rossi to share her glory. The critic of the *Athenaeum* expressed it succinctly: "In recording Madame Ristori's triumph, it is needful to record also that it has been won singlehandledly. The *Creusa* of the tragedy is tolerable—the other members of the company are wretched."(6)

From London Ristori went across the low countries and Germany to Warsaw, then returned to Italy, where at the beginning of 1857 she visited Naples for the first time. The permanent company at the Fiorentini had a monopoly on prose performances in the city but the Bourbon government gave Ristori a special dispensation to mount a short season at the Teatro del Dondo, normally an opera house. She opened with *Médée* but managed to obtain permission from the censor (though with many cuts) to offer *Fedra* as well, a play which had hitherto been totally banned in this city.

Everything seemed to conspire in the following years to solidify Ristori's position as Europe's best-known actress. Aside from her undisputed gifts and her indefatigable zest for travel, two external factors contributed enormously to her growing renown. First was the decline and death of her only possible rival, Rachel, who collapsed on her American tour and returned to Europe, never to act again. She died in January of 1858. The other was the staggering political success of Cavour and military success of Garibaldi, which created an Italian state almost overnight at the end of the decade and focussed European attention on this new power to the south.

The two external forces coalesced in 1860 when Ristori appeared in Paris in the final year of her three-year contract and her most successful one. Rachel was now gone and while Ristori was in Paris the victorious army of Napoleon III returned from its victories against Austria at Magenta and Solferino, won in collaboration with the new Italian kingdom. This spring Ristori opened her season at the Comédie in a benefit for Racine's grandniece. She presented the fourth act of *Phèdre* in Italian and delivered in French a poem written for the occasion by Legouvé. This experiment proved so successful that she agreed to prepare an entire play in French, though Legouvé was prudent enough to make the heroine of his *Beatrix* (1861) an actress with an Italian accent. The play, premiered at the Odéon, was well received and the *Illustration* observed that Ristori could now be called "the greatest of *our* artists."(7) Still, neither Ristori nor her supporters were sufficiently encouraged to pursue further the suggestion of a permanent position at the Comédie and it was, in fact, four years before the actress played in Paris again.

During the early 1860s she covered most of Europe—Germany, Spain, Portugal, Russia, Holland, Belgium, Greece and Austria—adding a tour in 1864 to Egypt, Smyrna and Constantinople. Students in Holland and in Russia held demonstrations to honor her and the new Italy. She gave private command performances for the Dutch, Prussian and Portuguese rulers and she planned with the King of Greece a performance in the Theatre of Dionysius on a Greek theme, which unhappily did not come to fruition. After each tour she returned to Italy, performing in all the major cities of the new nation. Her most famous Italian appearance during this period was in the spring of 1865 when Florence was celebrating the sixth centenary of Dante. The mayor of the city invited Ristori, Rossi and Salvini, the three most renowned names in the Italian theatre, to make a unique joint appearance in Florence to present Pellico's *Francesca da Rimini* for the celebrations. The site of this memorable occasion was the Teatro Cocomero, which in 1860 had been rechristened the Teatro Niccolini in honor of its major native playwright and had begun hosting Italy's leading prose companies. Ristori and Rossi repeated the leading roles they had performed together with such success a decade before at the Reale Sarda and in Paris and Salvini supported them in the role of Lanciotto. The audience was enraptured and so large that the play had to be repeated the following night to accommodate all who wished to see it. A marble slab with letters of gold was erected in the lobby to commemorate this performance.

The following year Ristori vastly expanded the sphere of her activities by embarking on an American tour. In this, she was essentially breaking new ground, with a venture far riskier than it might appear. The American public was of course long since accustomed to touring English stars and more recently to leading performers of Italian opera, but actors presenting spoken drama in languages other than English was another matter. Rachel was the single precedent and her tour ten years before had not been a signal success. The most astute observers frankly predicted that the entrepreneur Maurice Grau was courting financial disaster by offering an Italian actress the staggering sum of $50,000 for an American tour. But Grau, an apt pupil of the methods of P.T. Barnum and the great opera impresarios of the 1850s, Maurice Strakosch and Max Maretzck, confounded his critics by launching a publicity campaign as unprecedented as his investment. For months before Ristori's arrival the public was treated to reports on the new actress and Grau was extremely sensitive to the matters which would be most interesting to the "gilded age"—that period of new wealth which followed in the wake of the Civil War. Interest in the tours was generated on three levels: financial, as Grau stressed the sumptuousness of the actress' wardrobe and the expense of bringing her; social, since she could truly be billed as having played "before the crowned heads of Europe" and was herself a Marchesa (a Roman nobleman had defied his family to make this romantic match in 1847); and artistic, since as the successful rival of the great Rachel she could be considered a sort of world champion of the theatre.

Thanks to such preparation, Ristori's opening engagement in New York was the greatest triumph she had yet experienced. She performed *Medea, Maria Stuarda, Elisabetta regina d'Inghilterra* (created for her by Giacometti in 1853), *Fedra, Giuditta,* and *Macbeth.* All were performed in Italian and most of the audience purchased libretti to follow the action. The theatre was plagued by mechanical difficulties, the orchestra was pitiful and Ristori's supporting actors as usual wooden and unconvincing, but the actress triumphed over all. All performances sold out and tickets traded hands at enormously inflated prices. Grau's initial investment was repaid before Ristori even left New York, with many performances still ahead. In a single performance at the Brooklyn Academy of *Maria Stuarda* the income was $3,900, surpassing the $3,600 she had gained in Moscow, itself the largest amount ever recorded for a single evening in a European theatre. During her American tour, Ristori would break that record many times.

From New York the actress went on to Boston, then to Baltimore, Washington and Philadelphia. She added several modern Italian works in her repertoire, but these were not particularly successful. American audiences naturally preferred the familiar classics (even a *Macbeth* extensively rewritten to focus on Lady Macbeth) or epics dealing with English history to Marenco's *Pia dei Tolomei*, which the *Tribune* called "ponderous and solemn nonsense" and Montanelli's *Camma*, dismissed in similar terms. In such works even Ristori's much-vaunted realism occasionally came under attack, especially in the extended death scenes which she particularly favored. Thus in *Pia dei Tolomei* the *Tribune* complained of her "long and detailed death," during which the actress "gives malarious wheezes, turns up the whites of her eyes, flings her arms about, gasps and struggles for breath and sinks down, then collapses. She revives and is carried to a green baize rock to repeat the process." Similarly, in *Adrienne Lecouvreur:* "Never was so much dying given for the same amount of money. We have seen Forrest die in *Hamlet,* when it appeared as if he meant to make a night of it, and die all over the stage in every known style, but he was not at all equal to Ristori."(8) Only when Ristori returned to *Elisabetta, Medea* and *Maria Stuarda* did the chorus of unqualified approbation resume.

Early in 1867 the actress struck out into truly new territory, the expanding American West, for even Rachel had only toured a few cities on the eastern seaboard. Many major cities were now easily if not entirely comfortably accessible by railroad and the Italian company headed west to Detroit, Cincinnati and Chicago, then south to St. Louis, Memphis and New Orleans, where they remained for a month, through the carnival season. They then retraced their steps to New York, giving a total of 370 performances in thirty cities over a period of eight months and gaining a total income of $430,000.

Everywhere Ristori had been welcomed as a conquering hero, the greatest dramatic artist of the age and the living symbol of the new Italian nation. As part of her publicity, American papers would sometimes reproduce a letter written to her in 1861 by Cavour praising her for her patriotic service in Russia and France and concluding, "I applaud in you not only the first artist in Europe, but the most skillful co-operator in diplomatic negotiation."(9) Ristori would always carry with her something of this patriotic glamor but her triumph as an international star, especially in America, was of course due to many other things as well—her unquestionable talent, her particular style, her useful combination of aristocracy and Victorian maternal respectability, and the new social configuration in America itself, which made that society so receptive to the cultural prestige of hosting an international star. The message of this success was not lost on Ristori, nor on other stars in her generation. Inevitably she would return, and others would follow. The age of the international star, to which the Italians would be leading contributors, was truly launched by Ristori's first American tour.

Scarcely had Ristori left America in the spring of 1867 when the publicity began for her return that fall. Her second tour lasted until the following spring and was spent largely in New York and cities of the northeast, with a two-month trip in mid-winter to perform in Cuba. Few complaints had been voiced during her first tour about Ristori herself, but the relative weakness of her supporting actors and the unimpressive scenery and costumes had been frequently condemned, especially by the New York critics. The impresario Grau had profited sufficiently from the first tour to address these problems. He remodeled his theatre in New York to improve both stage and auditorium and contracted a new leading actor, Michele Bozzo, to play opposite Ristori. Bozzo (1825-1905), born in Palermo, was enrolled at the Naples Fiorentini in 1840 but dismissed after a season due to his heavy Sicilian accent. "When Signor Bozzo learns to speak Italian," said the director, "he may return to the Teatro dei Fiorentini."(10) In fact Bozzo returned, a year later, with accent little improved and nevertheless made himself one of the most popular actors of Naples by means of his fiery and passionate delivery and his dashing physical presence. In America where neither accent nor his inclination to random vocal emphasis for effect created any problem, he was universally praised.

Perhaps most significantly, Grau arranged on this second tour for Ristori to be accompanied by a large number of settings and costumes, mostly connected with a new historical spectacle, *Maria Antoinetta,* which Giacometti created especially to be premiered on this tour. The settings were designed by the leading theatre artists of Italy. From Naples came designs by Pietro Vernieri and Giuseppe Castagna, the leading designers of the Fondo and San Carlo and directors of the San Carlo school of scenography, who numbered among their previous works the settings for Verdi's Neapolitan premieres, *Alzira* and *Luisa Miller.* From Florence came a setting by Giannini, the leading designer for the Pergola, and from Genoa one by Colvin, designer for the Teatro Carlo Fenice. The costumes were designed by

Wrotz of Paris and were dominated by eight magnificent and frequently photographed robes for Ristori. There was even a special main curtain for the production, painted by du Cerri of the Paris Opera.

The new production proved crucial to the success of this tour. Before it opened, attendance was good but hardly outstanding. Then, with *Maria Antoinetta*, the New York papers reported, the old "Ristori fever" returned. Audiences overflowed the seats into the aisles, the orchestra, onto the stage. All traffic stopped for blocks for every direction because of the press of carriages. The huge production lasted from 7:30 until 1:15 but the enraptured audience showed no sign of fatigue and praise was universal for Ristori and Bozzo and perhaps even more enthusiastic for the visual spectacle. This dazzling success assured that *Maria Antoinetta* would be Ristori's staple work on this tour as *Elisabetta* had been the season before and guaranteed more significantly that later traveling stars, most notably Sarah Bernhardt, would rely on historical spectacle with lavish scenery and costume as an important part of their appeal to American audiences.

The following season Ristori spent touring Italy, presenting *Maria Antoinetta* for the first time there at the recently built Teatro Brunetti in Bologna. The play was at first denied permission, for the authorities feared that a drama concerning the French Revolution might arouse the populace to anarchist demonstrations. At last a permit was obtained, but the evening was indeed a turbulent one, and not at all for the reasons feared. The Bolognese patriots were furious at the sympathetic portrayal of the royal family and only when Ristori stopped the play and made a plea for a tolerant hearing was their anger cooled. Once this first crisis was past, the play proved as popular throughout Italy as it had been in America.

After tours to South America and through Europe to Russia, Ristori returned in 1873 to England, her first visit there in fifteen years. She had in her repertoire a new Giacometti play, *Renata di Francia*, but essentially she continued to rely on proven favorites—*Maria Stuarda, Medea* and *Maria Antoinetta*. For her last two performances in London she attempted the sleepwalking scene from *Macbeth* in English. The experiment was long anticipated and when the moment finally came, after a performance of *Maria Stuarda,* the *Athenaeum* reported "a hush such as is seldom known in a theatre." Ristori had some problems with final *e*'s and with words like Arabia, but her general interpretation was judged "subtle and powerful" and the ovation was tumultuous. The experiment was of course repeated the following year in America, which the actress crossed as part of a tour around the world. Everywhere she was received with respect, even with awe, but with little of the frenzy that had characterized her earlier tours. Her style and her repertoire had been assimilated into the international theatre consciousness. The *New York Herald* went so far as to call her "a dramatic curiosity—a famous relic of a storied past," and continued, "Nothing that she does now presents either her nature or her art in a new aspect; and everything that she does has been many times canvassed and described."(11)

It seemed that the time for retirement had come. Ristori indeed planned to retire in Rome following her world tour but the call of the stage remained too strong. She made what was billed as a final tour to Spain and Portugal in 1876, then another to Scandinavia in 1879. She then in fact left the stage, but two years of retirement proved more than she could bear and in 1882 she set forth again, with a project calculated to reawaken the enthusiasm of those English and American audiences who felt they had experienced all she had to offer. She learned the whole of *Macbeth* in English, along with an English translation of *Elisabetta* for good measure, and opened with them in July of 1882 at Drury Lane. Her experiment won high praise from the critics, though most had to admit that her English tended to become confusing in moments of high emotion and that while individual words were clear, she lacked a feeling for the natural rhythm of the language. The enthusiasm of the general public was unqualified and once again, in her sixties, Ristori filled the theatre with cheering spectators. She followed this London appearance with a final American tour lasting seven months and gaining her the greatest financial rewards of her phenomenally successful career. For her final performances, in May of 1885, she participated in two memorable experiments, presenting *Macbeth* with Edwin Booth at the Brooklyn Academy and *Mary Stuart* at New York's Thalia Theatre with her speaking English and the rest of the cast German.

Following this tour the great actress began her true retirement in Rome, but she never faded from the public view. She gave *Macbeth* with Rossi at the Teatro Apollo in 1887 and occasionally thereafter gave recitations for special events in Rome and Turin. For her eightieth birthday in 1902 all the major theatres in Italy gave performances in her honor, led by the Valle in Rome with Salvini as the leading artist, and telegrams of congratulations poured in from around the world and from most of the sovereigns of Europe. Four years later came her death. Salvini wrote: "She is the last ray of the sun of dramatic art which has gone."(12)

Salvini

The second of Italy's great international stars, Salvini, began his touring career, like Ristori and Rossi, with an engagement in Paris. In 1856, when he had achieved some measure of his goals as an actor in *Zaïre, Saul* and *Otello*, he persuaded his company leader Dondini to follow the example set by Ristori and present these plays to the Parisian public. Accordingly the Salle Ventadour, which by this time had witnessed Ristori in three successive seasons, was booked for Salvini and the Dondini company in the fall of 1857. Clementina Cazzola, fearing the inevitable comparisons with Ristori, refused to go and the young Alfonsina Aliprandi from Milan's Teatro Re was substituted for her. In Paris Salvini opened with Voltaire's *Zaïre,* in Italian of course, which proved an unfortunate choice. Ristori had prudently remained away from the French classics until her reputation in Paris was firmly established, though by 1857 she was able to win accolades even in Marivaux. Salvini paid for his boldness by receiving respectful but somewhat cool and occasionally condescending reviews. The *Illustration,* for example, praised his handsome figure and his delicate style, even his boldness in "wishing to introduce to Parisians Voltaire's Orosmane translated into energetic verse by Count Gozzi," but suggested that "Mr. Salvini does not yet merit being called the *Ristori* of the Salle Ventadour."(13) Alfieri's *Saul* was even more coldly received, but *Otello* proved a great triumph. Shakespeare, still strange and alien in Italy, had become since the romantic revolt a modish playwright on the French stage and Salvini's interpretation drew the first genuine acclamations of the tour. The season was saved for the Dondini company.

Perhaps discouraged by the near failure of this experiment, Salvini did not, like Ristori, commit himself to further foreign touring at this time. It was more than a decade before he performed outside of Italy again, though during that time his fame at home grew to rival hers. He returned to Naples in 1860, to the Fiorentini, where he had performed fifteen years before. When he had departed, the theatre was directed by a triumvirate, but in 1860 only one of the three directors remained, Adamo Alberti (1809-1885), who had joined the theatre in the early 1830s as a young actor and comic author. He had developed under the tutelege of F.A. Bon and always kept Bon's Ludro trilogy as an essential part of his repertoire. Under Alberti the Fiorentini had maintained its reputation as a leading theatre of the spoken drama, though its political and geographical separation from the northern

Italian state encouraged there an isolation which often made the importing of new talents difficult. During Salvini's early years in Naples Maddalena Pelzet, despite her success in Florence, had been forced to leave Naples when her style of playing and her Tuscan accent proved unacceptable to the Fiorentini audiences. In 1860, Salvini reported, a "Chinese wall" still existed between his company and others in the north, so that if an actor left Naples for Florence, for example, he might be asked whether he was going to Italy!

Nevertheless, Alberti persevered in improving his company by importing actors whenever possible. When Salvini arrived in 1860 only young Luigi Monti (1836-1903) among the leading actors at the Fiorentini had actually been trained there. Others had with varying degrees of difficulty acclimatized themselves to the demands of the Neapolitan stage. The leading lady was Fanny Sadowsky, formerly of the Battaglia-Bon Lombard company. She introduced *La signora dalle camelie* to Naples in an interpretation memorable despite extensive rewriting by the royal censors. The year of Salvini's arrival she married Achille Majeroni (1824-1888) who had accompanied Ristori on her European tours in the late 1850s. Another Fiorentini actor, Michele Bozzo, would accompany Ristori on her second American tour in 1867. Angelo Vestri, son of the great Luigi, had been at the Fiorentini thirteen years when Salvini arrived, but departed the following year. Luigi Taddei, who had been with Internari in Paris and subsequently at the Reale Sarda, attempted to join the Fiorentini company in 1848 and was poorly received, but returned with success in 1851 and remained.

Salvini was well received by the demanding public, first in *Pamela*, then in *Zaïre, Amletto* and *Saul*, and in a memorable production of *Francesca da Rimini* with Sadowsky and Majeroni. During this period Garibaldi and his troops conquered first Sicily, then the mainland portion of the Neapolitan kingdom. With the freeing of Naples Gustavo Modena, long banned from the city, arrived for a visit and Salvini undertook to arrange a series of performances for him. The old monopoly had disappeared with the Bourbon government and many actors now arrived in the city to take advantage of this freedom. Salvini gathered a company of them at the Teatro del Fondo, but Modena, after some hesitation, decided that his failing health would not permit him to appear there.

Though this project fell through, the Fondo did soon emerge as a rival of the long-protected Fiorentini. Salvini had departed to tour in the north, but Sadowsky, Majeroni and Taddei next withdrew from the Fiorentini to settle at the rival house and took with them many of the aristocratic subscribers who had long been the base of support for Alberti's venture. The desperate director appealed to Salvini to return to Naples and rebuild the Fiorentini. Salvini agreed and returned in 1864, bringing with him Clementina Cazzola and a repertory of forty plays never before seen in Naples. The Fondo immediately felt the impact of this competition and Majeroni only made his situation worse by attempting to rival Salvini in the production of new works. Many of those works selected by Majeroni were in fact older plays previously unproduced in Naples because of censorship. The aristocratic patrons who had followed him from the Fiorentini were sufficiently conservative to be offended at this fare and the Fondo declined more rapidly still. In 1866 Majeroni gave up the competition and took his troupe to tour in northern Italy.

Salvini and the Fiorentini now reigned again unchallenged as the Neapolitan prose theatre, even without the protection of an official monopoly. Only the San Carlo, which after 1860 began presenting hitherto forbidden Verdi works such as *La battaglia di Legnano* and *Un ballo in maschera,* along with the popular French romantic operas of Auber and Meyerbeer, surpassed the Fiorentini in popularity. Salvini stimulated unparalleled enthusiasm with his *Otello* and revived with great success Giacometti's *La morte civile,* which the Dondini company, now headed by Rossi, had premiered with only indifferent results in Fermo in 1861. Giacometti wrote in 1866 his first play created especially for Salvini, *Sofocle,* and though it was another considerable success, it was *La morte civile* which Salvini kept in his permanent repertoire. Doubtless it was the histrionic possibilities in the role of the suffering husband that appealed to him in this contemporary tragedy and not its realist concerns or its thesis. Still, his interest in it gave Giacometti his one important success in the genre of the modern thesis play being developed at this time in France by Dumas *fils* and Augier. Perhaps Giacometti, like the younger Ferrari and Torelli, would have made a more significant contribution to the development of this type of drama in Italy had not the stars for which he normally wrote preferred historical spectacles for their touring vehicles.

When Salvini's contract with the Fiorentini expired in 1867 he did not renew it, despite his great popularity in Naples, but organized a new company for touring. His beloved leading lady Cazzola was now suffering her terminal illness and her roles were assumed by Virginia Marini (1842-1918), who had been playing younger romantic roles at the Fiorentini. The high point of their tours through northern

Italy was the summer season of 1868, spent at the new Politeama Fiorentino in Florence.

They arrived in Florence in the midst of its brief period of political glory as the new capital, shortly after the assimilation of Venetia. An English tourist visiting the city at this same time found it a place of great beauty and interest, but also of upheaval and confusion "very much in the condition of a boy who has outgrown his clothes, which are far too small for his limbs, and consequently extremely uncomfortable."(14) The narrow streets were crowded with unaccustomed traffic, splendid new stores were opening all over the city, a huge new central market was being built and everywhere there was bustle and excitement.

The new prominence of Florence was naturally reflected in its cultural life and during the 1860s a dozen or more theatres offered the Florentines every variety of dramatic entertainment. Since the city had been for many years without a strong native theatre tradition, it had to rely for its best work on visiting performers, but as the new capital, it was assured the presence, as least from time to time, of most of the leading talents of the period. The European and American craze for Italian opera was now so great that a minor capital like Florence could not compete financially for a popular star like Adelina Patti (1843-1919), who did not even sing in Italy during the first seven years of her triumphant career, but it could still attract her for an occasional brief appearance on the basis of national pride. The Pergola, the great traditional opera theatre of the city, was the natural location for such appearances, but except for special guest attractions, its productions were indifferent. The direction, unable to afford the best singers or musicians, attempted to compensate by novelty, so that in two seasons in the early 1860s no less than forty-five new operas were offered, all of the most ephemeral sort. The public responded in the traditional way, by regarding the opera as a social rather than an artistic event. "All through the opera, the buzz of conversations is audible in the Pergola,"(15) one visitor complained.

Nevertheless, operas were regularly offered not only at the Pergola but at the Leopoldo, renamed the Nazionale in 1861, at the Borgognissanti, which favored opera buffa and renamed itself the Rossini in 1866, in the Pallacorda, and in the Pagliano, which opened in 1854 with *Rigoletto* and which during the 1860s offered the first Italian performances of certain works of Meyerbeer. The traditional leading Florentine theatre for the spoken drama was the old Cocomero, renamed the Niccolini in 1859, and the 1860s were perhaps this old theatre's greatest period. Here the famous Dante Centenary performance of *Francesca da Rimini* with Ristori, Salvini and Rossi was held, and each of these leading artists, and others such as Alamanno Morelli and Luigi Bellotti-Bon, appeared here with their companies to offer the Italian classic and modern authors, Shakespeare and such contemporary French dramatists as Augier, Scribe and Sardou. Since Florence was during this decade an obligatory touring stop for all major Italian companies, there were often two or more troupes here at the same time. Thus spoken drama could be found not only at the Niccolini but at the Alfieri, the Goldoni, the Logge and, most important, the Politeama Fiorentino Vittorio Emmanuele II, which opened in 1862 and at which the King and the leading figures in the new government were regular attendants.

Only the Pergola, however, received a modest subsidy from the court and Vittorio Emmanuele seemed disinclined to give further support to his capital's theatres except by his presence and by occasional gifts to the leading performers. Salvini, summoned to a private audience, discreetly raised the question of governmental support for the arts, but the King assured him that he need not fear for the future of the theatre, when his own great example would inevitably inspire new artists. "In fine," Salvini concluded, "with these praises he closed my mouth, and went back to politics."(16) After a tour in Spain and Portugal in 1869, Salvini returned to Florence for a season at the Niccolini and enjoyed a brilliant success in Stanislao Morelli's (1828-1881) *Arduino d'Ivrea*, the sentiments of which precisely suited the contemporary political situation.

Salvini was now nearing the end of his triumphant career in Italy. Since his Parisian tour in 1856 he had resisted the temptation to follow the profitable route of international touring established by the great operatic stars of the period and by Ristori, but now, feeling neither in the public nor in the government the support he considered the art of theatre deserved, Salvini embarked on the international phase of his career. At the invitation of an impresario in Buenos Aires, he assembled a company for a tour of South America in 1871. His leading actress was Isolina Piamonti, who had played young lovers with him in Naples ten years earlier before departing to tour with Majeroni. Despite the language barrier, the unfamiliar repertoire and an epidemic of yellow fever, Salvini was received with rapturous enthusiasm by the Latin American public and was not long in planning further touring. He returned to Italy only briefly, to appear at Rome's Teatro Valle for the carnival season and to present Alfieri's *Oreste* in Florence, with Rossi as Pylades.

The next major international tour was to North America, under the sponsorship of Maurice Grau and Charles Chizzola. Grau's uncle had sponsored the first two Ristori tours and was negotiating in Vienna for a tour by Rubenstein at the time of his death in 1892. Maurice, who had already begun to build a reputation and a fortune with the importing of French operetta companies, inherited the Rubenstein negotiations and brought the musician to America in the spring of 1873 for an unparalleled success. Considering his uncle's sponsorship of Ristori, it was almost inevitable that Maurice should contract Slavini, whose international reputation was now rapidly growing. Browning, who had seen him in Florence as early as 1859 in *Otello*, considered him the greatest living actor and later called his Oedipus "absolutely the finest effort of art" he had ever beheld, "not only in the field of acting, but in any art whatsoever."[17] Charlotte Cushman called him "the greatest Othello the world has even seen."[18]

These and similar commendations in the New York papers heralded Salvini's first appearance there in the fall of 1873. *Otello* was his first and most successful offering, with Piamonti playing Desdemona as usual and Salvini's brother Alessandro as Iago. The version which he presented had little in common with the traditional English interpretation, but only a few conservative critics faulted it on this score. The vast majority of critics and public alike were as dazzled by the range and power of the interpretation as Cushman had been. For most theatre goers of this generation it became the definitive Othello.[19] The opening acts he played quietly, building gradually to the overwhelming passion and fury of the conclusion. His most striking moments were those of great force and power—throwing Iago to the stage and raising his foot as if to crush his skull; the murder of Desdemona, mercifully hidden behind the bedcurtains and indicated by animal-like growls from Salvini; the final suicide, with a swift cut of a scimitar across his throat. Still these were not moments of technical abandon, but carefully calculated. The "symmetry" of Salvini's acting is often mentioned in the reviews and the most frenzied moments were apparently often carefully set off by quiet, relaxed, even lightly comic passages. The critic of the *Times* felt that the essence of Salvini's style could be found "in gradual or swift transition from declamation or action of overwhelming power to utterance of extreme gentleness or *vice versa*, and in exhibitions of the immense force which his marvelous physique enables him to throw into scenes where they are admissable."[20] The terms "animal-like" or "tiger-like" were often applied to his playing of these intense scenes. Yet despite the effect of complete spontaneity, even of abandon, every inflection and gesture was carefully studied and those who saw several perfomances of a single play were sometimes astonished to find how exact was Salvini's repetition of each moment.

Otello was followed by two modern plays—*Ingomar*, from a drama by the German Friedrich Halm, a costume piece which allowed Salvini to portray another noble barbarian and *La morte civile*, Giacometti's rather melodramatic attempt at a modern social drama. These unfamiliar works, presented in Italian, filled scarcely a third of the theatre. Salvini's Italian *Hamlet* attracted a larger audience, but few critics had anything positive to say about his bold and physical interpretation of the contemplative prince. Piamonti's Ophelia, delicate, natural and touching, was much more favorably received. Other modern plays followed, better received by the critics but not particularly attractive to the public at large. The pattern established in New York was repeated as Salvini toured the eastern seabord and went inland as far as Chicago and south to New Orleans and Havana, following much the same itinerary as Ristori's 1866-67 tour. Everywhere his Othello received ecstatic praise but enthusiasm for the rest of his repertoire was generally confined to the cultural elite. In Boston he dined with Longfellow, chatting in Tuscan, and delighted the party by reading scenes aloud from *Saul* after dinner,(21) but such delights were not for the general public, who never flocked to Salvini as they had to Ristori. He gave somewhat fewer than half the number of performances she had given during her first tour and gained only about one-third the income. The *Times* reported that once Grau had paid the actors and covered other expenses, he received nothing at all for himself from the tour. In any case, he did not invite Salvini to return, though he did arrange for a return by Ristori.

Salvini followed his United States tour with another trip through South America, then went on to Paris while his company returned to Italy. In Paris he was contacted by the British impresario Mapleson, who proposed that he offer his Othello and Hamlet at Drury Lane itself in the spring of 1875. Drury Lane was at this time under the general administration of F.B. Chatterton, who had begun his directorship in 1866 with dreams of Shakespeare but who soon found that to attract audiences he was forced instead to offer spectacular pantomimes, acrobatic acts, and variety entertainment. Musical offerings were an important part of this mixture and were under the supervision of Mapleson, who found imported Italian singers a profitable addition to the repertoire. Then he, like Grau in America, moved naturally from the importing of Italian singers to Italian actors, probably less on artistic grounds than in the hope of appealing to the London public's thirst for novelty. It could hardly have been the repertoire Salvini brought which he hoped would prove attractive, for Chatterton himself once said "Shakespeare spells ruin and Byron bankruptcy." Still, Shakespeare did find an audience on this occasion, and the experiment proved far more profitable for Mapleson and Drury Lane than it had for Grau. Older theatregoers compared his triumph to those of Kean and Rachel and both critics and public were more enthusiastic than they had been in America. The focus of the praise shifted, too. The violent final act of *Othello*, widely acclaimed by American critics, was frequently condemned in England for its excessive, even gross realism. The earlier, quieter acts won more praise. Much more striking was the generally favorable response to Hamlet, a role almost universally faulted in America. George Henry Lewes, though admitting that Salvini's Hamlet was not Shakespeare's and that it omitted many aspects of the complex character, went on to call this interpretation the "least disappointing" of any he had seen, and the one which contained the "most excellences."[22] Browning, as enthusiastic as ever, sent the actor a note praising his performance as one in which "the entire lyre of tragedy resounded magnificently."[23] William Poel called this Hamlet the "only perfect one within living memory" and looked back on the Salvini performances of 1875 as the experience which decided him to devote his life to the theatre.[24]

Naturally after such a success Mapleson arranged with Salvini for a return to London the following year, coupled with a tour through the major cities of England, Scotland and Ireland. For this, Salvini put together a new company, keeping only Piamonti as his leading lady and featuring Carlo Romagnoli (1820-1882), a veteran of the Reale Sarda and of Naples' Fiorentini, for such major supporting roles as Iago. This time he opened in London, not at Drury Lane, which Chatterton, anxious to exploit the new vogue for Italian stars, had reserved for Ernesto Rossi, but at the less prestigious Queen's. Still his Othello continued to attract large audiences and Salvini hoped to gain a new triumph with a new Shakespearean offering, *Macbeth*. A serious illness struck him just before the opening however and he was forced to disband his company and return to Italy. His *Macbeth* was premiered in Vienna during his 1877 tour to Germany and Austria.

Later that same year he undertook his second tour to Paris, after an interval of more than twenty years. He offered *Otello*, *Macbeth* and *Ingomar*, but achieved his most dazzling success with *La morte civile*, which had been rather indifferently received elsewhere. The

leading critics of the 1870s in Paris were championing the new school
of realism and they suddenly found in the interpretation of this work
by Salvini and his company a brilliant illustration of what they were
seeking in the theatre. Salvini's *Morte civile* was to the realists what
the touring English players had been to the romantics in 1827, a model
and a rallying point. Zola in "Le Naturalisme au théâtre" called *La
morte civile* an excellent example of the sort of play he had been attempting, in vain, to popularize in France: "M. Giacometti has no
pretentions of rivalling Shakespeare. His work may be even considered essentially mediocre despite its happy freedom from formula.
Yet it is of my own time, it moves in the air I breathe, it touches me
like an event which happened to my neighbor. I prefer life to art, as I
have often said, and a masterpiece frozen by the centuries is in sum
only a beautiful corpse."(25) His praise was higher still for the acting—for the simplicity, the subtlety, the finesse, the variety, but
above all the truth of Salvini's performance. In the last scene, for
example, "he moved gradually through the final moments of a dying
man with such truth that the audience was terrified. He was really
dying, with eyes become veiled, features growing pale and blank limbs
becoming stiff." The supporting company too Zola found worthy of
high commendation:

> They did not once look at the audience. The auditorium did not seem to
> exist for them. When they listened they kept their eyes fixed on the
> person speaking and when they spoke they addressed themselves most
> realistically to the person listening. None of them edged up to the
> prompter's box like a tenor getting ready to launch into his major
> aria. They turned their backs to the orchestra, entered, said what they
> had to say and left, naturally, without the slightest attempt to attract
> attention to themselves. All this may seem minor, but it is enormous,
> especially for us in France.(26)

In this respect Salvini proved a model for the direction
European acting in general was to take during this generation. In the
Italian tradition, his approach may be seen to have developed from
that of Modena, but Modena was generally unknown outside Italy,
while Salvini was seen around the world and admired not only by the
public, but by the great actors of his era—Booth in America, Irving in
England, Sonnenthal in Austria, Stanislavski in Russia. The Chicago
Tribune during his first American tour did not exaggerate in claiming,
"Of the school of realists he is the prophet, for he has revealed to us
the sweeping, irresistable power of that school."(27)

After a season in Florence Salvini toured Russia and eastern
Europe and returned to Florence to find there the agent of an
American impresario with a novel idea for another tour. The im-

presario was John Stetson, owner of the Globe Theatre in Boston, who proposed bringing Salvini to America alone to perform in Italian with a supporting company of American actors. At first Salvini treated the idea as a joke, but eventually he accepted. On November 15, 1880, he arrived in New York to meet the actors with whom he would open a polyglot *Othello* in Philadelphia only two weeks later. His supporting players had been rehearsing for several weeks and Salvini was delighted to find that they were already quite secure without a prompter. He, on the other hand, found it impossible to remember his lines under these conditions until he mentally numbered them and repeated them in order. As time passed, he gradually began to recognize words and phrases in his cues and thus to interact with his American companions even though he still had little knowledge of the English language.

As Stetson had hoped, this experiment proved much more attractive than Salvini's earlier, purely Italian performances. The company covered essentially the same territory as before—the cities of the northeast, Chicago and New Orleans—and offered essentially the same plays—*Othello, Hamlet, The Gladiator, Ingomar, Morte civile*, along with a new production, *Macbeth.* Yet in just over half as many performances (86 in all) the tour's total income was greater than before. Indeed, public enthusiasm ran so high that Salvini remained after the official tour for a supplementary engagement in New York, Washington, and Baltimore. After this success, his regular return to America was assured, as were mixed language productions featuring other stars. In Cincinnati Salvini was asked if his experiment might be repeated. He felt not, in view of "the strain in concentration and thought" on the leading player. "I am the first artist who has essayed a long series of bi-lingual performances," he concluded, "and I think I shall be the last."(28) The inaccuracy of this prophesy was clearly demonstrated before the year was out, when Ernesto Rossi arrived in Boston to follow Salvini's example even to the extent of using most of the same supporting actors.

The season of 1881-1882 Salvini spent on tour in Egypt and in Russia with a company of Italian actors and following the Italian pattern of changing the play each evening instead of playing a single role, as he had done in America, for weeks at a time. Thus the strain of constantly changing parts must have offset in some measure the easier task of performing with a company in his own language. Stanislavsky in Russia described with wonder and admiration the steps Salvini would go through each evening in working himself gradually into playing a role like Othello—a process lasting several hours.(29) No sooner had the actor returned to Florence from this exhausting tour than he embarked on a new project, studying *King Lear* for performance in England and America. He premiered his *Re Lear* at Florence's Teatro alle Logge, which ten years before had been renamed the Teatro Salvini. Although Salvini opened the new season in New York, he first played Lear in America at the Boston Globe Theatre, which was again serving as sponsor for the tour and providing most of his supporting company. His interpretation was well-received, especially in comparison with Rossi's unsuccessful attempt at the same play the previous year. In general, critics considered that Salvini created a brilliant picture of power and nobility, but that he was less successful in the weaker side of Lear. His gesture of seizing a branch from a realistic tree on stage and using it as a substitute sceptre was universally praised. During his final performances on this tour, Salvini was joined by one of America's leading actresses, Clara Morris.

Salvini had now adopted the pattern of alternating major tours with periods of rest and recuperation in Florence, where he would develop his new roles, usually Shakespearean. Thus 1883 found him again in Italy, this time preparing *Coriolanus*. His performances were now done almost exclusively abroad, though in 1883 he did give nine performances in Rome and appeared briefly on the Trieste and Florence stages. Items from his regular repertoire were offered, but not the new Shakespearean work, which he considered beyond the capacity of the Italian stage, "since it demands too costly a stage setting, and it was impossible to secure in the great number of assistants that artistic discipline without which the grandiose easily merges in the ridiculous."(30)

Only in America could Salvini obtain these conditions, so the play was not offered in London on his 1884 tour there either. Salvini suggested some bilingual productions on this tour, but Rossi had given London its first experience of this two years before and with so little success that Salvini's impresario insisted on a wholly Italian company. Even so, Salvini was received with much less enthusiasm than on his previous visit. His Otello was praised, as always, but his Lear and Macbeth, now seen in London for the first time, were considered to contain few new insights, and his supporting actors and staging were now thought much inferior to what Irving had led London audiences to expect. The *Athenaeum* remarked that "the appearance of Lady Macbeth, obviously in full attire beneath her night-dress, was disenchanting, and the escape beneath the table of the phantom of Banquo in the grave-clothes in which the body had not yet been shrouded, caused an outburst of merriment."(31)

Salvini's *Coriolanus* opened at New York's Metropolitan Opera in the fall of 1885 and Salvini as usual was praised for his naturalness, his power and finish, though the work never competed in popularity with the leading works of his previous seasons. The supporting company was not brilliant, but the crowd scenes were carefully managed and controlled and this, at a time when the Meininger had focussed attention on such matters in Europe, drew much favorable comment. This season for the first time Salvini crossed the continent, appearing in San Francisco early in 1886. On alternate nights, when Salvini was not performing, his son Alexander (1861-1896) offered *Romeo and Juliet*, entirely in English, with the promising young Viola Allen. Minnie Maddern, later one of America's leading actresses, was also a member of this company. Back on the east coast, Salvini appeared for several evenings in New York, Philadelphia and Boston with Edwin Booth. Their *Othello*, with two of the greatest living tragedians in the leading roles, was a magnificent occasion in the theatre of the period. They also appeared together in *Hamlet*, with Salvini modestly assuming the role of the Ghost.

The exhausting demands of touring began during this trip to take their toll even on Salvini's powerful constitution and an entire week of performances in California were lost because of illness. He returned to Italy this time not for a matter of months but for three years. He greatly reduced his activity, but he did not leave the stage, so his countrymen were able to see more of him than they had for many years. He gave *Otello* and *Saul* at Rome's Valle in 1887 and appeared once more with Rossi in *Saul* the following year in Florence. By 1889 he was sufficiently rested to essay a final tour to America, though without a major new play. His one novelty was *Samson*, produced in Italian during his first American tour but now done for the first time with an English supporting cast, in a translation made especially for this tour by William Dean Howells.

His last major appearance in Italy was appropriately in his home city of Florence, where during the season of 1890-1891 he performed at the Teatro Niccolini, playing the role of Iago, a new creation for him, to the Othello of Andrea Maggi (1850-1910), a leading actor of the new generation. Maggi followed Salvini's example to a certain extent, touring Austria, Poland, Russia and especially South America in the roles of Hamlet and Othello and in French social drama, but he was ultimately best remembered as the greatest Italian Cyrano de Bergerac. A few months after his appearance with Maggi, Salvini retired from the stage, though he returned on occasion for special celebrations and in 1901 made a final tour to Russia. He died in Florence in 1915.

Rossi

Although he had already achieved a solid reputation in his years with Leigheb and the Reale Sarda, Rossi's great years began in 1855 and 1856 when he accompanied Ristori to Paris and, upon his return to Itlay, presented *Otello* and *Amleto* at Milan's Teatro Re. In the years that followed he would rival Ristori and Salvini as an international star and would rely much more exclusively than either of them upon Shakespearean works. The productions at the Teatro Re were presented by a company of young actors which Rossi, clearly influenced by Modena, assembled himself and subjected to rigorous training, working with them from eight to four daily and performing each evening. In 1858 they added to their repertoire *Mercante de Venezia* (in Milan), *Romeo e Giulietta* (in Trieste), *Macbeth* (in Venice), and *Re Lear* (in Turin). These were received with interest but without great enthusiasm. To audiences trained on Alfieri, these new works were still alien and confusing. The company toured to Vienna in 1859 and found the public there far more receptive, but on his return to Italy Rossi encountered much antagonism for having performed for Austrian audiences. "I went to make art, not politics," he responded, which did little to mollify the patriotic audiences of Trieste and Venice.

Rossi hoped to establish his company permanently in Milan, but the Archduke's project for a state theatre fell through and Rossi disbanded his company, going himself to assume leading roles in the company of Cesare Dondini. These were the same roles recently played in that company by Salvini, including of course Hamlet and Othello, to which Rossi soon added Coriolanus. His training with Modena had also prepared Rossi for working with the new realistic school of playwriting now emerging in Italy and especially favored by Dondini. The Dondini productions of Ferrari's *Prosa* in 1860 and of *La bottega del cappellaio* in 1862 with Rossi in the leading roles quite eclipsed the earlier Domeniconi productions of these works.

In 1864 Rossi left Dondini to establish a new company in his own name, and for the rest of his career headed his own troupe or toured alone. Shakespeare remained at the heart of his repertoire, but during the next several years he added an impressive number of other works from a wide range of authors: Alfieri, Pellico, Niccolini,

Dumas, Corneille, Hugo, Scribe, Goethe, Iffland, Laube, Byron, Calderon. Contemporary Italian authors were also represented, with selections from most of the major schools for the period. Historical spectacle was provided by Giacometti (*L'ultimo dei duchi di Mantova,* 1864) and his followers, the most important of which was Angelo De Gubernatis (1840-1913) with his *Pier delle Vigne* (1860) and *Don Rodrigo ultimo re dei Visigoti* (1861). De Gubernatis as a youth of seventeen was inspired by Rossi's Hamlet in Turin to write his first play, and fittingly, it was eventually Rossi who first offered De Gubernatis' works to the public. His *Pier delle Vigne*, attacking the temporal power of the papacy, was his most popular work for the theatre, but among savants De Gubernatis, a highly-regarded professor of Sanskrit first at Florence and later in Rome, was much more praised for his pageants of Indian history and myth: *Mâyâ* (1868), *De Nala* (1869), *Re Desarata* (1869) and *Buddha* (1872). Most of these were presented only before learned societies, but Rossi did mount *Re Desarata* in Florence, with modest success, in 1871.

Another sort of drama was provided by Ferrari, who had begun his career with Goldonian comedies and more recently turned to realistic social dramas inspired by contemporary French authors. Parmenio Bettoli (1835-1907) showed an almost identical range in his work, from the Goldonian *Il Boccaccio a Napoli* (1865) to the influential Dumas *fils* adaptation, *Le idee della signora Aubray* (1867). Other French genres were also represented both in their original forms and in Italian imitations—the farces of Labiche inspired the works of Francesco Cameroni (d. 1878) and the proverbs of Musset were echoed in such plays as Francesco Coletti's (1821-1878) *Quel che l'occhio non vede il cuor non crede* (1865) and Francesco de Renzi's *Un baccio dato non e mai perduto* (1867).

Though Rossi toured throughout northern Italy during the 1860s, many of these works were premiered at the Teatro Gerbino in Turin, where he appeared frequently and where he remained almost six months in 1865-1866, an extremely rare occurence at this period. Since the disbanding of the Reale Sarda, Turin like most Italian cities, had to rely upon traveling companies for its theatre, and these rarely remained longer than a few weeks. Still, as the new capital, Turin attracted the best companies in sufficient numbers that the Sarda's Teatro Carignano could not always accommodate them. Thus the Gerbino, a former circus, was converted into an alternate prose theatre and housed Modena, Dondini and Salvini on occasion as well as Rossi.

It was during the mid-1860s that Rossi established himself as an artistic rival of Ristori and Salvini, first by being invited to appear with them in the famous Dante Festival of 1865, and then by undertaking a successful tour to Paris. At the Salle Ventadour he was billed as the "Italian Talma," a claim calling discreet attention to the fact that the French stage was then seriously deficient in serious actors of any stature able to present the classics. Rossi's reception was far more favorable than Salvini's had been, for a variety of reasons. Salvini had appeared only a few months after Ristori and suffered some reaction from the fervent welcome accorded her, but after Salvini's tour nine years elapsed before Rossi arrived in Paris. It was a politically opportune moment—Piedmont and France had just become military allies in a struggle against the Austrians. Moreover, Rossi stirred fond memories in French theatre goers who recalled him as the dashing young man who had supported Ristori on her first triumphant visit. He did not, like Salvini, take the risk of beginning with a French work, but with Shakespeare—*Hamlet*, followed by *Othello*—to the universal acclaim of the French critics. Opinion was divided concerning the visual aspect of the productions, some critics calling the scenery "poor and mean," and others praising it as "similar to what Shakespeare himself would have used." The latter apparently confused a certain primitiveness with authenticity, since Rossi used a good deal of furniture and machinery, even if his settings were Spartan by French standards. Reservations were also expressed about the supporting cast, but Rossi himself was hailed as magnificent, unapproached by any contemporary French actor. Several critics expressed the hope that he might lead the French back to the classics after their recent "debauch of drama and comic opera."(32) In acknowledgment of the 260th anniversary of Corneille's birth in June, Rossi's company was invited to present three acts of *Le Cid* at the Comédie. It was a work he had already offered in Italy, most successfully at Florence in 1863, and like Ristori he gained a new triumph in this citadel of the French theatre. From Paris Rossi toured to Bordeaux and Marseilles, where he offered *Le Cid* in French (he had played entirely in Italian in Paris), then he went on to Spain, where he presented the first Shakespeare seen in Barcelona and Madrid.

While on tour, Rossi received an offer from Fanny Sadowsky, who had recently left the Teatro Fiorentini in Naples to become the impresario of the rival Fondo. Alberti's Fiorentini had an enviable record of stability even in these turbulent times and Sadowsky hoped that this indicated that Naples could support a second prose theatre. Rossi accepted and even created a popular comic opera, *Colpe e speranze* (1867) for the Fondo, but such successes were few, the Fiorentini audiences remaining generally faithful to the theatre. Also at that time Naples suffered from an epidemic of cholera, then Garibaldi's march on Rome added new tensions to the already unstable political situation. In 1868 Sadowsky gave up the Fondo and Rossi returned to Paris and to Spain.

Henceforth Rossi, like Salvini, performed only occasionally in Italy, between tours. He spent three years beginning in 1871 touring throughout South America, then appeared in Austria, Hungary, and Germany. In 1874 Maurice Grau, who had just sponsored Salvini's first American tour, invited Rossi to follow, but though the contract was signed, Rossi, disturbed by a grave illness which had striken his son, decided not to leave Europe. Forfeiting a heavy penalty to Grau, he began a six-month season in Paris. He offered *Amleto, Lear, Macbeth* and *Romeo e Giulietta* and was warmly praised for the variety and richness of his characterizations. To close his season he selected a contemporary Italian work, an experiment Salvini had not attempted. This was *Nerone*, by Pietro Cossa (1830-1881), a major work of the neoromantic school and a favorite with most of the leading Italian actors for the rest of the century.

Like the sprawling historical pageants that Giacometti created for Ristori, *Nerone* had little plot but was rather a series of striking theatrical scenes. The French critics were, in general, baffled by it. Some felt it showed the influence of Sardou, others felt it a corruption of the tradition of Alfieri, still others noted, more accurately, the influence of Shakespeare. But there were other influences closer at hand conditioning Cossa's work. Like Giacometti he responded to the contemporary taste for historical visual spectacle, but between the 1860s, the decade of Giacometti's most important works, and the 1870s, when Cossa made his major contributions, important changes had occurred. Politically, of course, the house of Savoy had established itself as the dynasty of Italy, with Rome as its symbolic if not yet its actual capital. Thus the generalized taste for historical spectacle tended to turn toward the classical Roman heritage. Another force was the growing interest in realism, apparent in such authors as Ferrari, which encouraged historical dramatists also to place more stress on psychology and local color. Only in *La morte civile,* not, strictly speaking, a historical play at all, had Giacometti clearly reflected these concerns, but all of Cossa's work was strongly influenced by the new style. He wrote in verse, as a concession to his conservative auditors and to tradition, but his Nero was treated in contemporary realistic and psychological terms. Cossa ingeniously mixed old and new, as in the opening of his play, which was a classic prologue but was delivered by a clown standing before the curtain, who promised a new Nero, not a towering Caesar but an intimate figure "seen in the taverns and the backstreets." Indeed the entire second act was a much-admired tavern scene, the high point of which was a realistic scene of drunkeness involving Nero, his clown and his freed slave. All this was considered dazzling in Italy—the historian Costetti called the tavern act worthy of Shakespeare—but French critics raised on the Nero of *Britannicus* were not impressed. The lack of focus, the episodic structure and worst of all the jumble of comedy, tragedy and drama left them confused and irritated. Individual scenes were praised but the whole was considered in the words of one critic "a meal of piquant hors-d'oeuvres."(33) Rossi, as always, was lauded for his realism but the French seemed to feel that this should be restricted to Shakespeare.

Before he left Paris, Rossi was approached by F.B. Chatterton with an offer to perform at Drury Lane. Salvini's London tour the previous year had been sufficiently successful to encourage the importation of another Italian star and letters from Englishmen in Italy and Paris had been extolling Rossi's Shakespearean interpretations ever since Mary Crowden Clarke had first championed him in the pages of the *Athenaeum* in 1873. Chatterton's codirector, Mapleson, had already arranged for Salvini to return in 1876 but Chatterton, convinced that the novelty of Rossi would make him a bigger draw, booked him for Drury Lane and demoted Salvini to the Queen's Theatre.

The simultaneous appearance of Italy's two most famous actors in London, both offering Shakespeare, should have provided an excellent opportunity for critical comparison, but circumstances thwarted this. Salvini returned to Italy after performing only his *Otello* (because of illness, he says in his autobiography, though the London papers speculated that he had simply found his demotion to the Queen's unacceptable). Rossi remained, but did not attempt Othello, perhaps fearing to challenge comparison in the role acknowledged as Salvini's greatest. His Hamlet and Lear in any case were rather indifferently received by the London critics, who praised his technical skill but felt that the interpretations lacked intellectual and emotional depth. Some even speculated that such "northern" characters were beyond the grasp of Italian actors, who should stick to the passionate Othello. Rossi, stung, replied in a letter to the *Times:* "There are vivacious Northerns and apathetic Southerns; the point is to seize the character of the man Hamlet and express it as the artist, whatever his own temperament may be, would express the emotions incident to such a character were they his own.''(34) Nevertheless he apparently made a strong effort to modify his style for the more conservative English taste, even though, unhappily, this seems only to have made it more flat and uninteresting. The London productions were clearly not the success those in Paris had been and doubtless Rossi returned to France with relief that summer.

In the fall of 1876 he went north again, across Germany to Russia, at the invitation of the Emperor. His company toured Russia that winter with such success that they returned again in 1879 and 1881, with intervening trips to Austria, Roumania, Poland and Egypt. The assassination of Alexander left them stranded in Moscow, but fortunately an invitation came from Berlin, where they rebuilt their resources with a highly successful three-month engagement. Rossi now decided, despite his cool reception to England, to undertake at last an American tour. Salvini's success the previous year with an American company provided the impetus. In the fall of 1881 Rossi arrived in New York, hoping to repeat Salvini's success. His opening in Boston as Lear was a triumph, local critics calling this and the Hamlet which followed the greatest ever seen in America. Unfortunately, his reception elsewhere was much more subdued. In New York he opened with *Otello*, and the inevitable comparisons with Salvini were not in Rossi's favor. His Romeo fared little better and not until he turned to Hamlet and Lear did he gain generally favorable reviews. In other eastern cities his reception was warm but never equal to that for Salvini and reviewers often remarked that he was playing to disappointingly small houses. By the time he appeared in Chicago, early in 1882, the owner of McVicker's Theatre refused to accept the usual percentage of profits and demanded a straight rental instead. In an effort to increase profits, Rossi's manager insisted that he perform on a far more exhausting schedule than Salvini's. Often in America Salvini would give a single play, *Otello*, three nights a week, with evenings between performances to rest. Rossi's schedule in Washington was typical of his entire tour: Monday, opening in *Amleto,* Tuesday *Edmund Kean*, Wednesday, *Re Lear*, Thursday *Otello*, Friday *Edmund Kean*, Saturday matinee, *Romeo e Giulietta*. Often there was a Saturday evening performance as well. Little wonder that Rossi on his departure from America expressed to a reporter from the *Times* his opinion that the tour had been not only exhausting but detrimental to his art.

The relative indifference with which Rossi was greeted in England and America was probably due in large part simply to the fact that he followed Ristori and Salvini (the latter by a single season) and thus found a public already somewhat sated with the Italian experiment. Nonetheless he had, far more than either of his predecessors, based his career on his interpretations of Shakespeare and the rebuffs he received in these two English-speaking nations clearly hurt him deeply. The suggestion by various English and American critics that he lacked a real intellectual grasp of Shakespeare was especially galling to him and was surely one of the major reasons that he undertook to publish a series of Shakespeare studies, first in *Studi drammatici e lettere autobiografiche* (Florence, 1885), then in *Quaranta anni di vita artistica* (Florence, 1887-1889). He never tried his fortune, however, in England or America again.

The idea of bilingual Shakespeare Rossi carried to other countries with rather more success. During the early months of 1885 he toured Germany playing Othello, Hamlet, Lear and Shylock with a German company. In May he repeated the experiment with a Swedish company in Stockholm. The following year he was invited back to Germany to participate in a Goethe festival at Weimar and he remained to play Othello, Lear and Hamlet with the famous company of the Duke of Saxe-Meiningen. During his later years he performed more often in Italy between tours, most often in Florence, where he offered Machiavelli's *Mandragola* in 1885 with a company of young actors and his own translation of *Julius Caesar* in 1886. The latter production toured through Italy with Rossi playing Brutus on some occasions and Anthony on others. His final tours were to Turkey, Greece and Russia. He was performing *Re Lear* in Odessa in 1896 when striken by the sudden illness which proved fatal. He was brought home to Italy, where he died soon after his arrival.

Verdi's Later Years

During this period, when the greatest names of the Italian theatre were more likely to be found in Paris, London or Petersburg than in Milan, Naples or Rome, even Verdi, a kind of living symbol of the Italian artistic soul at mid-century, was not an exception. Only three of his twenty-three operas written before 1860 were premiered outside of Italy, but between 1860 and 1880 not one was first offered in his homeland. *La forza del destino* (1862 was premiered in St. Petersburg, *Don Carlo* (1867) at the Paris Opera, *Aïda* (1871) in Cairo. The new Italian nation proved a disappointment to Verdi both politically and artistically, and during these years his official connection with it steadily declined. Except for a single performance in Rome, he withheld *La forza del destino* from any production in Itlay for seven years and he refused invitiations from Turin, Milan and Busseto to create some musical tribute to Vittorio Emmanuele. He did however accept an invitation in 1862 to represent the Italian musical world at the London Exhibition. For this he created a cantata, *Inno delle nazioni*, set to a text by young Arrigo Boito (1842-1918), who was introduced to Verdi in Paris where he had come after the success in Milan of his own first cantata, *Le sorelle d'Italia*.

Thereafter, for a time, Verdi and Boito's paths diverged. Verdi went to Russia for the premiere of *La forza del destino*. Boito returned to Milan, where he established a journal called the *Figaro* with the writer Emilio Praga (1839-1875), in which Boito championed German music, especially that of Beethoven. This gained him the reputation, undeserved, of being a disciple of Wagner, but he did seem determined to separate himself and his generation from Verdi. In 1863 at a dinner given to celebrate the opening at La Scala of *I profughi fiamminghi* with music by Faccio and text by Praga, Boito gave what became a notorious toast to Italian Art, hoping that it would soon "escape, young and healthy, from the clutches of the old and idiotic ways." The toast was published and the "old and idiotic ways" universally assumed to be those of Verdi. Faccio wrote at once to Verdi to apologize and Verdi seemed willing enough to forget the whole matter. Still, Boito was correct in his analysis that Italian opera was changing—that the older, more melodramatic arrangement of striking effects was giving way to works with more well-rounded and psychologically true characters. In short, realism was beginning to enter the opera as it was the regular drama. His error was to imply that Verdi himself was not involved in this process too, so that for a time many were led quite mistakenly to think of Verdi as the melodramatic old guard, to be inevitably replaced by the realists, headed by Boito. Verdi's great final works would demonstrate the extent of their error.

Faccio's next opera was an *Amleto,* with text by Boito, which was offered without success in Genoa in 1865. Thereafter Faccio turned his energies to conducting, for which he had far greater ability. He went on to conduct the first European performance of *Aïda* in 1872 and the premiere of *Otello* in 1887, becoming generally acknowledged as the greatest Italian conductor of his time. With Faccio no longer composing, the responsibility for the new movement then fell on Boito and the opening of his *Mefistofele* at La Scala in 1868 recalled the famous battle of *Hernani* a generation earlier in

Paris. The theatre was filled with patrons less interested in hearing the music than in demonstrating their support for or opposition to the "new music." As with *Hernani*, the confrontation had its nationalist as well as its artistic side, for the supporters of Verdi and the old music felt that they were also defending the Italian stage from the Germans and perhaps even from the mysterious and disturbing new menace, Wagnerism. In opposition to La Scala policy, the composer himself conducted, and despite the length of the work (it ended at 1:30 a.m.), audiences were so aroused that the performance was followed by a riot outside the theatre. It was repeated once, divided into two evenings, but further rioting resulted and the police ordered the work withdrawn. Boito then completely rewrote it, greatly reducing its length, and the modified version enjoyed a modest, tranquil success in Bologna.

The failure of Boito's work, in which La Scala had put high hopes, worsened the theatre's already severe financial problems since the new Italian government had refused to continue the subsidy the Austrians had always paid. The directors pleaded with Verdi to end his twenty-year estrangement from the theatre and allow them to premiere his revised version of *Forza del destino*. Verdi at last agreed, and the premiere was a great success, even though the work made little concession to Boito's demand for "new music." Verdi himself found this somewhat troubling, as we see in a letter he wrote to Antonio Gallo, the first producer of *Traviata:*

> It's a curious thing, and at the same time discouraging! While everyone cries out "Reform," "Progress," the public generally refrains from applause, and the singers only know how to be effective in arias, romances, and canzonettas! I know that they now also applaud scenes of action, but only in passing, as the frame of the picture.... It can't go on like this. Either the composers must take a step backward, or everyone else must step forward.(35)

The enormous success of *Aïda*, offered at Cairo in 1871 and La Scala in 1872, did not resolve this problem, for each faction saw in it what it wished to see—an imitation of French grand opera, a continuation of the Verdian love of melody and song, or an attempt by Verdi to adjust his art to the influence of Wagner! Some critics suggested that Verdi, like certain of his contemporaries in the spoken drama, was evolving toward a greater realism but in the sense that this was meant— psychological depth in the music or a concern with authenticity in setting and costume—Verdi had long been a "realist." Twenty-five years before, while preparing for the production of *Macbeth* in Florence he

had insisted that Perrone, the designer for the Pergola, observe
historical accuracy:

> Please let Perrone know that the era in which *Macbeth* takes place is
> much later than Ossian and the Roman Empire. Macbeth assassinated
> Duncan in 1040, and he himself was killed in 1057.
>
> In 1039, England was ruled by Harold, called Harefoot and of
> Danish extraction. He was succeeded in the same year by Har-
> dicanute, half-brother of Edward the Confessor.
>
> Don't forget to tell Perrone all of this, because I believe he is
> making a mistake about the period.(36)

Later the same month he wrote: "I want the costumes to be very well
made, and to ensure that they are authentic I have sent to London,
and I have consulted the foremost authorities on the period and the
costumes."(37)

During Verdi's absence from La Scala a new chief designer had
appeared, Carlo Ferrario (1833-1907), the only designer in the latter
half of the century whose fame and influence rivalled Sanquirico's in
the earlier half. Ferrario's designs paralleled the experiments of the
Scapigliatura, a group of contemporary Lombard painters whose concern with the picturesque and narrative possibilities of everyday scenes
led directly to the new school of realism. Ferrario, who began
designing at La Scala in the late 1850s, was thus credited with introducing realism to Italian operatic design, though in fact his work
still contained many elements of the grandiose and picturesque that
might be more properly styled romantic. The blend was in fact not
dissimilar to that which Verdi developed musically in his operas and
the Ferrario designs for Verdi became the standard model for much
Verdian production of the early twentieth century.

The conjunction of the work of these two artists, however, appropriate it seemed in retrospect, was not immediately apparent when
Verdi returned to La Scala. Though Ferrario was by this time well
established, having designed the settings for such major offerings as
Boito's *Mefistofele*, the directors of La Scala were unsure of his
ability to handle an assignment as important as the first European
staging of *Aïda*. In May of 1871 Verdi wrote to Giulio Ricordi:

> The management (which wants to stage *Aïda* in the best possible way)
> has determined to change the scenic designer, replacing Ferrario with
> some better artist. They have turned to me for advice in the matter. I
> remember that you spoke to me several times of a famous painter at
> the theatre in Parma, whose name I do not remember. Could we get
> him for La Scala?(38)

The painter was Gerolamo Magnani (1815-1889), professor of painting at Parma's Academmia. His style was rather more grandiose and

flamboyant than Ferrario's, but this seemed quite suitable for *Aïda*. Magnani accepted the commission and his designs for *Aïda* were pleasing to Verdi and the public alike. Still, Ferrario's power and reputation continued to grow, with the result that in 1877 when *Aïda* was revived, he was charged with the designs for it. These were successful enough to assure him the responsibility of designing the last two Verdi premieres, *Otello* and *Falstaff*.

The triumph of *Aïda* and the relative failure of *Mefistofele* demonstrated beyond a doubt that despite all the uproar about the "new music," Verdi remained the leading contemporary composer in Italy. Now that Verdi was reconciled with La Scala and experience had shown that Boito's skills as a librettist were greater than those as a composer, Ricordi and Faccio proposed to Verdi that he collaborate with Boito on an opera based on *Othello*. They suggested that the two artists in collaboration might find the way to the renewal of Italian opera both had been seeking in their individual ways. Composer and librettist indeed found each other compatible, so much so that they put aside the *Otello* project temporarily to complete a rapid but extremely successful reworking of *Simon Boccanegra*.

The collaboration went smoothly, but slowly, and *Otello* was not completed until 1887. It was Verdi's first new opera in sixteen years and once again there was widespread doubt whether the master could live up to his reputation. The premiere at La Scala was a triumphant vindication of Verdi and of the Italian operatic tradition itself. Both were shown to be still gloriously alive and unfailing in power. Boito began almost at once on a new libretto, for *Falstaff*, which was completed in 1893 and which was another and final great success for Verdi. The vision of "new music" that was to give new emphasis and attention to the dramatic element in opera was nowhere more triumphantly fulfilled than in these two final masterpieces by the composer once mistakenly thought the leading representative of the old guard.

Notes to Chapter V

1. Adelaide Ristori, *Memoires and Artistic Studies,* trans. G. Mantellini (New York, 1907), p. 19.
2. Eugène Delacroix, *Journal* (Paris, 1932), II, 360.
3. Ristori, *Memoires,* p. 26.
4. Letter printed in *Le Gaulois,* March 3, 1875, quoted in G. d'Heylli, *Journal intime de la Comédie française* (Paris, 1877), p. 83n.
5. No. 1458, June 7, 1856, p. 609.

6. No. 1493, June 7, 1856, p. 721.
7. Vol. XXXVII (1861), p. 200.
8. *New York Tribune,* Nov. 17, Nov. 19, Nov. 15, 1866.
9. *New Orleans Daily Picayune,* March 13, 1867.
10. Luigi Rasi, *I comici italiani* (Florence, 1905), I, 499.
11. March 15, 1875.
12. L.D. Ventura, *Biographical Reminiscences* (New York, 1907), p. 252.
13. Sept. 5, 1857, p. 147.
14. Charles Richard Weld, *Florence: The New Capital of Italy* (London 1857), p. 35.
15. Weld, *Florence,* p. 250.
16. Tommaso Salvini, *Autobiography* (New York, 1893), p. 134.
17. William Michael Rossetti, *Some Reminiscences* (New York, 1906), I, 189.
18. Quoted in *New York Times,* Aug. 24, 1873. Westland Marston in *Some Recollections of Our Recent Actors* (London, 1888), II, 82 reports that years later Cushman could describe with admiration every detail of Salvini's interpretation.
19. For a detailed study of Salvini's performance see Tuckerman Mason, *The Othello of Tommaso Salvini* (1890). A shorter description may be found in John Rankin Towse, *Sixty Years of the Theatre* (New York, 1916), pp. 157-65.
20. December 11, 1873.
21. H.W. Longfellow, *Final Memoires* (Boston, 1887), III, 212.
22. George Henry Lewes, *On Actors and the Art of Acting* (London, 1875), p. 275.
23. Salvini, *Autobiography,* p. 170.
24. Robert Speaight, *William Poel and the Elizabethan Revival* (Cambridge, Mass., 1954), p. 26.
25. Emile Zola, *Oeuvres complètes,* XLVII (Paris, 1927), 121.
26. Zola, *Oeuvres,* XLVII, 120.
27. January 11, 1874.
28. Quoted in the *New Orleans Times-Picayune,* Feb. 13, 1881.
29. Constantin Stanislavsky, *My Life in Art,* trans. J.J. Robbins (New York, 1956), pp. 273-74.
30. Salvini, *Autobiography,* p. 223.
31. *Athenaeum,* No. 2942 (March 15, 1884), p. 355.
32. For a summary of critical reactions to Rossi, see Renée Lelièvre, *Le Théâtre dramatique italien en France 1855-1940* (La Roche-sur-Yon, 1959), pp. 48-50.
33. Charles Dejob, *Etudes sur la tragédie* (Paris, 1896), p. 390.
34. May 9, 1876.
35. Giuseppe Verdi, *Letters,* trans. Charles Osborne (New York, 1971), p. 149.
36. Verdi, *Letters,* pp. 40-41.
37. Verdi, *Letters,* p. 41.
38. Hans Bush, *Verdi's Aïda* (Minneapolis, 1978), p. 161.

VI

Realism

The proclivity of its best actors for international touring and the lack of any theatre center with an established company and steady support continued to plague the Italian theatre through the end of the nineteenth century. The leading director to dedicate himself to the improvement of the Italian stage and to the development of a significant modern repertoire, Luigi Bellotti-Bon, was at last driven to suicide by the burden of artistic and financial frustration. Still the efforts of Bellotti-Bon and of a few other devoted actors, directors, critics and playwrights did eventually succeed in laying the foundations during this period of a modern Italian repertoire. By the end of the century Italian plays, along with Italian operas and Italian actors, began to make a real contribution to the European theatre tradition.

Though the particular political, cultural and artistic situation in Italy naturally conditioned the development of this repertoire, its various stages may in general be seen to correspond with those in other European countries at roughly the same periods. Thus the realistic dramas of Paolo Ferrari and Achille Torelli in the 1850s and 1860s, the former tending to emphasize moral and political questions, the latter more personal psychology, have much in common with the French Second Empire social dramas of Dumas *fils*, Augier, and Feuillet (all successfully translated and presented in Italy at this time).

To these succeeded the Italian verist movement, established in the early 1880s by Luigi Capuana and Giovanni Verga from Sicily and developed during the next decade by the Milanese authors Giacosa, Praga and Rovetta. This movement, indebted to scientific positivism and stoutly opposed to the intervention of the author in the work or to any "literary elaboration," clearly had much in common with Zola and the naturalist playwrights to the north. The spirit of verism entered the opera also, in the works of Mascagni, Leoncavallo and most notably Puccini, works which of course carried this movement far

161

beyond the borders of Italy. A more local but in the history of the
Italian stage equally important effect of verism was the encouragement of dialect theatres, presenting pictures of common life in
the language best suited to such portrayals. Led by Turin, Venice,
Milan and Naples, most major cities of Italy had at least one
significant dialect theatre by the end of the century.

In Italy as elsewhere the translation and presentation of the
plays of Ibsen provided another stimulus for young dramatists of the
late nineteenth century. Actors like Virginia Martini and Ermete Zacconi became particularly associated with productions of Ibsen and of
the Ibsen-inspired works of such Italian dramatists as Enrico Butti
and Roberto Bracco. Finally in the closing years of the century the
Italian theatre, like others in Europe, experienced a poetic and
idealistic reaction to the theatre of realism and naturalism. Some of
the realists themselves contributed to this reaction, as can be seen in
Rovetta's *Romanticismo* or Giacosa's *Come le foglie*, but the most
striking figure of reaction was the poet Gabriele D'Annunzio, whose
exotic, sensual writings and flamboyant persona made him the best-
known Italian playwright of his time. His reputation was aided in no
small measure by Eleanora Duse, the last of the great nineteenth-century international stars and D'Annunzio's sometime mistress, who
devoted much of her remarkable career to the promotion of his
dramas.

Morelli and Bellotti-Bon

During the 1860s and 1870s, while Ristori, Salvini and Rossi
were spreading the fame of Italian acting across the globe, actors and
companies of real stature were in fact rarely to be found in Italy itself.
The unstable political conditions and the disappearance of the court
subsidies which had helped to maintain the best troupes earlier in the
century combined to undermine the art. The few artists and companies to rise above the mediocre almost inevitably sought the more
lucrative arrangements offered by touring outside Italy and the
playwrights, as a rule, were forced to survive by writing potboilers for
indifferent local companies or vehicles for the international stars.

And yet in this unpromising soil the seeds for a new Italian
theatre were planted between 1850 and 1867 by a touring French company, led by Eugène and Hippolyte Menadier. Appearing with great
success in all the major cities of Italy just at the period when the

greatest Italian actors were going elsewhere, they offered to Italian audiences a level of performance that was a revelation. Even those cities like Turin and Florence fortunate enough to witness occasional performances by Ristori, Rossi or Salvini found something new and impressive in the French, whose approach to the art was entirely different. Not one of their company could approach the brilliance of the great Italian stars, but instead of offering a brilliant star supported by an often indifferent troupe, they presented a highly trained and polished ensemble, striving for a unity of effect. Their repertoire too was a revelation—the new social drama of Augier, Dumas and Sardou—which brought a fresh vision of realism to the Italian public as well as to authors and actors.

Despite the impact of the Menadier company, the generally depressed condition of the Italian stage at this time prevented them from stimulating much emulation among Italian companies. Two happy and extremely influential exceptions were the troupes of Alamanno Morelli and Luigi Bellotti-Bon (1820-1883), which offered to the Italian playwrights of the period a rare opportunity for the staging of significant new works. It is therefore hardly surprising that most of the leading dramatists of this generation were discovered or encouraged by these companies. Morelli we have already encountered as a member of the Lombarda troupe and a pupil of Modena. After leaving the Lombarda, he served for several years as director of the Accademia dei Filodrammatici in Milan. The arrival of the Menadier company in Milan inspired him to launch a new troupe of his own, which he did in 1860.

Bellotti-Bon was born Luigi Bellotti and adopted by the beloved actor-author F.A. Bon, who educated him in his craft. Appropriately, his first great success was as Bon's famous Ludro with the Tessari company. He worked with many of the leading directors of the 1840s and 1850s, first with Gustavo Modena, then, like Morelli, at the Lombarda under Battaglia, finally at the Reale Sarda, where he replaced Gaspare Pieri in youthful leading roles. In 1856 he accompanied Ristori to Paris, London, the Low Countries and Berlin and was often her leading man in later years when she returned to perform in Italy between tours. In 1859 with the financial backing of a Trieste banker, Bellotti-Bon established an excellent company and began actively seeking contemporary Italian plays for production.

Neither of the new companies relied to any great extent on the classic repertoire and even the basso romantico dramatists like Giacometti were rarely offered (the only Giacometti premiere by

either company was Bellotti-Bon's *L'indomani dell'ubbrico* in 1862).
Instead, the emphasis was on the new generation of realistic
dramatists inspired, like Morelli and Bellotti-Bon themselves, by the
contemporary school of social drama and comedy in France and freed
by the new social order to consider themes hitherto closed to them by
censorship. The leader of this school was Paolo Ferrari, whose
Goldoni e le sue sedici commedie and *Prosa* had been among the most
significant premieres of the 1850s. Goldoni was a strong influence on
Ferrari's early plays but contemporary French influence became much
stronger in the plays he wrote for the new companies. Echoes of
Goldoni can still be found, as in *Amore senza stima* (Morelli, Venice,
1868) or *Amici e rivali* (Bellotti-Bon, Florence, 1874), but even these
have a strong moral tone. Much more typical are the dramas and
thesis plays: *Il duello* and *Gli uomini seri* (both given by Morelli,
Florence, 1868) or *Il ridicolo* (Morelli, Rome, 1872).

The precise mixture of comedy, drama and didacticism varied a
good deal in Ferrari's work, much to the confusion of those critics
who have attempted to separate this work into distinct genres. Croce
more reasonably suggested that any division of Ferrari's work into
groups was artificial, since all of his plays, whatever their surface dif-
ferences, were driven by the same power, a concern with social issues:
"Ferrari had no other Muse; morality made him a dramatist, just as
love or indignation have made dramatists of others."(1)

Later realists attacked the work of Ferrari as highly selective
and biased and indeed he was demonstrably far less interested in painting the mores of Italian society, which was his claim, than in arguing
certain social causes by means of his plays. Of course this is a tension
which existed in much of the late nineteenth-century realistic theatre,
but Ferrari had another quality which eventually brought him under
even more severe attack. Unlike those realists whom we normally
associate with a certain amount of social didacticism, Ferrari was
anything but a rebel. His plays are as a rule directed against the persons who would challenge or disrupt the tradition or the status quo.
Of course, there is an element of this in Augier and Dumas *fils* also
but even French critics who praised the social drama of the Second
Empire were outraged by a play like Ferrari's *Il duello,* a defense of the
practice of duelling, and their criticism was gradually accepted by
Italian critics as well.

Nevertheless, Ferrari marked out a path which other dramatists
were quick to follow. Cuban-born Luigi Suñer (1832-1909), like
Ferrari, achieved his first success in the competitions held by Florence's Ginnasio Drammatico, which in 1859 offered *I gentiluomini*

speculatori. The new order in Italy inspired his second work, also given at the Ginnasio, *I legittimisti in Italia* (1861), which showed a young Italian freedom fighter's difficulties in winning a girl whose parents belonged to the old aristocracy. Suñer then became one of the standard authors for Bellotti-Bon, providing him with a series of satiric protraits of contemporary society and politics such as *L'ozio* (1863) and *Una piaga sociale* (1865). Valentino Carrera (1834-1895) was another dramatist discovered by the Florence Concorso drammatica, which after 1860 was sponsored no longer by the Ginnasio Drammatico, but by the government of Vittorio Emmanuele. Carrera's prize-winning play, *Quaderna di Nanni* (1870), condemning the Florentine passion for gambling, soon entered the repertoire of both Morelli and Bellotti-Bon.

There were also established dramatists who after 1860 shifted their style to follow the mode being popularized by Ferrari and others. Giuseppe Costetti (1834-1928), an important chronicler of the nineteenth-century Italian stage, began his career as an author of romantic dramas in the French style such as *La morte del conte di Montecristo* (1854), but as taste shifted from the style of the older to the younger Dumas in France, Costetti adapted, echoing the latter's *Fils naturel* in his *Il figlio di famiglia,* offered by Bellotti-Bon in 1864. His *Il dovere* (Bellotti-Bon, 1866) and *I dissoluti gelosi* (Morelli, 1871) were major contributions to the Italian thesis play.

Gherardi del Testa, whose career extended back a decade before Costetti's, still showed himself equally willing to adjust to the new style, so much so that the historian Roux called him in 1874 "the greatest painter of manners in the peninsula today."(2) The wit and polish which had hitherto gone into farces and light comedies were not turned to more serious studies of recent political and social conflicts, most notably in *Le coscienze elastiche* (1862), *Il vero blasone* (1863), and *La carità pelosa* (1879), all presented in Florence by Bellotti-Bon. Plays by Gherardi del Testa won both the last Concorso drammatica held in Turin (1864) and the first held in the subsequent capital of Florence (1860).

The next step in the evolution of the realist drama after Ferrari was taken by Achille Torelli (1841-1922), whose *I mariti,* premiered by Bellotti-Bon in Florence in 1867 won the Concorso for that year and achieved a popular success which quite eclipsed the rising fortunes of Ferrari. Costetti suggested that "every decade may be said to have a name by which it may be called. From 1850 to 1860 it was Paolo Ferrari; from 1860 to 1870, Achille Torelli."(3) In *I mariti* Torelli subordinated the political and moral concerns of Ferrari to a more neutral presentation of psychological studies. More striking still, he avoided the machinery of the French well-made play, still essential to Ferrari, and even the emotional debates which had already become a cliché of the thesis drama. Neither intrigue nor situation were stressed; the play was simply a study of six couples, in which various husband-wife relationships were amusingly contrasted. It came very close to the slice of life presentations soon to be advocated by the French naturalists. Croce called Torelli's work the first clear step beyond the concerns of the Risorgimento: "The political and civil mission no longer dominates in Torelli; his psychology is more varied and more delicate than the rather simplified psychology of Ferrari; the nerves are beginning to prevail over the muscles."(4)

The range of portraits in *I mariti* made it an excellent ensemble piece and for Bellotti-Bon and several of his actors it was among their most memorable creations. Particularly striking was Giacinta Pezzana (1841-1919), who had already been hailed for her interpretations of romantic drama, Shakespeare and Goldoni with the Dondini company. With this play she began a series of even greater achievements in the drama of realism. In the 1870s she toured through Europe and America and in 1879, at Naples' Fiorentini, created her most famous role, the old Madame Raquin in the naturalist classic, Zola's *Thérèse Raquin*. The young Eleanora Duse played the title role.

Though the realist social drama of Ferrari and Torelli and their followers dominated the offerings of Bellotti-Bon and Morelli, the alternate school of historical spectacle still formed an important part of the repertoire. The leading author of such works during the 1860s was Leopoldo Marenco (1831-1899), whose father Carlo had provided the highly regarded *Pia dei Tolomei* and other dramas for the Reale Sarda. Leopoldo began his career in his father's footsteps with two lyric tragedies in the same manner, both premiered by Ristori, *Piccarda Donati* (1855) and *Saffo* (1856). He then began to explore directions of his own and was instrumental in establishing two subgenres of the historical play which formed a significant part of the theatre of this period. First came the pastoral drama, inaugurated by *Marcellina* (premiered by Dondini in 1860) and developed in *Giorgio Gandi* (Dondini, 1861) and the "bucolic idyll" *Celeste*, offered by Morelli in 1866. The old Arcadian preciosity which Goldoni had satirized a century before enjoyed a brief renaissance and filled the theatre with oppressed maidens, virtuous brigands and philosophical shepherds. The critic Yorick lamented: "The stage became a nest of doves and pigeons, poetic language reduced itself to a continuous round of sonnets and madrigals, and on the boards of the stage there came into being a whole anthill of dramas, pretty childish things, full of baby lovers.''(5)

Somewhat more substance but little more reality was provided by Marenco's other innovation, the *dramma medievale*, triumphantly launched in 1871 with *Il falconiere di Pietra Ardena.* This melodrama of the tenth century, depicting the noble knight Aleramo who lives in disguise as a falconer in the Apennine gorges, the gruff but tender-hearted Emperor Otton, and his daughter Adelaide who flees to join the mysterious falconer, was first given by Bellotti-Bon in Milan, where its author was accorded twenty-seven curtain calls. Within the year another highly successful drama of the same type was offered in Milan, *I pezzenti,* by Felice Cavallotti (1842-1898). In the preface to *I pezzenti,* Cavallotti cited Hugo as his major inspiration, but this first of his works, like those which followed, was much closer to recent Italian authors of the basso romantico in the suggestions of political concerns and in the division of the action into innumerable brief scenes. Like Mareco, Cavallotti was interested in history primarily as a sort of scenic background to give an extra interest to his story, as he made clear in his preface to *Agnese* (offered by Morelli in 1872):

> The author may depart from history whenever he chooses, may invent on his own initiative situations, personages, episodes, just as the impressions of his mind and the contrasts of passions dictate; intent on representing on the stage more than historical facts, not an historical epoch, nor historical characters, but an "episodio intimo," one of those pitiful dramas of the heart which belong to all countries and all ages.(6)

This "humanizing" and seeking to protray the "intimate" in history clearly corresponded to the goals of Cossa in his popular *Nerone,* and between 1870 and 1880 Cossa was the outstanding author of this variety of historical drama. Bellotti-Bon premiered three of his most successful works, *Plauto e il suo secolo* (1873), *Cola di Rienzo* (1874), and *I Borghia* (1878). The example of Cossa evidently encouraged Cavallotti to consider classic as well as medieval subjects, resulting in *Alcibiade* (1875) and *La sposa di Mènecle* (1880), both first offered by Bellotti-Bon.

The author who would take the next step beyond Ferrari and Torelli into late-nineteenth-century realism or verism was Giuseppe Giacosa (1847-1906), who was discovered and encouraged by Bellotti-Bon. During his years with this company he remained safely inside the mainstream of light comedy and medieval spectacle. His first play, offered by Bellotti-Bon in 1872, was a one-act "Proverbio" in verse, *A can che lecca cenere non gli fidar farina.* He wrote a delicate medieval fable, *Una partita a scacchi,* at about the same time. This was first presented by a company of amateurs in Naples in 1873 and remained into the twentieth century a favorite with amateur groups and the best known and loved of Giacosa's early works. More ambitious but no more realistic medieval dramas followed—*Il trionfo d'amore* (1875) and *Il fratello d'armi* (1877), both offered by Bellotti-Bon. Like Marenco and Cavallotti, Giacosa saw such "historical" works as romantic fancies owing no debt to psychology, social concerns or historical reality. He dabbled also in Goldonian comedy and admitted in a poem written in honor of the eighteenth-century playwright that he and his colleagues felt no inclination to give way to the fashionable thesis play: "It used to be said that the theatre was to amuse. Social problems were not solved there, nor were theatres changed into hospitals for diseases of the mind."(7) It was a fair assessment and also an apologia for Giacosa's work at this time, but it was not a position he held long. Only ten years later the success of his *Tristi amori* in Rome would establish the new naturalist drama on the Italian stage.

The enormous success of Bellotti-Bon proved his undoing. In 1873 he split his popular company into three troupes, each of which possessed two or three members of the original group. The sense of ensemble he had so carefully developed was lost, and none of the troupes enjoyed much success. In an attempt to enlarge and enliven their repertoire they began to borrow more heavily from the French, thus undermining the new generation of Italian authors which Bel-loti-Bon had done so much to encourage. Critics, theatregoing public, and playwrights alike protested the new organization. Influential writers such as Pietro Ferrigni complained that Italian theatre was disappearing entirely amid the imitations of the Greeks, the Romans and above all the French.(8)

In 1875 the Bellotti-Bon companies entered a period of financial crisis which steadily worsened, though their director collapsed them back into two, then one. At last, overwhelmed with debts and with all reorganizational possibilities exhausted, the harried director committed suicide in 1883. The theatre world of Italy was profoundly shocked by this tragic conclusion to so important a career. For several years after Bellotti-Bon's death, articles and books analyzed the problems of the contemporary theatre, those problems he had struggled in vain to overcome. Certain of them were cited again and again—the lack of state support for the prose theatre, the inadequacy of the national repertoire, the inability of the theatre to develop a single generally acceptable Italian dialect. Unhappily, the solutions were not so clear as the problems and no specific lasting reforms of any sort were undertaken.

The Dialect Theatres

Despite the efforts of Manzoni and the romantics, the problem of dialect drama remained unsolved during the nineteenth century. The period of unification, which one might expect to have been the proper time for the final solidification of a single theatrical idiom, was on the contrary a period of a new flourishing for the theatres of various regional dialects. The Italians still generally thought of themselves as citizens of their city or region first and when foreign domination slackened and disappeared, the new freedom and national spirit was, perhaps not surprisingly, most strikingly manifested in many areas through regional drama.

The first major dialect theatre to be established during this period was for the Piedmontese dialect, in Turin. Dialect theatre was an ancient entertainment in this area and some early forms survived well into the nineteenth century. In mountain villages during the holidays ancient mystery plays were still given, many of them containing dialect characters, such as Sardevolo in the Passion and Gelindo in the Nativity. The dialect had been employed during the renaissance in a series of farces by Giovan Giorgio Alione (1460?-1521) and had resurfaced occasionally in more modern works, most notably the popular *'L cont Piôlet* (1784) by Giambattista Tana.

Still it was not until the period of unification that a permanent dialect theatre was established in Piedmont. Its founder was Giovanni Toselli (1819-1886), a disciple of Modena. The older actor admired Toselli's naturalness and spontaneity in dialect performance and encouraged him to dedicate himself to this type of theatre. Accordingly in 1859 Toselli began touring in the north with *Cichina 'd Moncalè,* a dialect version of Pellico's *Francesca da Rimini* created by himself and Federico Garelli (1827-1885).

According to the historian Dornis, the traveling French company of Menadier heard reports of Toselli's new venture, attended a performance, and were so dazzled that they invited the dialect troupe to perform in Turin's Teatro Angennes, which they had leased, while Menadier moved to the less prestigious Teatro Scribe. There is some doubt about this story, but Toselli did appear this spring at the Angennes with *Cichina 'd Moncalè,* and was so well received that the continuation of his venture was assured. Garelli provided him with a long series of plays beginning with *Guera o pas?* (1859), a comedy posing the question "whether Piedmont should or should not force Austria to declare war," and answering, of course, in the affirmative. Two other Piedmontese dramatists soon appeared—Luigi Pietracqua (1832-1901) and Giovanni Zoppis (1830-1876).

Critics in Turin were by no means certain that Toselli's experiment should be supported. Vittorio Bersezio (1828-1900), one of the most influential among them, wrote in the *Gazzetta Piemontese* of 1859: "You wish to create a Piedmontese theatre, with Piedmontese actors and Piedmontese artists? What a folly! What an anachronism! It has never been so necessary as it is today for us to become once and for all Italians! And at this point you wish to resuscitate the era of *'L cont Piôlet*. Don't you realize that a common tongue is the principle bond of nationality?"(9) Cavour himself expressed similar misgivings.

Toselli perserved, however, and gradually conquered this opposition. Cavour was forced to admit that the political tone of *Guera o pas?* and a whole series of similar subsequent works made a real contribution to the Risorgimento and Bersezio became more and more impressed with Toselli's skill and the power of his realism. Toselli himself explained, "on the stage one ought to speak as if at home, without thinking of making effects; the effect will spring from the honesty of free and impulsive expression from the heart."(10) Thus Toselli's experiment seemed justified both on political and artistic grounds. By 1861 Bersezio had been completely won over. His articles began to support Toselli's work and finally under the pseudonym of Carlo Nugelli he became the leading dramatist for Toselli's company. *Le miserie d'monssù Travet* (1863), a comic study of a small bureaucrat oppressed by superiors at the office and his wife at home, became one of the best known and most loved plays of the period and was translated not only into standard Italian, but into French and German, with continued popularity. Among the many praises heaped upon this work, the most famous is probably that from Manzoni, who after seeing it in Milan wrote to Bersezio, "you have created truth and not simply that which is called realism."(11)

The great years of Toselli's theatre were the 1860s, when his example inspired a number of dialect theatres elsewhere. He developed an excellent company, led at first by Adelaide Tessero (1842-1892), then by Giacinta Pezzana, both of whom subsequently contributed to the lustre of the Morelli and Bellotti-Bon companies. Toselli's third leading actress and the one most associated with the triumphs of Bersezio was Marianna Moro Lin (1831-1898). In 1868 her departure and that of several lesser actors brought Toselli's administration and this first period of Piedmontese dialect theatre to an end. The tradition was carried on until the early 1880s by two companies of lesser stature led by Tancredi Milone and Enrico Gemelli. A new dialect theatre was then launched by public subscription, with Milone, Gemelli and (for the first two years) Toselli serving as co-directors. A new and much more successful period followed, dominated by the farces of Eraldo Baretti (1846-1895), most notably the political satire *I fastidi d'un grand om* (1881), and the realistic dramas of Mario Leoni (1847-1931), whose Zolaesque *I mal nutrì* (1886), dealing with the sufferings of the rural peasantry, was considered one of the great dramas of the period.

Venetia, much more than Piedmont, possessed a rich tradition of dialect theatre, dominated of course by Goldoni and Gozzi. Isolated examples of dialect comedy appeared all through the early nineteenth century, with a particularly rich contribution from F.A. Bon in the 1820s and 1830s. Still, the establishment of a permanent dialect theatre had to await the union of Venetia to Italy. Not long after, the theatre founded by Toselli in Turin provided not only a model for Venice, but the founding personnel and even the basic repertoire for the new theatre. Toselli's leading actress, Marianna Testa, married a native of Venice, Angelo Moro Lin (1831-1898), who returned with her to Venice in 1870 to found a dialect theatre there. They established themselves in the Teatro Camploy (the former San Samuel), opening with one of the Piedmontese comedies created by Zoppis for Toselli translated into Venetian dialect.

The first new Venetian authors appeared in 1871—Riccardo Selvatico (1849-1901), with *La bozéta de l'ogio* and Giacinto Gallina (1852-1897), with *Le barufe in famegia*, both clearly in the tradition of Goldoni. Despite an overwhelmingly favorable reception, Selvatico withdrew from the theatre, writing only one more dialect play five years later. He left the field to Gallina, who became the major supplier of the new company. Gallina specialized in detailed studies of the foibles of his fellow Venetians, but an everpresent warmth and good humor separates his plays clearly from the darker life studies of the realists. Marianna Moro Lin seemed a perfect actress for Gallina's sentimental family studies and she contributed importantly to both the inspiration and success of such plays as *Una famegia in rovina* (1872) and *La mama no mor mai* (1879). Her sudden death in 1879 was a cruel blow to both author and company and ended the most productive period of this theatre. Angelo continued to serve as director for another three years, encouraging Gallina and other native playwrights, reviving Goldoni and offering translations into Venetian dialect of plays by Ferrari and Giacometti.

After 1883 Moro Lin's work was carried on by Emilio Zago (1852-1929), who for the rest of the century offered native Venetian authors and translations into the dialect not only in Venice but on tours through much of northern Italy. Gallina remained the favorite modern author, inspiring a number of disciples in the next generation. When he died in 1902 the Venetians inscribed on his tomb, "He was the man who received the soul of the Venetian people into his own great ingenuous soul, and has showed it, living, in his plays, which were inspired by genius and goodness."(12)

In Milan a dialect theatre had been the lifelong dream of the beloved actor Giuseppe Moncalvo, but the Austrian authorities, fearful of its political possibilities, thwarted his attempts. Moncalvo died in 1859, just as Milan at last achieved its freedom, but his dream was carried on by the journalists Camillo Cima (1827-1908) and Carlo Righetti (1830-1906). The example of Toselli in Turin provided a critical extra stimulus, especially after Toselli's troupe made a series of guest appearances in Milan. A number of individual vernacular works appeared during the 1860s, then in 1869 an Accademia del Teatro Milanese opened at the Teatro Fiando with Cima's *El zio scior*. The venture lasted only a single season and but for the determination of Carlo Righetti that might have been the end of the experiment. Against considerable odds, he continued to strive for a permanent dialect company. A fellow journalist later reported a conversation with the determined Righetti about this project:

> When one would observe, "There is no repertoire," he would answer, "I shall create one." To the response, "There are no authors," he would insist, "They will appear." "There are no actors", "I shall train them." "There is no location", "I shall find one." "There are no means", "I shall think about that."(13)

Indeed, with an inheritance of his own, supplemented by a public subscription, Righetti established his Teatro Milanese in 1870, found a performance space, began training actors and under the pseudonym Cletto Arighi began providing them with plays. The first, a Milanese version of Labiche's *Cagnotte*, had a disastrous reception but gradually won over the public and became a triumphant success. For the next ten years Milanese versions of French farces and vaudevilles, many by Righetti, dominated the repertoire but the native authors and actors Righetti promised made their appearance too.

The greatest of them, and perhaps the fullest embodiment of the ideals of the Italian dialect theatre, was Edoardo Ferravilla (1846-1916), who made his debut fittingly in the opening performance of the Teatro Milanese. In Ferravilla the old spirit of the commedia dell'arte seemed reborn. He was a brilliant actor who was able to create striking individual portraits which yet seemed instantly recognizable as Milanese types. These he placed in play after play which he wrote himself but within which he would freely improvise during the actual performance. Perhaps the greatest mark of his skill was that while his foolish lover Sur Pedris, his docile bourgeois dilettante Pastizza, his dimwitted scholar Massinelli and still others of his roles were considered by the Milanese hilarious satires of local types, Ferravilla toured through Italy arousing equal delight with them in Rome or Naples as in Milan. In 1876 he followed Righetti as director and remained the company's leading actor until 1890. The year of Righetti's departure the theatre gained its leading actress, Emma Ivon (1850-1899), whose Camille was one of the great creations of this theatre.

When the new Italian state was formed, Naples, of all the major Italian cities, had the most solid tradition of dialect drama. Here Pulcinella had been consistently featured at the Teatro San Carlino for more than a century. The San Carlino tradition was nevertheless near its end. Several of the leading actors and authors of the theatre died during the 1870s, among them the beloved Pulcinella Antonio Petito (1822-1876), and in 1880 the theatre closed its doors permanently. Two author-actors carried on its tradition, one closely following the old models, the other much closer to the new dialect theatres being established in the north. The older tradition, though seriously weakened by the losses of the 1870s and by a changing taste in the public, was continued by Giuseppe de Martino (1854-1918), who performed in Rome and at the Neapolitan Teatro Nuovo. The rival, more realistic and more modern style was championed by Eduardo Scarpetta (1853-1925), who began his career under Petito at the San Carlino. There he created the character on whom he built his reputation, Felice Sciosciammocca, who was developed in a series of plays by Petito himself.

After the death of Petito, Scarpetta joined a dialect troupe in Rome. He returned to the San Carlino once more before its closing, to present his popular *Don Felice* (1878), but he was finding the traditional masks and commedia presentation more and more restrictive. An author's note accompanying the published version of *Don Felice* insisted:

> reform is essential—Naples too must have its good dialect theatre, with written texts and scenes built up from within. We need to create truth and not juggling tricks; to want to be men and not marionettes. Ah, if I could only achieve it—I would, first, take away as gently as possible all those old worn-out scenes, all those tattered rags, all those machines for apotheoses, those flying devices, those resurrections, those appearances and disappearances—...(14)

A tour through northern Italy, where he performed in Milan with Ferravilla and Ivon, solidified these ideas and Scarpetta returned to Naples in 1880 to put together his own dialect company. It opened with his version of the French vaudeville *Bébé* by Najac and Hennequin, which was a revelation: "The public, astonished and delighted by the confidence of the company, the naturalness of the performance, the impeccable propriety of the costumes, laughed and applauded tumultuously."(15) There was no doubt about Scarpetta's success—he quite overshadowed his rivals performing traditional commedia—but critics disagreed on the value of his reforms. Some felt that he was working to dispossess the true Neapolitan dialect theatre to replace it with mere adaptations from the French. Others, admitting he had not become the Toselli or Moro Lin of Naples, nevertheless felt that he was preparing the way for such dramatists. Time proved the latter correct; the pioneer realist Achille Torelli created several plays in Neapolitan dialect and he was followed by dramatists who made such works their specialty. Foremost among these was the poet, playwright and theatre historian Salvatore Di Giacone (1860-1934), who created a series of somewhat sentimentalized but richly detailed studies of old Naples beginning with *'O voto* (1889).

The dialect theatres of Turin, Milan, Venice and Naples achieved the greatest renown during the final years of the nineteenth century, but their example was followed by other groups in every region and every major city of Italy. A dialect theatre was proposed for Bologna as early as 1877 and was established in 1888 by Alfredo Testoni (1856-1931), who served not only as its director but as its major playwright. His light comedies of domestic life were considered insubstantial by those enamoured of the new thesis plays, but they enjoyed continued success, not only in Bologna, but in translation into other dialects. The spirit of the new movement was brought to Rome by the poet Giggi Zanazzo (1860-1911), who visited Milan and Turin to gather ideas for the revival of dialect theatre. Yet despite some thirty works by Zanazzo and despite the popular dialect comedies and vaudevilles of Pippo Tamburi (1840-1915) during the 1880s, a regular dialect theatre in Rome was long in coming. Finally in 1907 a contest for dialect works was established, followed the next year by the founding of a permanent company of the Teatro Quirino.

An equally lengthy campaign was necessary to establish a vernacular theatre in Florence. Bersezio's *Fratellanza artigiana* was offered in Tuscan as early as 1870, but it was not until 1892 that Augusto Novelli (1867-1927) took up in the pages of his journal *Il Vero Monello* the cause of dialect theatre. The Teatro Fiorentino was at last established in 1908 at the Teatro Alfieri. The opening performance, an immense success, was of Niccoli's *L'acqua cheta.*

One of the most famous of the dialect theatres developed in Sicily under the leadership of Giovanni Grasso (1873-1930), whose father and grandfather had since mid-century been popular producers of marionette plays in the Sicilian dialect. Giovanni began in the 1890s mixing performances of live actors with the puppet plays, so successfully that Ernesto Rossi, performing in Sicily, urged him to devote himself fully to live theatre. Grasso took the advice and founded a company in 1899. His repertoire was small at first, with a few plays from the marionette theatre and Sicilian translations of Verga, but with a theatre devoted to this dialect established, native playwrights soon appeared.

In the early years of the new century the company began to tour, first to Rome and then to Milan, Florence and Naples, with dazzling success. Ristori and Salvini joined Rossi in their praise; Bracco called Grasso "the greatest artist in the world." Critics joined these artists in enthusiasm. Rome's *La Capital* called Grasso equal to Rossi, Salvini, Zacconi or Novelli, the greatest stars of the period, "with the difference that in these great artists constant study has refined their natural genius, while with Grasso, the natural works prodigies."(16) Similar praise was heaped upon Grasso and his company as they began to tour outside Italy, to North and South America, Paris and London, bringing the Italian dialect theatre its greatest renown and providing new support of the theatre of realism in its competition with new styles, particularly with symbolism. Thus city by city and region by region the modern dialect theatre spread, contributing in no small way to the richness of the Italian theatre and to the development of realism but contributing at the same time to the artistic dispersion and the continuing linguistic problem which still troubles the Italian playwright today.

Verismo

The interest of certain of the dialect dramatists of the 1870s and 1880s in French farces and vaudevilles obviously involved a certain contradiction in aesthetic aims, but these authors were in a sense simply following what had for most of the century been a main current in Italian theatre. Hugo, Dumas and Vigny, then Musset and Ponsard, then Augier and Dumas *fils*—each generation of French

dramatists had immediately inspired successful and influential adaptations and translations south of the Alps. "Today," wrote the critic
Ferrigni in 1885, "we are witnessing the inauguration of a new system;
the system of causes without effects, of premises without conclusions,
of naked ideas without facts, of theses without consequences. We no
longer wish to discuss, we seek only to enunciate a problem, to pose a
question.... This is the system of the modern French theatre; it is the
school of Alexandre Dumas."(17)

It is clear that the verist movement which appeared in Italy in
the 1880s indeed owed an important part of its inspiration to the French
realists but, as with each preceding wave of French influence, this
was importantly qualified in Italy. Indeed there was a kind of con-
vergence of Italian and French artistic concerns at this period so that,
paradoxically, the champions of a distinctly Italian literature provided
much of the critical foundation for the verists who looked to Zola and
Balzac for specific models. As we have seen, realism was throughout
the century a more central concern in the Italian theatre than in the
French. It was the realism of Sanquirico which caused him to be
praised above Ciceri by the *Revue de Paris*. Modena's realist heritage
had influenced most of the major Italian actors since his time and after mid-century, when the emphasis was often on the individual star,
playwrights creating vehicles for Rossi, Ristori, Salvini or Sadowsky
were naturally influenced by the realistic bias in the style of such actors. When these artists traveled outside Italy, their realism was often
noted by critics, adding new evidence to a feeling long held, especially
in France, that the Italians as a people were basically more realistic in
their literary and theatrical expression. Typical is Sainte-Beuve's
comment in 1839 on the author Xavier de Maistre, who was born in
Savoy when it was still part of Piedmont: "If he belongs to France by
his language, one can say that he already belongs to Italy by his manner of telling a story. All is *true* in his work; nothing literary; his anec-
dotes copy reality with an exact resemblance."(18) Thus at mid-
century the French critics who championed Ristori over Rachel
stressed the realism in her style and as the century closed the same
note was struck in Parisian comparisons of Duse with Bernhardt.

Creation of the new Italy almost inevitably reinforced what
tendency Italian artists had toward preoccupation with reality. The
present, with its problems and its potential, occupied everyone's attention, and those artists and critics seeking suitable expressions for the
new nation naturally turned away from the subjects of ancient myths
and legends, pastoral scenes and remote history as too far removed

from their present concerns (even though there was a tradition of employing such subjects for their parallels to contemporary situations and even, more recently, examples of realism applied to the historical subjects themselves, as in Cossa's *Nerone*). As in France, the painters showed the way. Telemaco Signorini (1835-1901) and his colleagues in Florence spurned the traditional subjects of art in the 1860s to go out into the streets and countryside with their sketchbooks to capture contemporary reality. Already by 1873 Francesco De Sanctis had observed that this painterly concern had begun to affect literature as well: "The ideal, which has ruled for so many centuries, is disappearing even from terminology and today, for instance, the ideal is no longer mentioned and they say 'take from nature' instead of the old 'idealize.'"(19)

Thus we find that certain tendencies within the Italian tradition itself led naturally to an increasing interest in artistic realism during the nineteenth century. The Risorgimento writers were focussed toward the future, though the ubiquitous censorship generally forced them to express this interest through subjects of the past. When the Italian state was at last created, the present became a central concern and realism the dominant mode. The dialect theatres were an important part of this reaction and those critics were seriously mistaken who saw in their sudden growth after 1860 nothing but an unfortunate reversion to outmoded forms.

Despite these distinctly Italian influences, the verist movement was attacked by many Italian critics as simply another manifestation of Italian subservience to French models. There is no question that the French too contributed significantly to the new style, as can be clearly seen in the writings of Luigi Capuana (1839-1915), the first major spokesman of the new movement. Born in Sicily, Capuana decided early to devote himself to literature and in 1863, recognizing that he must make his reputation in one of the major cities on the mainland, he settled in Florence, just before that city became the new capital of Italy. He remained there until 1868, during the period of great artistic excitement, and himself contributed in an important way to the scene as drama critic for the Florence *Nazione*. He quickly absorbed the major currents of the time. "I plunged into the philosophy of Hegel," he says, "and lived on scientific positivism."(20) He read Balzac, Flaubert, and Zola, Comte, Taine and Renan and made many friendships in the intellectual and artistic world of Florence, most importantly one with Giovanni Verga (1840-1922), whose background and interests closely paralleled his own. Verga was a fellow Sicilian of

Capuana's age who had arrived in Florence at almost the same time and with much the same motives.

When Rome became the new capital, the intellectual community of Florence began to disperse. Verga, with many others, was attracted to Milan, which became the center of the new realist movement. Capuana was forced by illness to return to Sicily, where in 1872 he published his collected drama reviews, *Il teatro contemporaneo*. In the preface he bade farewell to the drama as incompatible with the progress of contemporary human thought. The short story and the novel now received his undivided attention. He joined Verga in Milan and the friends encouraged each other in the completion of the first two major novels of Italian naturalism, Capuana's *Giacinta* (1879), dedicated to Zola, and Vergas *I malavoglia* (1881), considered by many the greatest Italian novel since *I promessi sposi*.

In Milan Verga met Giacosa, who encouraged him to try his abilities in the drama. Unfortunately, Verga's major creative period was past. The three plays he wrote before 1900 were all rather unimaginative adaptations from his earlier novellas, with only essential changes made to adjust them for stage presentation. Still *Cavalleria rusticana* (1884), the first of these, was the first major dramatic work in the verist style and as such played a key role in the development of modern Italian drama. It was first offered in Turin by Cesare Rossi (1829-1898), a leading actor from the Bellotti-Bon company who carried on that tradition in the production of French drama and the encouragement of realist experiments. Rossi had left Bellotti-Bon in 1877 to form his own company, hoping to settle it in a permanent home.

Following the creation of the Italian state, Salvini and others had called for a system of permanent subsidized theatres, with little result. It was not until after 1900 that his hope began to be realized. Still, by the late 1870s occasional tentative steps in this direction were being taken and Rossi was an important pioneer. He obtained a municipal subvention and free use for six months of the Teatro Carignano in Turin, the former home of the Reale Sarda. His organization proved one of the longest lasting "permanent" theatres in Italy during this period, performing in the Carignano from 1877 until 1885.

The leading members of Rossi's "Città di Torino" company came from the Fiorentini in Naples, where the wealthy Princess Santobuono subsidized a troupe during the 1870s directed by Giovanni Emanuel (1848-1902), an actor who had played leading roles with

Salvini and Bellotti-Bon. The leading actress was Giacinta Pezzana, supported by the young Eleanora Duse (1858-1924). Duse, after a number of years of indifferent efforts, achieved her first real success at the Fiorentini in such roles as Ophelia, Desdemona, Elettra (in Alfieri's *Oreste*) and most importantly as Therese Raquin in 1879. Soon after this last creation, the Princess decided to change her support to opera and the company was left without a sponsor. Rossi was quick to invite the leading actors to join his new company in Turin and Duse, Emanuel and Pezzana were soon playing leading roles there. Rossi advertised his new acquisitions with a delight that soon changed to despair. Emanuel and Pezzana departed almost at once on tours and Duse seemed incapable of recapturing the success she had achieved in Naples. She seemed unable to catch the spirit of the sophisticated French roles she inherited from Pezzana and she was desolated by an unhappy love affair she had experienced before leaving Naples. She performed indifferently; audiences were disappointed and Rossi was furious. Duse considered abandoning the stage.

Then came a turning point in her career—a visit to Turin by Sarah Bernhardt, at the peak of her fame and power. She presented three plays by Dumas *fils,* and Duse attended every performance, dazzled by the French actress' achievement. "Here is one," she said, "who elevates the profession, who brings to the public a reverence for the beautiful and forces them to bow down before art."(21) Duse was more than impressed, she was inspired to become the Bernhardt of Italy. To the astonishment of Rossi, Duse announced her desire to follow the Bernhardt performances with her own series of Dumas plays. Rossi naturally hesitated, knowing that this would provoke inevitable and surely unfavorable comparisons with the French star. He attempted to convince Duse to present instead a safe and tested comedy by Gherardi del Testa, but when she insisted he finally gave way and allowed her to prepare *La Princesse de Bagdad*, a Dumas play Bernhardt had not offered.

The Turin papers were, as Rossi feared, filled with scorn for Duse's presumption but curious spectators who filled the theatre were astonished at her new power and inspiration. Her success was so great that she was able to continue with Bernhardt roles just seen in Turin—*La Femme de Claude* and even the greatest Bernhardt creation, Marguerite Gautier in *La Dame aux camélias,* to continuing public acclaim. In one magnificent season, Duse had established herself as Italy's most promising new actress. Flavio Andò (1851-1915), the new leading man who had replaced Emanuel, played Armand, a part in which he had already achieved a certain renown, and provided a brilliant partner for the new star.

With these successes Duse, Rossi and Andò attracted the attention of the entire Italian theatre world. When Verga completed his *Cavalleria rusticana* it was almost inevitable that Giacosa, his dramatic mentor, should urge that it be submitted to Rossi. Giacosa himself undertook the negotiations, but encountered difficulties. Rossi seemed disinclined, after the triumphs with Dumas *fils*, to gamble on a new Italian work with a markedly different tone. In November of 1883 Giacosa wrote to Verga:

> I spoke to Rossi, who thinks it would be impossible to present your play successfully.... I do not agree with him, but Duse has a great influence on her director and she forecasts a failure. What is to be done? ... I shall in any event keep trying. As for the opinion of Rossi and Duse, I do not take it seriously. Rossi is a creature of habit. Duse, who is clever and daring enough as an actress, is extremely timid in the judgment of an unpresented work and lacks the courage to assume responsibility.(22)

Blocked from one direction, Giacosa tried another, and urged the play on Andò, himself a Sicilian with some sympathy for the regionalism of the work. At a dinner held by Giacosa, Andò promised Verga that he would get Rossi to present his play if Verga would bear the expenses of costumes and give up his author's customary share of the first evening's income. On these terms the play was presented, with Andò playing Turiddu and Duse playing Lola. The third leading part, Lola's husband Alfio, should have gone to Rossi, but he remained sufficiently opposed to the work to give the role instead to Teobaldo Checchi (1844-1918), an actor of modest ability who had become Duse's husband in real life in 1881.

The play was, contrary to Rossi's expectations, quite well received. It enjoyed the unusual honor of a second performance the following evening. It was then taken up by other companies, and even translated into German and French. In Paris it was accepted at that citadel of the new drama, Antoine's Théâtre-Libre. Thus Verga made his mark as a leader of the new naturalist style in the drama as well as in the novel. It was a leadership which he maintained only briefly. Few theatres were able to repeat the success of Rossi's company with *Cavalleria rusticana* and at the Théâtre-Libre it came close to outright failure. What in fact assured the work and its author a lasting reputation in the theatre was that it was selected as a libretto by the young composer Pietro Mascagni (1863-1945), who created from it the first major work of *verismo* in the musical theatre.

During the 1870s, as Faccio and Boito's musical reputation declined, the candidate most favored to replace the aging Verdi was Amilcare Ponchielli (1834-1886). The success of his operatic version of *I promessi sposi* at Milan's Teatro del Verme in 1872 opened to him La Scala, for which he created four extremely popular operas between 1876 and 1885. The first of these, *La Gioconda*, remains his best-known work. Though based on Victor Hugo's melodramatic *Angelo, Tyran de Padoue*, the libretto, created by Boito, nevertheless had certain elements which looked forward to realism. Perhaps Ponchielli would have developed further in that direction had he lived longer, but he was still much under Verdi's shadow when he died in 1886, the year before Verdi's *Otello* showed him still master of the Italian operatic world. The hints of a new direction in *La Gioconda* thus had to be developed by a new generation of composers, but significantly, the most important of these—Mascagni and Puccini—were both students of Ponchielli.

A prize contest for one-act operas sponsored by the Milanese music publishing house of Sonzogno provided the impetus for Mascagni's *Cavalleria rusticana*. It won first place and was premiered soon after, in 1890, at Rome's Teatro Costanzi. Its success was immediate and overwhelming. Within two years it was presented in all the major cities of Italy and in Berlin, New York, London and Paris. Verdi himself remarked: "Now I can die content; here is one who can worthily continue the Italian opera."(23) Unfortunately, Mascagni never again equalled the achievement of *Cavalleria rusticana*. With the continual encouragement of Sonzogno he created operatic versions of two Erckmann-Chatrian novels, *L'amico Fritz* (Rome, Costanzi, 1891) and *I Rantzau* (Florence, Pergola, 1892), which were warmly, but not enthusiastically received, then went on to La Scala with even less distinguished works.

By the mid-1890s it was becoming clear that Mascagni was not in fact destined to be the long-awaited successor to Verdi, nor was Ruggero Leoncavallo (1858-1919), who was inspired by the success of *Cavalleria rusticana* to create another classic of *verismo* opera, *I Pagliacci*. This too was sponsored by Sonzogno and premiered in 1892 at Milan's Teatro del Verme. After this triumph Leoncavallo, like Mascagni, created a long series of distinctly lesser works, while the leadership of the new school passed to the greatest of the verists, Giacomo Puccini (1858-1924). His first opera, *Le villi*, was submitted to the first Sonzogno competition and did not even receive honorable mention. Then, thanks to the efforts of Boito and Ponchielli, it was given a performance at the Teatro del Verme with such success that it was revived at La Scala. It was another decade before the promise of this beginning was fulfilled, but then came the dazzling trio of *Manon Lescaut* (1893), *La Bohème* (1896), both premiered at Turin's Teatro Regio, and *Tosca* (1900), premiered at Rome's Teatro Costanzi. The librettos for each of these masterpieces were in part the work of Giacosa, who in his final years as a playwright created some of the most significant works of the verist theatre.

In the spoken theatre Verga, following *Cavalleria rusticana,* turned from Sicilian peasant life to a drama of Milan slum-dwellers, *In Portineria.* The play was offered in the new Teatro Manzoni, the same theatre where Bellotti-Bon just before his death had offered works by such dramatists as Ferrari and Torelli. The Manzoni patrons were thus accustomed to realism, but Verga's cruelly ironic new work proved too extreme for them, and the news of *Cavalleria rusticana's* failure in Paris, coming at this same time, discouraged Verga from attempting another theatre piece for a number of years. Capuana fared little better with the stage version of his major novel *Giacinta,* which was offered by Rossi but without Duse, who refused to perform in it.

The distinction of creating the first unqualified success in the new style was gained not by the writers who had pioneered *verismo* but by Giuseppe Giacosa, who had established his reputation in more traditional styles. Giacosa's friendship with Verga naturally led him to attempt experiments of his own in the new style, beginning in 1879 with *Luisa.* This odd play, with the subject matter of a realistic social drama but cast in verse (somewhat in the manner of Augier's *Gabrielle*), was not particularly effective, but Giacosa continued to work this vein and in 1887 created the first great success of verism in the spoken theatre, *Tristi amori.* Its theme was a familiar one in realistic drama, a husband's discovery of his wife's adulterous love, but Giacosa treated it in a strikingly new manner. The characters were developed objectively—not as fools, victims or villains, but as weak, suffering, average human beings. Action and setting were commonplace, even sordid, but without the French naturalists' grim irony.

The play was premiered in Rome, at the new Teatro Drammatico Nazionale. In several of the major Italian cities the 1880s saw attempts to found prose theatres on the model of the Comédie Française, and the Nazionale was one of these, subsidized by a group of Roman aristocrats and opened in 1886 under the direction of the dramatist Paolo Ferrari from Milan. The experiment was short-lived with Giacosa's work one of the few important offerings before the theatre shifted from prose to the more popular lyric theatre. The premiere, attended by Queen Margherita and the cream of Roman society, was a disaster. Indifferently performed, it received hisses and boos. In the Roman papers the critics opposed to the new realism condemned the play as "photography and not art." Those in favor of it upbraided Giacosa for departing from the practice of French dramatists like Becque by giving the play a happy ending.

Other companies planning to produce the play became wary but fortunately Rossi in Turin, despite his frequent timidity in such matters, continued with his plans for a production there with both Duse and Andò in the leading roles. Its success in Turin was immediate and overwhelming, and was followed soon after by a similarly warm reception in Milan. The victory was won for Giacosa and for the new style and *Tristi amori* was established as one of the major dramas of its time. The verist goal that Capuana articulated in the 1890 preface to his *Giacinta* had been in fact more fully and more successfully carried out by Giacosa in *Tristi amori*:

> In writing this comedy I intended insofar as possible to simplify the conduct of the action and the form of the dialogue of contemporary dramatic art; and insofar as possible to develop a more intimate collaboration between actors and public for the success of a theatrical work. Simplifying the action meant for me disencumbering it of most of those conventions which through long use or abuse even in writers of the greatest skill have become so inextricably mixed with that which truly constitutes dramatic art that they have become erroneously regarded as being of the same nature and of equal respectability with it.
>
> Simplifying the form of the dialogue meant for me putting aside all vain ornament, all the elaboration which is falsely called "literary," arising from the intervention of the personality of the author in the manifestation of the thoughts and feelings of the characters; and, instead, employing a tightly-knit, rapid, straightforward, economic style, capable of giving the illusion of spoken dialogue without sacrificing any more than necessary of its artistic quality.(24)

Tristi Amori opened a period of major achievement for the verist theatre, centering at Milan's Teatro Manzoni. The Manzoni, like Rome's Nazionale, had been erected in the hope of establishing a permanent national home for spoken theatre, but this had proven no more possible in Milan than in Rome. Bellotti-Bon attempted, but failed, to establish a prose troupe here, and since his suicide the Manzoni had sheltered touring companies presenting both musical and spoken theatre. Still, it remained the house most associated with the new drama. Verga's *In Portineria* was premiered here in 1885, and here were given the first Milan productions of *Cavalleria rusticana* and *Tristi amori*. In the early 1890s the develop-

ment of a school of verist playwrights in Milan brought the Manzoni
close to achieving the aim of its original founders.

The most successful dramatists of this school were Marco
Praga (1862-1929) and Gerolamo Rovetta (1851-1910), whose best
works followed directly the path opened by *Tristi amori*. Rovetta
wrote several unsuccessful plays in the 1870s before achieving significant popular and critical acclaim with his *Trilogia di Dorina,*
presented at the Manzoni in 1889. This work, depicting a poor girl
who becomes a governess, loses her honor and ends as a cruel adven-
turess, was, like most of Rovetta's works, strong on milieu and rather
weak on characterization. Nevertheless its realistic depiction of three
class levels in contemporary society and its bitter cynicism, actually
closer to the French than to Giacosa, made it ideally suited to the taste
of the period, and it enjoyed a wide if not enduring success. Equally
well received was *I disonesti*, premiered in Turin in 1892, one of the
best developments of the theme, highly popular with the realists, that
men are made good or evil by circumstances not by principles. The
French critic Taine's expression of this idea is the most famous: "No
matter if the facts be physical or moral, they all have their causes;
there is a cause for ambition, for courage, for truth, as there is for
digestion, for muscular movement, for animal heat. Vice and virture
are products, like vitriol and sugar."(25) As one of Rovetta's characters comments, "One is not born dishonest."

Praga even more strikingly than Rovetta departed from the
touches of the didactic and the sentimental which could still be found
in Giacosa. He sought, like Verga and many of the French, to observe
human actions coldly and objectively. In a letter of 1890 he wrote
"What is my aim? To portray the truth; life as it is lived; to create
drama of character, drama of milieu, but never drama of intrigue. I
detest Sardou; I love Augier."(26) In practice this aim often led him,
as it did many of the French, to create a dramatic world of dark rather
than neutral tones, with no possibility of a noble action or of disin-
terested motives. Praga's fame was established with *Le virgini*, presented at the Manzoni in 1889, a grim tale of a girl's inability to escape
from a home environment which has compromised her sexually.

Le virgini, I disonesti, and *Trilogia di Dorina* were all
premiered by the same company, headed by Virginia Marini (1842-
1918). Marini achieved her first successes in Goldonian comedy at the
Fiorentini in Naples during the early 1860s, while Salvini and Cazzola
were performing there. Later she built her repertoire with such French
adaptations as *Adriana Lecouvreur* and *La signora dalle camelie*. In

1868 she appeared with Salvini in Florence before the King and the next year accompanied Salvini on his tour of Spain and Portugal. From 1870 to 1876 she was with Morelli and from 1876 to 1881 with Bellotti-Bon, at the time when these two companies were the center of the new realistic drama. During the 1870s, indeed, she rivaled Adelaide Tessaro for the position of leading interpreter of this drama. After leaving Bellotti-Bon, Marini continued to pursue this direction, first in the troupe directed by Ferri and later with Cesare Rossi. In 1888 she formed her own company, which naturally favored the verist drama. Many of its members had achieved their reputation in other genres but a few, like Marini, were primarily associated with this style of theatre and two of these, Italia Vitaliani (1866-1938), who played secondary roles to Marini, and the leading man Ermete Zacconi (1857-1948), would carry on the emphasis of this company into the new century.

In Italy, as elsewhere in Europe, a major new impetus was given to the realist drama by the coming of Ibsen, and Marini and her actors played a central role in the introduction of the Scandinavian dramatist. They did not, however, present the first Ibsen in Italy. That step was taken by Duse, who offered his *Doll's House* at the Milan Filodrammatici in 1891. The seven years since the success of *Cavalleria rusticana* had been extremely eventful ones for her. In 1885 the Rossi company had taken a tour of South America, in the course of which the relationships depicted in Verga's drama were strikingly repeated in the real lives of the actors who had taken those roles. Duse became increasingly involved with Flavio Andò and her husband increasingly aware of this and increasingly furious. Italian law allowed no divorce but Duse and her husband returned to Italy agreeing to a permanent separation and Duse organized a new troupe, headed by herself and Andò, the "Compagnia Drammatica della Città di Roma." As the passionate lovers in plays by Dumas and Sardou, they went from success to success and Duse was hailed as the new leading actress of Italy. The company was invited to perform in Russia by Alexander III. There Duse first offered *A Doll's House*, to great acclaim, reviving it upon her return to Italy. The role of Nora tempted Duse, as it did most of the leading actresses of the period, even though it was rather removed from the sophisticated French heroines found in most of her repertoire. Clearly it was the role and not the Ibsen style of drama that attracted her, for this was Duse's only Ibsen premiere and before the end of the century she appeared in only two other Ibsen works, *Rosmersholm* in 1895 and *Hedda Gabler* in 1898, clearly both also selected for their leading roles.

In the meantime a host of other Ibsen productions were mounted by actors and companies who found the Ibsen style itself more congenial. Chief among these were Virginia Marini and Ermete Zacconi, who produced Italy's second Ibsen premiere, *Ghosts (Gli spettri)* at the Teatro Manzoni in 1892. It was Zacconi, in the role of Osvald, who dominated the production and this became his most famous creation. For the accurate depiction of Osvald's insanity he read the leading psychological texts of the period and visited hospitals and clinics to study symptoms for use on stage. The result was a degree of realism new to the Italian theatre, though some critics felt the production as a whole suffered:

> He [Zacconi] undoubtedly studied the reality of that illness which leads Osvald to imbecility and he has truly reproduced it on stage, with terrifying effect. But he has shown too quickly the symptoms of this malady which is destroying him to achieve the theatrical effect that develops from reality. Preoccupied with his own character, he has too much forgotten the rest. How can it be that Mrs. Alving becomes aware only at the end of the grave illness that has striken her son when from the beginning of the last act his speech is the babbling of a paralytic and an imbecile? In order to be real, scrupulously real, Zacconi has ceased to give the illusion of reality.(27)

The following year Marini and Zacconi presented their own version of *A Doll's House*, along with other important works of the new drama, *Pane altrui* from Turgenev and *Potenza delle tenebre* from Tolstoi. They also began presenting dramas by young Italian playwrights working under the new inspiration Ibsen provided. One of the most open in his homage to the Norwegian was Enrico Butti (1868-1912), whose *L'utopia* Marini offered early in 1894. In the preface to this play Butti (speaking of himself through a pseudonym) says:

> He boasts of his debt to Ibsen; he says and demonstrates that he has understood perfectly the aesthetic conception of the author of *Ghosts* and *The Master Builder,* and since this conception pleased him and he found it in conformity with his own artistic tendencies and those of the intellectual age through which we are passing, he seized upon it and produced a work in which he tries to point out some of the great contradictions of our stormy contemporary spirit.(28)

What Butti found in Ibsen which so pleased him was a concern with the personal problems of members of modern society, especially when those problems reflected a conflict between the new scientific spirit and the weight of tradition. Butti also noted the frequent defeat of the new spirit in Ibsen's plays, and took up this theme with such grim determination that he often alienated the public and caused critics to see in him a champion of reactionary social ideas. *L'utopia* was typical of his works. It showed a rationalistic modern doctor who preaches the elimination of weak and unfit children even though this leads to his social ostracism. Then, as if by divine retribution, his own child is born hideously deformed and he finds his ideals impossible.

Not long after offering *L'utopia,* the Marini-Zacconi troupe dissolved, but its two leaders continued to champion the new drama, Zacconi founded a new company of his own and Marini joined another being formed by Francesco Gazes (1848-1894), which took as its specific aim the continuation of the reform of Italian prose theatre begun by Bellotti-Bon. Gazes did indeed introduce several important reforms; he abolished the prompter, did away with footlights, and sought a distinctly greater degree of realism in scenery, but his goal of following Bellotti-Bon was grimly and all too accurately fulfilled within a year when he too, under great financial pressure, committed suicide. The major event of his brief administration was the Italian premiere of Ibsen's *Rosmersholm,* with Marini as Rebecca West. After his death, Marini retired from the stage, leaving the leadership of the new school to Zacconi and others.

At the end of 1894 Zacconi returned with his company to the Manzoni and remained there through the following spring, offering during these few months a repertoire rivalling that of any of the avant-garde Free Theatres in Europe. He gave Ibsen's *Ghosts, Enemy of the People,* and *Little Eyolf* (the latter for the first time in Italy), and revived the Turgenev and Tolstoi works from Marini's repertoire. He also revived works from the previous generation he felt compatible with the new repertoire—Giacometti's *Morte civile,* Cossa's *Nerone,* and several works by Dumas *fils*—but he favored new plays, both imported and domestic. He was keenly aware of the new dramatists of the Free Theatre movement in northern Europe and introduced Milan audiences to such plays as Hauptmann's *Einsame Menschen,* Théodore de Banville's *Gringoire,* Maeterlinck's *L'Intruse,* and Daudet's *L'Obstacle.*

No director of this period was more receptive than Zacconi to the new works of Italian realism. In 1894 he offered Giacosa's *Diritti dell'anima,* a work heavily influenced by Ibsen, and Camillo Antona-Traversi's (1857-1934) *Danza macabre,* a study of the helplessness of young aristocrats in the real world (the same theme later used by Giacosa for his masterpiece *Come le foglie*). In 1895 came Rovetta's *Realtà,* with a dark view of society similar to but more bitter than Ibsen's *Enemy of the People.* A new disciple of Ibsen appeared in Roberto Bracco (1860-1943), a Neapolitan critic who championed Ibsen and Wagner in the pages of the *Corriere di Napoli* before turning to direct imitation of Ibsen in the one-act *Maschere,* which Zacconi premiered in 1894. Clearly works of this sort appealed strongly to Zacconi but his repertoire was a varied one, including Racine, Goldoni and even Sheridan's *The School for Scandal.*

Zacconi's casting policy, like his repertoire, showed the influence of contemporary experimentation in Germany and France, as an article in the *Illustrazione italiana* pointed out in 1894:

> The actor who plays the protagonist today will tomorrow be a minor character actor of the second rank; and this evening's extra may well be applauded tomorrow as Fedra or Fernanda. It seems that Zacconi wishes to do here what Antoine the director of the Théâtre-Libre has done in France, create an interpretation which is perfect not only in major roles but also in the minor ones.(29)

In fact, Zacconi seems to have had little interest in establishing a permanent theatre in the Théâtre-Libre style in Milan, or it may be that he simply could not stimulate sufficient support. In any case his experiment here lasted only a single season. He then resumed his touring with a repertoire dominated by realist drama but offering few premieres. He did not attempt to build an ensemble either but changed his supporting actors constantly, in the manner of Salvini and Rossi. In the late 1890s he left Italy for two years to tour to Vienna, Berlin, Petersburg, Budapest, Spain and Portugal.

Aside from Zacconi, the two actor-managers who contributed most to the encouragement of the new drama in the 1890s were Ermete Novelli (1851-1919) and Duse's partner Flavio Andò. Novelli gained his first significant success as a member of Bellotti-Bon's company, where he played opposite Marini and was much praised, especially in comic roles, for his ability to create extremely varied and clearly defined characters. After the death of Bellotti-Bon he joined Ferri's Drammatica Compagnia Nazionale but after a year departed to establish his own company. He toured Italy with a repertoire composed largely of French comedies by such authors as Bisson, Feydeau, Valabrégue and Hennequin, gaining universal praise for his comic touch and for his ability to achieve brilliant effects by the most economic means. In 1886 and 1887 he toured to Spain and in 1890 to South America.

Upon his return, Novelli formed a new company with Claudio Leigheb (1848-1903), another veteran of Bellotti-Bon's company who had worked with Cesare Rossi, Duse, Andò and Marini. Without forsaking his interest in comedy, Novelli now turned as well to the new realist drama, creating a repertoire that was in this respect similar to Zacconi's—including Giacometti's *Morte civile*, Cossa's *Nerone*, and Ibsen's *Ghosts* and *The Master Builder*. He premiered *The Wild Duck* in Italy in 1891, finding in Hjalmar Ekdal an Ibsen character whose comic touches were particularly suited to his special skills. He also premiered works by the Italian realists: Praga's *Alleluja* (1892), a rather foolish tragedy of heredity; Bracco's *Don Pietro Caruso* (1895), a moving little one-act Neapolitan tragedy; and Antona-Traversi's *Il signor Lecocq* (1895), on which Novelli collaborated. Novelli's total repertoire was much larger than Zacconi's, embracing not only many more comic works, but a larger number of classics—Goldoni, Beaumarchais, Molière and above all Shakespeare. Shylock became his particular specialty as Othello was Salvini's. From 1894 to 1899 he left Italy again to tour but returned in 1900 hoping, like many of his generation, to establish a permanent Italian Comédie. His Casa di Goldoni, established at Rome's former Teatro Valle, was the most promising of these attempts and made important contributions in staging and in the presentation of new works. Still, it suffered the inevitable financial crisis and disappeared after only two seasons.

During the decade after the establishment of their Città di Roma company, Duse and Andò enjoyed great success, especially in foreign tours, but Duse remained suspicious of the new Italian realistic drama. Rovetta and Bracco were not offered and though Duse premiered one Giacosa play, this was a rather flamboyant neoclassic drama, *La signora di Challant* (1891), originally written in French as a vehicle for Sarah Bernhardt. The only important work of the new drama premiered was Praga's *La moglie ideale* (1890), another play clearly chosen for its excellent leading female role. Duse's repertoire dominated by the works of Dumas *fils*, and her favorite roles were Marguerite Gautier and Shakespeare's Cleopatra. The latter she created in an adaptation by Boito, her new lover, for her relationship with Andò was now strictly a professional one. "He was beautiful but stupid," she observed later, and she found in Boito a much more compatible soul.

Early in 1894 the Città di Roma company dissolved and Andò whose interest in realistic drama was clearly stronger than Duse's became much more involved with its encouragement. He was associated for two years with Claudio Leigheb, then in 1897 formed a new company with Tina di Lorenzo (1872-1930) that became famous for its interpretations of verist theatre. Among their first premieres was Butti's *La fine d'un ideale* (1898), another of its author's studies of a defeated revolutionary. In this, a liberated young woman leaves her husband, only to find she is too weak to survive alone in the outside world. Butti next undertook his most ambitious project, a trilogy of plays called *Gli Atei* which continued to portray both liberal and conservative ideas as equally productive of disillusion and unhappiness. Only the first work of the trilogy was given by Andò, *La corsa al piacere*, in 1900.

The hopelessness and gloom of dramatists like Butti inevitably sparked a reaction, even among some of the verists themselves. The most striking and most successful manifestation of this reaction was Rovetta's *Romanticismo*, presented by Andò in Turin in 1901. In an article in the *Rassegna Nazionale*, Rovetta explained that he had written the work "in the hope of reviving the feeling in our national life during the Venetian-Lombard revolution." Even he had been at first surprised by its success, he admitted, but in fact:

> It is a very understandable reaction. The novel and the historical drama are not being reborn by a renewal of love for history itself but because of an idealist reaction. The public supports the dramatists in this new infatuation as they once supported the naturalists against that cardboard romanticism which they had been offered for twenty-five years. They had had enough of seeing fictions on the stage instead of applauding living humanity there. When this humanity was offered—speaking, acting, suffering—they applauded it and were right to do so. But truth has fallen today into too vulgar a reality and the public wants something new; that is, they wish to be brought truth still, but this time enveloped in a certain poetic idealism.... They have had enough in the theatre of those *platitudes* added to what they inevitably encounter in everyday life.(30)

This reaction may thus be seen as similar to the "idealist" reaction in France, which supported the symbolist experiments of Fort and Lugné-Poë and the Neo-romanticism of Rostand. *Romanticismo's* great and unexpected success most closely corresponds with that of *Cyrano de Bergerac*, though its subject was drawn from a much more immediate source—the Italian war of liberation and a patriotic idealism which at least some members of the audience could remember as firsthand experience.

Significantly, the other great popular dramatic success at the end of the century was another, if milder, reaction to the verist theatre by one of the masters of that genre, Giacosa. Throughout his career, Giacosa had been extremely successful in crystallizing the dominant new trends as each appeared in the theatre. He had gained the first great victories for the verist drama and now he contributed importantly to the reaction to that genre as it came to be established. On the occasion of the inauguration of a bust of Paolo Ferrari in 1898 he called for reform in these terms:

> Adultery and the love interest have been far too exclusively the subject of drama. Let us mix in our plays ambition and anger, avarice, pride, revolt, the sorrow of fathers and mothers, betrayals of friendship, humiliations coming from physical information and those still more biting coming from moral informities and intellectual tares. Then you shall see whether or not the stage will be rejuvenated and will become more living and real than at the time when amorous perversions triumphed.(31)

Proclamations of this sort by artists are not always successfully carried into parctice, but Giacosa stunningly demonstrated his new ideas in *Come le foglie*, premiered by Andò at Milan's Teatro Manzoni in 1900. The love interest was indeed completely subordinated in this story of the inability of a once-wealthy family to adjust to altered circumstances, and the play was universally praised and widely produced. It has been called the Italian *Cherry Orchard,* more, doubtless, for its theme than for the depth of its evocation or the richness of its texture. Nevertheless, Giacosa's work as the new century began enjoyed a prominence in the Italian theatre not unlike Chekov's in the Russian. Once again he had indicated with a major work a new direction for the Italian theatre.

Virgilio Talli (1858-1928), who played Massimo, the hero of *Come le foglie,* formed his own company soon after this success and carried on into the new century the support of the realist drama Andò had provided during the late 1890s. His company premiered Giacosa's final work, *Il più forte,* in 1904 and Rovetta's new "idealist" drama, *Re Bulone,* in 1905 but the emphasis of the repertoire remained in the verist mainstream—Praga, Bracco, Antona-Traversi and the final two works of Butti's *Gli Atei* trilogy, *Lucifero* (1900) and *Una tempesta* (1901). Dramatists with similar interests from other nations were also represented—Donnay, Brieux, Jullien, Hervieu, Sudermann, Przybysewski, Wolff, Lavedan.

Realism was also given continued support as the new century began in the dialect theatre, most importantly in Sicily. Capuana returned to playwriting, still serving the realist cause but this time in dialect drama. Like many others, he was at first suspicious of the dialect theatre, but was eventually won over by its clear popularity and effectiveness. During the first decade of the twentieth century he created a series of popular dialect works and between 1911 and 1921 published five volumes of dialect plays with a preface in which he defends such drama against those who continued to hope for a linguistically unified Italian theatre. Thus the influence of the Verga-Capuana tradition was still powerful, in both dialect and standard lingua theatre, when the first great Italian playwright of the new century, Luigi Pirandello, began writing, and his early plays were deeply indebted to this example.

Duse and D'Annunzio

As in most of Europe, realism in Italy successfully withstood the assaults of the various alternative modes pitted against it at the close of the nineteenth century, but as the century ended the outcome of the conflict was uncertain. Rovetta's success with the new idealist drama seemed to open the possibility of a new theatre, more lyric and more exalted than the dominant realist one. The writer of the period who saw himself and was seen by his contemporaries as the obvious leader of this new movement was Gabriele D'Annunzio (1863-1938), whose life and works were the fullest and most flamboyant embodiment in Italy of the strange and exotic final flowering of romanticism which in the north of Europe gave rise to the symbolists and the decadents.

D'Annunzio began his literary career as a poet under the influence of Giosuè Carducci (1835-1904), the leading poet of the years just after unification. D'Annunzio's was a new and unique style, though it drew on both classic and romantic sources. To this generation it seemed classic in its concern with carefully wrought images and subjects from antiquity, but the intensity and passion it brought to these concerns owed much more to romanticism. D'Annunzio's first volume of verse appeared in 1879, while he was still a student, and caused a major stir by its brilliant language and strong eroticism. In subsequent volumes these qualities became more striking. D'Annunzio was widely acclaimed as a genius, if a somewhat decadent and ultrasophisticated one, a histrionic image that he worked assiduously to develop. His verses were those of a *poète maudit*, his novels were steeped in the ethics of Nietzsche and the *fin de siècle* luxuriousness of Huysmans or Wilde.

D'Annunzio's reputation, built on his poems, his novels and his flamboyant personal life, was well established not only in Italy but in France and England by 1894, when he first met Eleanore Duse in Venice. The locale was particularly appropriate, since Venice at the end of the century was once again becoming artistically fashionable, not despite its decay but in large part because of it. The particularly Venetian mixture of luxury and decadence precisely suited the *fin de siècle* taste and writers from many countries came here to sample this spirit.

The Duse-Andò company had just dissolved after a tour to America and England which had not been a particular success. Duse was now at a turning point in her career, seeking a dramatist who could give her the scripts of poetic power she desired, and seeking to establish the major international reputation which had so far eluded her. The year 1894 saw the beginning of the fulfillment of both of these dreams. She signed an eight-year contract with the impresario Joseph Schurmann, who arranged before the end of the year a tour to Germany, where she was for the first time hailed as a greater actress even than Ristori, and to London, where she competed directly and successfully with Sarah Bernhardt herself. Duse won the preference of many London critics, led by Bernard Shaw (32), and was even invited to perform *La locandiera* at Windsor Palace. She toured through eastern Europe the following year and in 1896 returned to America, this time as a conquering star. Performances were sold out weeks in advance and theatre receipt records were broken as they had been in the days of Ristori. In Washington President Cleveland and his cabinet attended every night of Duse's performances, filling her dressing room with white roses and chrysanthemums. Duse was even invited to tea at the White House, an unprecedented honor for an actress.

Her repertoire in America was composed of works Duse had made her specialty for years—*La locandiera, Cavalleria rusticana, La signora dalle camelie*—with one more recent addition, Sudermann's *Magda*. Despite its success, she found this repertoire more and more unsatisfying, both emotionally and artistically. She wrote to Boito from London that she now rarely felt "that *depth* of life I was once able to grasp." She longed for plays which could provide this instead of the banal realism which dominated the theatre now. "What an offense to the soul is this aping of life! And yet I see around me, despite all these papier-mâché trees padded with green cloth, so many people clutching at this chimera of chimeras!"(33)

It was probably this feeling, rather than artistic cowardice, as Giacosa suspected, that made Duse so unreceptive to the new realistic drama while she was acting with Rossi. And yet the more poetic, more idealistic drama of which she dreamed had not yet appeared. Discouraged with the present, she turned to the past, and above all to

Shakespeare. She urged Boito in vain to provide her with more translations like *Antony and Cleopatra,* and finally obtained from the
critic and Shakespearean scholar Giulio Piccini (1849-1915) a new and
rather indifferent adaptation of *Romeo and Juliet.* Under the circumstances, her interest in D'Annunzio, the rising star of Italian poetry,
was almost inevitable, even though he had as yet written nothing
for the theatre. Not long before her encounter with him in Venice she
read his *Trionfo della morte* and wrote to Boito: "We poor women
think we have found the words we need, but this infernal D'Annunzio
also knows them all. I would rather die in a corner than love such a
soul.... I hate D'Annunzio and yet I adore him."(34) Then came the
fateful meeting and the instant recognition of a harmony of vision:
"One dawn, I was alone after a sleepless night," wrote Duse. "Suddenly I saw him in front of me emerging from a gondola.... We spoke
of art ... of the poverty of art in the theatre of today... We said nothing
which bound either of us, but between us, tacitly, a *pact* was
signed."(35)

It was a pact both spiritual and physical. They met again in
Venice in February and September of 1895 and became lovers—most
of their biographers feel on September 26, 1895, a date marked in
D'Annunzio's notebook as "sacred to love and sorrow." At the same
time they dreamed together of the new spiritual drama which the poet
would write and the actress create. D'Annunzio's visit that summer to
the recently discovered site of ancient Mycenae suggested a subject.
Three days before the famous entry in his Venetian notebook, the poet
wrote to George Hérelle, his French translator who had accompanied
him to Greece, that he was planning a major drama with the title *La
città morta.* Soon after, Duse left for England and America with new
inspiration and the vision of returning in the spring to her new lover
and her long-sought new drama. When she returned, in June of 1896,
she found she had been betrayed by both lover and poet, a portent of
her stormy relationship with the erratic D'Annunzio. In her absence
he had actively pursued an affair with a younger artist (which despite
his best efforts remained platonic) and in perhaps deeper betrayal had
offered *La città morta,* still unfinished, to Sarah Bernhardt.

Duse discovered the unconsummated love affair first and
forgave D'Annunzio, but it was several months before she discovered
the artistic betrayal. She was still putting together a new company and
the poet led her for a time to believe that once this obstacle was past
the play would be hers. Finally in the fall, when her company was
assembled and the final version of the play complete, D'Annunizio
could dissemble no longer and informed her of what he had done.

Duse broke off all communication with him and departed from Italy with her company. Far from being disturbed, D'Annunzio utilized all this as inspiration for his autobiographical novel, *Il fuoco*, which he had begun the previous summer and which he planned to publish in the *Revue de Paris*.

Though she had appeared in many of the European capitals, Duse had never yet attempted Paris, the citadel of her great rival. In April of 1897 Schurmann announced a series of Duse performances in that city at Bernhardt's own theatre, the Renaissance. Rumors flew about this remarkable development. Some said that Sarah had offered her theatre as a gesture of professional generosity, others that the French actress was anticipating a disastrous showing which would silence her upstart challenger forever. Schurmann hinted that the whole matter was merely commercial and that he had paid Bernhardt a huge sum for the theatre expecting the publicity would allow him to recoup it. Whatever the truth, the choice of theatre reinforced the image of Duse as Bernhardt's rival and Duse's choice of plays made this even clearer. She would present *La locandiera* and *Cavalleria rusticana*, but also *Magda, La moglie di Claudio*, and *La signora dalle camelie*, Italian versions of the central works of Bernhardt's own repertoire.

A play by D'Annunzio would also be offered, thanks to the efforts of Count Primoli, who brought the estranged artists together at his villa in April to effect a reconciliation. Duse pleaded with D'Annunzio to give her *La città morta* for her Paris performances and when he still refused, insisted that she would not appear in Paris without one of his plays in her repertoire. Thus he promised and completed within a week the one-act *Sogno d'un mattino di primavera*, which was published in French translation this same spring in the *Revue de Paris*, along with a summary by Primoli of Duse's career and the background of this particular work.(36)

Duse opened in Paris at the beginning of June in *La signora dalle camelie*, with Bernhardt highly visible in one of the boxes. Duse's obvious nervousness qualified critical praise, but when she appeared in *Madga* the following week she had clearly grown in assurance and effectiveness. She now drew warm praise, though most critics were careful to note that the style of Bernhardt and Duse was so different that the two could not really be compared. Once more, as with Salvini and Ristori, French critics were most impressed by the realistic quality of Italian acting. Francisque Sarcey wrote in *Le Temps*: "Mme Duse, through her simplicity and sincerity, carries to its highest level the the illusion of reality.... She does not seem to *play* a role but to *live* it.

One forgets the actress to see only a woman who loves and suffers and it is not an actress that one sees dying, it is a woman."(37) How far this approach was from the contemporary French mode represented by Bernhardt may be seen from the observation on Bernhardt's acting made in Moscow by the young Anton Chekov: "Every sigh, all her tears, her convulsions in the death scenes, the whole of her acting is nothing more than a cleverly, faultlessly learned lesson. A lesson, readers, simply a lesson....! When she acts, she is not trying to be natural, but to be unusual. Her aim is to strike the audience, to astonish and to dazzle them...."(38)

The two actresses appeared on stage together on June 14, 1897, in an extraordinary program put together as a benefit for a monument to Dumas *fils,* who had died two years before. Bernhardt presented the final two acts of *La Dame aux camélias* and Duse the second act of *La moglie di Claudio.* The evening was a grand occasion for both though once again the realism of Duse was particularly praised, the critic of the *Gil Blas* reporting that she had "communicated the breath of life to something we thought had never lived."(39) The new D'Annunzio play was premiered two nights later and warmly applauded, though all the praise went to Duse. The script itself was dismissed as lyric rather than dramatic and as a pale imitation of Maeterlinck. Duse did not repeat the work, but returned to *La signora dalle camelie,* which she gave three more times with steadily increasing power and assurance. Andò, who had joined her for the opening performances and received poor notices from the French critics, returned to Italy and was replaced by Carlo Rosapina (1853-1921), who became Duse's favored leading man during the years that followed.

For her final performance Duse offered the complete *Moglie di Claudio* and *Cavalleria rusticana,* but she had by now so fascinated the Parisian theatre world that they insisted on another evening. Every one of her ten performances had been totally sold out and Sarcey in an open letter in *Le Temps* begged her to appear one final time at the large Porte-Saint-Martin theatre. Accordingly Duse gave there a matinee on July 3 of *Cavalleria rusticana,* the second act of *La moglie di Claudio* and the final act of *La signora dalle camelie* and returned to Italy with the cheers of the artistic and literary world of Paris ringing in her ears.

Back in Italy Duse, reconciled with D'Annunzio, took up again one of their first dreams, the establishment of an open-air festival theatre with a company headed by Duse presenting the poet's work. D'Annunzio, who at one point in *Il fuoco* portrayed himself as a Latinate Wagner, clearly saw this project as his Bayreuth. In interviews in the *Gazzetta di Venezia* and the Paris edition of the *New York Herald* D'Annunzio outlined his plans. The theatre would be built on the shores of the lake at Albano, near Rome. Three more plays, each based on a different season, would be created as companion pieces to *Sogno d'un mattino di primavera*. *La città morta* would, of course, be in the repertory, along with new adaptations by D'Annunzio of *Agamemnon* and *Antigone*. Count Primoli collected funds among the Roman aristocracy and the *Herald* proposed a joint stock venture to finance the project, but in vain. The Italian Bayreuth, announced for the opening of 1889, never materialized.

In the meantime, Duse premiered *Sogno* in Italy at the Rome Valle, along with Goldoni's *La locandiera*. The result was a bitter defeat for D'Annunzio, whose play was received in disappointing silence, while *La locandiera* generated shouts of Viva Duse and Viva Goldoni. He left soon after for Paris, relying upon Bernhardt to finally establish his reputation as a major dramatist with *La città morta*. Once again he was disappointed. Although Bernhardt was praised without qualification, the play was generally viewed as an interesting but ultimately unsuccessful experiment in the revival of classic tragedy. Some critics found the passions of Greek drama offensive in a modern setting and suggested that if one were to deal with incest one might at least employ verse. Others more legitimately noted that the play was almost completely lacking in drama, conflict, even a clear sense of character, and possessed only those qualities which D'Annunzio obviously possessed as a lyric poet—brilliant and original use of language and intense emotional expression. "As a play," the critic Faguet concluded, "it doesn't exist."(40)

Duse spent this spring and summer on tour in France and Portugal, then rejoined D'Annunzio in Italy. After his experience with Bernhardt, the poet was ready to commit his work exclusively to Duse and they signed a contract promising to her his entire dramatic output. The Albano project showing little signs of development, Duse arranged with Zacconi to establish a new company for which D'Annunzio would be resident dramatist. Poet and actress then departed for a tour to Greece and Egypt. From Corfù D'Annunzio sent back to Zacconi the script for his new play *La gioconda* to be distributed to the players and promised another play, *La gloria*, to follow. *La gioconda* was well received at the Teatro Bellini in Palermo in April of 1899 and during the next three months was taken to most major Italian cities by the Duse-Zacconi company. Poetry still dominated this drama and some objected to its ethical message, since the play, reflecting D'Annunzio's interest in Nietzsche, featured an artistic genius who seemed justified in sacrificing all others to his superhuman ideals. Still, *La gioconda* was unquestionably D'Annunzio's best realized theatrical work to date. *La gloria*, on the other hand, was so disastrously received in Naples soon after that no further performances were even attempted. D'Annunzio dedicated *La gioconda* to Duse and *La gloria* to "the dogs in Naples who booed it." In the fall, the Duse-Zacconi company disbanded. Zacconi returned to Ibsen and Tolstoi and Duse remained faithful to D'Annunzio, taking on a new leading man, Luigi Rasi (1852-1918), and departing for Vienna and Berlin with *La gioconda*.

The publication of D'Annunzio's clearly autobiographical *Il fuoco* in 1900, with its extremely intimate and often unflattering portrait of Duse, was thought by many to mark an end of the relationship of actress and poet but if these intimate revelations pained her Duse made no complaint. The most productive and successful years of D'Annunzio-Duse collaboration in fact lay just ahead. Duse realized her dream of touring Italy with *La città morta* in 1900-1901, though once again the audiences gave more praise to the actress than to the play. D'Annunzio's theatrical skill was nevertheless improving, as his new work, *Francesca da Rimini* (1902), demonstrated. It was a huge historical pageant (with settings costing 400,000 lire) in the tradition of Giacometti, but with the intense passion that was D'Annunzio's specialty and in rich, swiftly moving verse. None of D'Annunzio's previous plays had been so well received and for Duse this was proof that she could devote herself to his works alone. During 1902 and 1903 she toured Europe, then the United States, offering only *Francesca, La città morta*, and *Gioconda*, to the despair of her sponsors, for only *Francesca* proved even moderately attractive.

For her faithfulness, Duse was once again betrayed by D'Annunzio in the production of his only unqualified theatre success, *La figlia di Iorio* (1904). This was a pastoral lyric tragedy, a kind of *Cavalleria rusticana* on a far more ambitious scale. The central character was presumably created for Duse, but D'Annunzio became concerned that the delicate, somewhat ethereal actress would not be effective as the more substantial and earthy country prostitute of his tragedy. He therefore gave the role, which Duse had already prepared, to Irma Gramatica (1873-1956), a young actress already well known for her realistic interpretations of Giacosa, Bracco and Verga, on the pretext that Duse's health would not allow her to do the role. The premiere at Milan's Teatro Lirico was one of the great successes of the period and a revival soon after by Lugné-Poë at the Théâtre de l'Oeuvre in Paris was another triumph. D'Annunzio had apparently at last discovered how to develop his poetic gifts in theatrically effective terms.

He had betrayed Duse for the last time, however. She sent him a bitter note of farewell, saying that henceforth she would be as if dead to him. D'Annunzio, predictably, seemed unconcerned, but apparently he needed Duse more than he realized. Nothing that he created afterward for the theatre would rival the works he had written during the stormy artistic and personal relationship with Duse. The actress, with her health rapidly fading but her reputation, especially after she turned to dramatists other than D'Annunzio, steadily growing, continued to tour. She found in the works of Ibsen — *A Doll's House, Rosmersholm, Hedda Gabler, The Lady from the Sea* — the triumphs she had hoped in vain to achieve for D'Annunzio. She was forced to retire from the stage in 1909, but she remained, despite her letter, faithful to her faithless lover to the end. Whatever her success and fame in other works, there was always at least one play by D'Annunzio in her repertoire.

Notes to Chapter VI

1. Benedetto Croce, *La letteratura italiana* (Bari, 1957), III, 345.
2. Amedée Roux, *La Littérature contemporaine en Italie 1883-1896* (Paris, 1896), p. 192.
3. Giuseppe Costetti, *Il teatro italiano nel 1800* (Rocca San Casciano, 1901), p. 341.
4. Croce, *Letteratura,* III, 354.
5. Pietro Ferrigni, *La morte di una musa* (Florence, 1885), p. lxv.
6. Quoted in Lander MacClintock, *The Contemporary Drama of Italy* (Boston, 1920), p. 24.
7. Quoted in MacClintock, *Contemporary Drama,* p. 41.
8. Ferrigni, *Morte,* pp. l-lii, lxvii-lxix.
9. Jean Dornis, *Le Théâtre italien contemporain* (Paris, 1903), p. 59.
10. E. Ferdinando Palmiero, *Il teatro veneto* (Milan, 1948), p. 17.
11. Quoted in Guido Mazzoni, *L'ottocento* (Milan, 1934), p. 1014.
12. Quoted in MacClintock, *Contemporary Drama,* pp. 206-7.
13. F. Gabrielli, *Vent'anni di giornalismo,* quoted in Severino Pagani, *Il teatro milanese* (Milan, 1944), p. 121.
14. Eduardo Scarpetta, *Don Felice* (Naples, 1883), pp. 125-26.
15. Eduardo Scarpetta, *Dal San Carlino al Fiorentini* (Naples, 1899), p. 332.
16. No. 10-12, May 18, 1903.
17. Ferrigni, *Morte,* pp. l-li.
18. C.A. Sainte-Beuve, *Les Grands Ecrivans français: le XIX siècle* (Paris, 1930), I, 13.
19. *La letteratura italiana nel secolo XIX* (Bari, 1953), II, 323.
20. Luigi Capuana, *Spiritismo?* (Catania, 1884), p. 130.
21. Olga Signorelli, *Eleanora Duse* (Rome, 1938), p. 46.

22. Ciavarella, Aurelio, *Verga-De Roberto-Capuana* (Catania, 1955), p. 198.
23. According to the *Enciclopedia della Spettacolo*, VII, 226, though I have been unable to find this enthusiastic endorsement elsewhere. Edoardo Pompei, in *Pietro Mascagni nella vita e nell'arte* (Rome, 1912), reports nothing from Verdi on this subject more enthusiastic than "He is a young man who will go far. *Cavalleria* has all the elements of a success." (p. 433).
24. Alfredo Barbina, *Capuana inedito* (Bergamo, 1974), p. 183.
25. H.A. Taine, *History of English Literature* (trans. H. Van Laun, New York, 1879), p. 6.
26. To Jarro, critic of the *Nazione* in Florence, quoted in Giorgio Pullini, *Marco Praga* (Rocca S. Casciano, 1960), pp. 41-42.
27. Achille Tedeschi, *Illustrazione Italiana*, January 13, 1895, p. 27.
28. Quoted in MacClintock, *Contemporary Drama*, p. 135.
29. February 25, 1894, p. 119.
30. Vol. CCIV, quoted in Dornis, *Théâtre*, pp. 206-7.
31. Piero Nardi, *Vita e tempo di Giuseppe Giacosa* (Verona, 1949), p. 821.
32. See "Duse and Bernhardt" in Bernard Shaw, *Dramatic Opinions and Essays* (New York, 1916), I, 134-42.
33. Piero Nardi, *Vita di Arrigo Boito* (Verona, 1944), p. 603.
34. Nardi, *Boito*, p. 606.
35. Guglielmo Gatti, *Vita di Gabriele D'Annunzio* (Florence, 1956), p. 148.
36. *Revue de Paris*, III (May-June, 1897), 453-532.
37. No. 13150, June 3, 1897.
38. From the article *Opyat' o Sare Bernar*, quoted in Harvey Pitcher, *The Chekov Play* (New York, 1973), p. 18.
39. June 16, 1897.
40. Emile Faguet, *Journal des Débats,* January 24, 1898.

Conclusion

At the end of the nineteenth century the greatest concern in the Italian theatre was the establishment of a permanent company or companies to give focus and stability to the Italian stage. Between 1898 and 1918 a whole series of such theatres, primarily inspired by the independent theatres or art theatres of other countries, were launched in Milan, Rome and Turin, without achieving their goal. The coming of Fascism finally brought significant national support to the theatre, but with it a rigid control that made the theatre simply a tool for propaganda. Not until 1947 and the founding of the Piccolo Teatro of Milan did Italy at last regain the sort of permanent company it had possessed a century before with such troupes as the Reale Sarda.

Despite the idealist and symbolist reaction in drama at the end of the century, realism remained in Italy as elsewhere in Europe the dominant mode, the new classicism against which the more radical new romanticisms of the twentieth century would revolt. Despite the great impact of D'Annunzio, poetic drama did not become a dominant mode in the Italian theatre after 1900, though it achieved, in such authors as Benelli, a greater popularity and success than it did in the same period in England, France or Germany, where similar poetic revivals were attempted.

The reactions against realism in Italy as elsewhere were often as much philosophic as artistic. The realism of the late nineteenth century was based on the philosophy of scientific positivism and as the authority of that system became eroded, the literature of fact and objective presentation based upon it suffered accordingly. New dramatists sought to portray a world in which values, even individual personalities, were in constant flux and to which the application of reason and intellectuality was at best futile and perhaps actually counterproductive. D'Annunzio's dramas, as celebrations of hedonism and the primacy of the senses, may be seen as early manifestations of the abandonment of the intellect. The drama of futurism, appearing early in the new century, was another reaction, celebrating noise, speed and sensory impulse. A third was the theatre of the grotesque, which focussed on the illogical and capricious in the human condition. These various anti-realist reactions culminated in the major works of the greatest Italian dramatist of the new century, Luigi Pirandello.

With the international success and influence of Pirandello, the Italian theatre, having demonstrated during the nineteenth century its ability to produce operatic composers and singers, actors and stage designers worthy of being ranked among the best in Europe, was now able to claim that distinction in playwriting as well. The power and the assurance of the Italian stage grew with the triumphs of Pirandello and his successors and the establishment at last of a series of state-supported theatres in the major cities. Later in the twentieth century, as the director achieved ever greater prominence, Italian theatre again could be counted among the leaders in Europe, thanks to such artists as Strehler, Squarzina, Visconti and Zeffirelli. From being the artistic stepchild of France at the beginning of the nineteenth century, Italian theatre came to more than fulfill the visions of the eighteenth-century reformers and in modern times has reasserted its position as one of the great theatre nations of Europe.

Bibliography

General

Acton, H. *The Bourbons of Naples*, London, 1956.

Adami, G. *Cento anni di scenografia alla Scala*, Milan, 1945.

Alberti, A. *Quarant'anni d'istoria del Teatro dei Fiorentini in Napoli*, 2 vol., Naples, 1878-1880.

Allevi, G. *Teatro milanese*, Milan, 1931.

Andrei, V. *Gli attori italiani da Gustavo Modena a Ermete Novelli*, Florence, 1899.

Antona Traversi, C. *Le grandi attrici del tempo andato*, Turin, 1929.

Apollonio, M. *Storia del teatro italiano*, 4 vol., Florence, 1950.

Arrigoni, R. *Notizie e osservazioni intorno all'origine e al progresso dei teatri e delle rappresentazione teatrali in Venezia*, Venice, 1840.

Berengo, M. *La società veneta*, Florence, 1956.

Bernini, F. *Storia di Parma*, Parma, 1954.

Bertana, E. *La tragedia*, Milan, 1905.

Bonaventura, A. *Saggio storico sul Teatro musicale italiano*, Leghorn, 1913.

Bottura, C. *Storia aneddotica e documentata del Teatro Comunale di Trieste*, Trieste, 1885.

Bragaglia, A. *Storia del teatro popolare romano*, Rome, 1958.

Bragaglia, L. *Shakespeare in Italia,* Rome, 1973.

Brocca, G. *Il Teatro Carlo Fenice*, Geneva, 1898.

Brockway, W. and H. Weinstock. *The World of Opera*, New York, 1962.

Brunelli, B. *I teatri di Padova,* Padua, 1921.

Bustico, G. *Il teatro musicale italiano*, Rome, 1924.

Caffi, F. *I teatri di venezia*, Venice, 1868.

Calzoni, A. *Per la storia di alcuni minori teatri milanesi*, Milan, 1932.

Cambiasi, P. *La Scala 1778-1906*, Milan, 1906.

Cametti, A. *Il Teatro di Tordinona poi di Apollo*, Tivoli, 1938.

Carrieri, R. *La danza in Italia*, Milan, 1946.

Cauda, G. *Chiaroscuri di palcoscenico,* Savigliano, 1910.

_____. *Lo spirito meneghino altraverso i tempi*, Milan, 1950.

Ciampi, I. *La commedia italiana*, Rome, 1880.

Cibrario, L. *Storia di Torino*, Turin, 1846.

Collison-Morley, L. *Shakespeare in Italy*, Stratford, 1916.

Corradi-Cervi, M. *Cronologia del Teatro Regio di Parma*, Parma, 1955.

Costetti, G. *I dimenticati vivi della scena italiana*, Rome, 1886.

203

_____. *Il teatro italiano nel 1800*, Rocca San Casciano, 1901.

Cristini, C. *Cento anni di vita del Teatro San Carlo*, Naples, 1948.

Croce, B. *L'ottocento*, Bari, 1957.

_____. *I teatri di Napoli dal rinacimento alla fine del secolo decimottavo*, Bari, 1926.

Curiel, C. *Il Teatro San Pietro di Trieste*, Milan, 1937.

Cusani, F. *Storia di Milano dall'origine ai nostri giorni*, Milan, 1861-1884.

Dalla Brida, E. *Il costume storico nel teatro*, Milan, 1954.

Damerini, G. *Scenografi veneziani dell'ottocento*, Venice, 1962.

D'Amico, S. *Epoche del teatro italiano*, Florence, 1954.

_____. *Storia del teatro drammatico*, 4 vol., Milan, 1958.

_____. *Tramonto del grande attore*, Milan, 1929.

D'Auria, V. *Il Teatro del Fondo*, Naples, 1894.

De Angelis, A. *La musica a Roma nel secolo XIX*, Rome, 1935.

_____. *Scenografi italiani di ieri e di oggi*, Rome, 1938.

De Felice, F. *Storia del teatro siciliano*, Catania, 1956.

De Filippis, R., and R. Arnese. *Cronache del Teatro di San Carlo*, 2 vol., Naples, 1963.

_____. *Napoli teatrale dal Teatro Romano al San Carlo*, Milan, 1962.

Della Corte, A. *L'interpretazione musicale e gli interpreti*, Turin, 1951.

De Sanctis, F. *Storia della letteratura italiana*, 2 vol., Turin, 1962.

Devoto, G. *Il linguaggio d'Italia*, Milan, 1974.

Di Giacomo, S. *Storia del Teatro San Carlino*, Milan, 1935.

Di Stefano, C. *La censure teatrale in Italia*, Rocca San Casciano, 1964.

Doglio, F. *Il teatro pubblico in Italia*, Rome, 1969.

Donadoni, E. *A History of Italian Literature* (trans. R. Monges), New York, 1969.

Dovretti, G. *Storia del teatro piemontese*, Turin, 1956.

Enciclopedia dello Spettacolo, 9 vol., Rome, 1954-1968.

Ferrari, G. *La scenografia*, Milan, 1902.

Ferrari, P. *Spettacoli drammatico-musicali e coreografici in Parma dall'anno 1628 all'anno 1883*, Parma, 1884.

Ferrarini, P. *Parma teatrale ottocentesca*, Parma, 1946.

Ferrero, F. *Livorno e i grandi letterati da Petrarca a D'Annunzio*, Leghorn, 1948.

Ferigni, P. *La morte di una musa*, Florence, 1902.

Fleres, U. *Teatri di Roma nell'ottocento*, Rome, 1931.

Gallina, G. *Dal Goldoni al Gallina*, Cividale, 1904.

Galvani, V. *La Fenice gran teatro di Venezia*, Milan, 1876.

Gandini, A. *Cronistoria dei teatri di Modena dal 1539 al 1871*, Modena, 1873.

Garnett, R. *History of Italian Literature*, London, 1898.

Gatti, C. *Il Teatro alla Scala*, Milan, 1964

Gatti, H. *Shakespeare nei teatri milanesi dell'ottocento*, Bari, 1968.

Ghilardi, F. *Storia del teatro*, Milan, 1961.

Grabinski-Broglio, A. *I teatri d'Italia*, Milan, 1907.

Gutierrez, B. *Il teatro Carcano*, Milan, 1914.

Hall, R. *A Short History of Italian Literature*, Ithaca, 1951.

Labande-Jeanroy, T. *La Question de la langue en Italie de Baretti à Manzoni*, Paris, 1925.

Lianovosani, L. *Saggio di drammaturgia veneziana*, Venice, 1879.

Lonzo, G., *et al. La Fenice*, Milan, 1972.

Mangini, N. *I teatri di Venezia*, Milan, 1974.

Manzella, D. and E. Pozzi. *I teatri di Milano*, Milan, 1971.

Marangoni, G. and C. Vanbianchi. *La Scala*, Bergamo, 1922.

Mariani, V. *Storia della scenografia italiana*, Florence, 1930.

Masi, E. *Sulla storia del teatro italiano nel secola XVIII*, Florence, 1891.

Mazzoni, G. *L'ottocento*, 2 vol., Milan, 1953.

Mezzanote, P., *et al. Cronache di un grande teatro: il Teatro Manzoni di Milano*, Milan, 1952.

Miragoli, L. *Il melodramma italiana nell'ottocento*, Rome, 1924.

Molmenti, P. *Storia di Venezia nella vita privata dalle origini alla caduta della Repubblica*, Bergamo, 1929.

Molussi, L. *Diario del Teatro Ducale di Parma*, Parma, 1841.

Monaldi, G. *Cantanti Celebri*, Rome, 1928.

_____. *La regine della danza*, Turin, 1910.

_____. *I teatri di Roma negli ultimi tre secoli*, Naples, 1928.

Monteverdi, M. *Italian Stage Designs*, London, 1968.

Mori, F. *Il Reale Teatro di San Carlo*, Naples, 1835.

Morini, V. *La Reale Accademia degli Immobili e il suo teatro La Pergola*, Pisa, 1926.

Mugnier, F. *Le Théâtre en Savoie*, Paris, 1887.

Mussi, V. *Notizie e ricerche storica sul Reale Teatro Alfieri di Firenze*, Florence, 1896.

Nivellini, V. *Il Teatro del Filodrammatici*, Milan, 1948

Nulli, S. *Shakespeare in Italia*, Milan, 1918.

Pagani, S. *Il teatro milanese*, Milan, 1944.

Palmeriero, E. *Il teatro veneto*, Milan, 1948.

Pandolfi, V. *Antologia del grande attore*, Bari, 1954.

_____. *Storia del teatro*, Turin, 1964.

Papini, G. *Il Teatro Carignano dal 1608 ai giorni nostri*, Turin, 1935.

Piccini, G. *Il teatro della Pergola*, Florence, 1912.

Rasi, L. *I comici italiani*, 3 vol., Florence, 1897-1905.

Repaci, L. *Teatro di ogni tempo*, Milan, 1967.

Ricci, C. *La scenografia italiana*, Milan, 1930.

Righetti, F. *Teatro italiano*, Turin, 1828.

Rolandi, V. *A proposito del bicentenario del Teatro Valle*, Rome, 1927.

Roux, A. *Histoire de la littérature contemporaine en Italie*, 4 vol., Paris, 1870-1896.

Russo, L. *Gli scrittori d'Italia*, 2 vol., Florence, 1951.

Sacerdote, G. *Il Teatro Regio di Torino*, Turin, 1892.

Salvioli, G. *Teatri di Venezia*, Venice, 1878.

Sanesi, I. *La commedia*, Vol. II, Milan, 1925.

Sanguinetti, L. *Storia del Teatro Re*, Milan, 1967.

_____. *Il teatro dialettale milanese dal XVII al XX secolo*, Milan, 1967.

Schlitzer, F. *Mondo teatrale dell'ottocento*, Naples, 1954.

Simoni, R., *et al. Il Teatro Manzoni di Milano*, Milan, 1952.

Sismonde de Sismondi, J. *Historical View of the Literature of the South of Europe* (trans. T. Roscoe), London, 1846.

Strunk, O. *Source Readings in Music History*, New York, 1950.
Tardini, V. *I teatri di Modena*, Modena, 1900.
Tegani, U. *La Scala nella sua storica e nella sua grandezze*, Florence, 1946.
Toldo, P. *L'Oeuvre de Molière et sa fortune en Italie*, Turin, 1910.
Tonelli, L. *L'evoluzione del teatro contemporaneo in Italia*, Palermo, 1913.
_____. *Storia del teatro italiano*, Milan, 1924.
_____. *Il teatro italiano dalle origini ai giorni nostri*, Milan, 1924.
Toschi, P. *Storia del teatro italiano*, Turin, 1956.
Valeri, D. *Il teatro comico veneziano*, Venice, 1949.
Vallebona, G. *Il Teatro Carlo Felice*, Geneva, 1928.
Vergani, O., and F. Rosti. *Teatro milanese*, Parma, 1958.
Viale, M. *Tempi e aspetti della scenografia*, Turin, 1954.
Vianello, C. *Teatro, spettacoli, musiche a Milano nei secoli scorsi*, Milan, 1941.
Viviani, V. *Storia del teatro napoletano*, Naples, 1969.
Wilkins, E. *A History of Italian Literature*, Cambridge, 1954.
Zambaldi, S. *Il teatro milanese*, Milan, 1927.

Eighteenth Century

Ademollo, A. *Una famiglia di comici italiani nel secolo decimottavo*, Florence, 1885.
Alfieri, V. *Lettere edite e inedite*, Turin, 1890.
_____. *Memories* (trans. anon.), London, 1961.
_____. *The Prince and Letters* (trans. B. Corrigan and J. Molinaro), Toronto, 1972.
Andrieux, M. *Daily Life in Papal Rome in the Eighteenth Century* (trans. M. Fitton), New York, 1968.
_____. *Daily Life in Venice in the Time of Casanova* (trans. M. Fitton), New York, 1972.
Apollonio, M. *Alfieri*, Milan, 1930.
_____. *Metastasio*, Milan, 1930.
Arullani, V. *L'opera di Vittorio Alfieri e la sua importanza laica nazionale e civile*, Turin, 1907.
Astaldi, M. *Baretti*, Milan, 1977.
Bacchelli, R., and R. Longhi. *Teatro e immagini del settecento italiano*, Turin, 1953.
Baretti, G. *An Account of the Manners and Customs of Italy*, London, 1768.
Bartoli, F. *Comici italiani*, Padua, 1782.
Bencini, M. *Il vero Giovan Battista Fagiuoli e il teatro in Toscana a' suoi tempi*, Turin, 1884.
Berengo, M. *La società veneta alla fine del settecento*, Florence, 1956.
Bertana, E. *Il teatro tragico italiano del secolo XVIII prima dell'Alfieri*, Turin, 1901.
_____. *Vittorio Alfieri studiato nella vita, nel pensiero e nell'arte*, Turin, 1904.
Borghesani, E. *Carlo Gozzi e l'opera sua*, Udine, 1904.
Bouvier, R., and A. Laffargue. *La Vie napolitaine au XVIIIe siècle*, Paris, 1956.
Branca, V., and N. Mangini. *Studi Goldoniani*, 2 vol., Venice, 1960.
Burney, C. *Metastasio*, London, 1796.
Caprini, G. *Carlo Goldoni, la sua vita, le sue opere*, Milan, 1907.

Cerlone, F. *Commedie,* Naples, 1778.

Cestaro, B. *Carlo Gozzi,* Turin, 1932.

Chatfield-Taylor, H. *Goldoni: A Biography,* New York, 1913.

Chiari, P. *Commedie da camera,* Venice, 1771.

Cochrane, E. *Florence in the Forgotten Centuries,* Chicago, 1973.

Colagrosso, F. *Saverio Bettinelli e il teatro gesuitico,* Naples, 1898.

Collison-Morley, L. *Guiseppe Baretti,* London, 1909.

Copping, E. *Alfieri and Goldoni: Their Lives and Adventures,* London, 1862.

Courville, Xavier de. *Un Apôtre de l'art du théâtre au XVIIIe siècle,* Vol. I, Paris, 1943.

Crinò, A. *Le traduzioni di Shakespeare in Italia nel settecento,* Rome, 1950.

Croce, B. *La letteratura italiana del settecento,* Bari, 1949.

De Brosses, C. *Lettres écrites d'Italie à quelques amis en 1739 et 1740,* Paris, 1836.

Della Corte, A. *L'opera comica italiana nel '700,* Bari, 1923.

Fehr, M. *Apostolo Zeno und seine Reform des Operntextes,* Zurich, 1912.

Ferrante, L. *Goldoni,* Milan, 1971.

Freeman, R. *Opera without Drama,* unpub. thesis, Princeton, 1967.

Galanti, F. *Carlo Goldoni e Venezia nel secolo XVIII,* Padua, 1882.

Galbiati, G. *Il teatro della Scala degli inizi al 1794,* Milan, 1929.

Galletti, A. *Le teorie drammatiche e la tragedia in Italia nel secolo XVIII,* Cremona, 1901.

Gentile, A. *Carlo Goldoni e gli attori,* Trieste, 1951.

Giordano, G. *Alfonso Varano e le sue opere,* Naples, 1889.

Goethe, J. *Travels In Italy* (trans. C. Nesbit), London, 1883.

Goldoni, C. *Mémoires,* Paris, 1822.

Gozzi, C. *Memoires* (trans. J.A. Symonds), 2 vol., New York, 1939.

Guerzoni, G. *Il teatro italiano nel secolo XVIII,* Milan, 1876.

Holme, T. *A Servant of Many Masters,* London, 1976.

Jonard, N. *Giuseppe Baretti: L'Homme et l'oeuvre,* Clermont-Ferrand, 1963.

_____. *La vita a Venezia nel XVIII secolo,* Milan, 1967.

Kennard, J. *Goldoni and the Venice of His Time,* New York, 1920.

Lalande, J. *Voyage d'un Français en Italie,* Paris, 1769.

Lee, V. *Studies of the Eighteenth Century in Italy,* London, 1880.

Logan, O. *Culture and Society in Venice 1470-1790,* New York, 1972.

Longworth, P. *The Rise and Fall of Venice,* London, 1974.

Lucchesi, D. *Kulturgeschichtliche Betrachtung von Pietro Chiaris commedie,* Munich, 1938.

Magrini, G. *I tempi, la vita e gli scritti di Carlo Gozzi,* Benevento, 1883.

Malamani, V. *Il settecento a Venezia,* 2 vol., Turin, 1891-1892.

Masi, E. *Studi sulla storia del teatro italiano nel secolo XVIII,* Florence, 1891.

Megaro, G. *Vittorio Alfieri,* New York, 1930.

Monnier, P. *Venice in the Eighteenth Century* (trans. anon.), London, 1910.

Montanelli, I., and R. Gervaso. *L'Italia del settecento,* Milan, 1970.

Napoli-Signorelli, P. *Storia critica dei teatri,* Naples, 1813.

Natali, G. *La vita e le opere di Pietro Metastasio,* Leghorn, 1923.

Ortolani, G. *Della vita e dell'arte di Carlo Goldoni,* Venice, 1907.

_____, et al. *La riforma del teatro nel settecento e altri scritti,* Venice, 1962.

Pagani-Cesa, G. *Sovra il teatro tragico italiano,* Florence, 1825.

Porena, M. *Vittorio Alfieri e la tragedia,* Milan, 1904.

Portinari, F. *Di Vittorio Alfieri e della tragedia*, Turin, 1976.
Prota-Giurleo, U. *Paisiello e i suoi primi trionfi a Napoli*, Naples, 1925.
Rabany, C. *Carlo Goldoni*, Paris, 1896.
Radicotti, G. *Giovanni Battista Pergolesi, vita, opere e influenza sull'arte*, Rome, 1910.
Rho, E. *La missione teatrale di Carlo Goldoni*, Bari, 1936.
Riccoboni, L. *Histoire du Théâtre Italien*, Paris, 1731.
Richard, Abbé. *Description historique et critique de l'Italie*, Paris, 1769.
Schiedermair, L. *Simon Mayr*, Leipzig, 1907-1910.
Scrivano, R. *La natura teatrale dell'inspirazione Alfieriana*, Milan, 1963.
Serao, M. *La vita italiana nel settecento*, Milan, 1896.
Sharp, S. *Letters from Italy in the Years 1765 and 1766*, London, n.d.
Sommi-Picenardi, G. *Un rivale del Goldoni*, Milan, 1902.
Vaussard, M. *Daily Life in Eighteenth-Century Italy*, London, 1962.
Zardo, A. *Teatro veneziano del '700*, Bologna, 1925.
——————. *Un tragico padovano del secolo scorso*, Padua, 1884.

Early Nineteenth Century

Allason, B. *La vita di Silvio Pellico*, Milan, 1933.
Allocco-Castellino, O. *Alberto Nota*, Turin, 1912.
Arcari, P. *Gian Battista Niccolini e la sua opera drammatica*, Milan, 1901.
Ashbrook, W. *Donizetti*, London, 1965.
Avitabile, G. *The Controversy on Romanticism in Italy*, New York, 1959.
Baldini, M. *Il teatro di Gian Battista Niccolini*, Florence, 1907.
Baretta, P. *Camillo Federici e il suo teatro*, Vicenza, 1903.
Barr, S. *Mazzini, Portrait of an Exile*, New York, 1935.
Bazzi, G. *Primi erudimenti dell'arte drammatico*, Turin, 1845.
Bertolotti, A. *Giuseppe Moncalvo*, Milan, 1889.
Binni, W. *Preromanticismo italiano*, Bari, 1974.
Bonazzi, L. *Gustavo Modena e l'arte sua*, Città di Castello, 1884.
Bonfio, G. *Cenni Biografici di Antonio Sografi*, Padua, 1854.
Borgese, G. *Storia della critica romantica in Italia*, Milan, 1920.
Borgomaneri, T. *Il romanticismo nel teatro di Gian Battista Niccolini*, Milan, 1926.
Branca, E. *Felice Romani e i più reputati maestri di musica del suo tempo*, Turin, 1882.
Branca, V. (ed.). *Il Conciliatore, figlio scientifico letterario*, Florence, 1953-1954.
Brazzi, A. *Il teatro giacobino ed antigiacobino in Italia*, Milan, 1887.
Buckingham and Chandos, Duke of. *Private Diary*, 3 vol., London, 1862.
Calvi, C. *Notizie biografia di Carolina Internari*, Florence, 1859.
Cantù, C. *Il "Conciliatore" e i Carbonari*, Milan, 1878.
Chiappori, G. *Il teatro milanese nei secolo XVIII-XIX*, 4 vol., Milan, 1818-1825.
Chiomenti, V. *Vincenzo Monti nel dramma dei suoi tempi*, Milan, 1968.
Ciampi, I. *Vita di Francesco Augusto Bon*, Trieste, 1866.
Cimino, M. *Il teatro di Silvio Pellico*, Naples, 1925.
Citanna, G. *Il romanticismo e la poesia italiana dal Parini al Carducci*, Bari, 1935.
Colet, L. *L'Italie des Italiens*, Paris, 1862-1863.
Colquhoun, A. *Manzoni and His Times*, London, 1954.

Corona, M. *La fortuna di Shakespeare a Milano, 1800-1825*, Bari, 1970.

Cosentino, G. *Modena, Lombardi, e Vestri a Bologna*, Bologna, 1900.

Costetti, G. *La Compagnia Reale Sarda e il teatro italiano dal 1821 al 1855*, Milan, 1893.

Cotta, A. *Camillo Federici e il suo teatro*, Assisi, 1906.

Croce, B. *Alessandro Manzoni*, Bari, 1930.

Cutore, M. *La fortuna dell'Alfieri dai tempi del poeta fino alla prima guerra del risorgimento*, Catania, 1921.

Deabate, G. *I comici di Sua Maestà*, Turin, 1905.

De Angelis, A. *Il Teatro Alibert o delle Dame*, Tivoli, 1951.

Dejob, C. *Mme de Staël et l'Italie*, Paris, 1890.

De Simone, J. *Alessendro Manzoni: Aesthetics and Literary Criticism*, New York, 1946.

De Staël, Mme. *Corinne ou l'Italie*, Paris, 1833.

Doglio, F. *Teatro e risorgimento*, Rocca San Casciano, 1960.

Ferrari, M. *La preparazione intellettuale del Risorgimento italiano*, Milan, 1923.

Flori, E. *Il teatro di Ugo Foscolo*, Biella, 1907.

Florimo, F. *Bellini: memorie e lettere*, Florence, 1882.

Fulchignoni, P. *Il dramma romantico*, Salerno, 1907.

Galletti, A. *Alessandro Manzoni, il pensatore e il poeta*, 2 vol., Milan, 1927.

Ghislanzoni, G. *Gli artisti da teatro*, Milan, 1845.

Giuria, P. *Silvio Pellico e il suo tempo*, Voghera, 1854.

Griffith, G. *Mazzini, Prophet of Modern Europe*, London, 1932.

Grimaldi-Grosso, G. *Pietro Giacometti nella vita e nella opera*, Genoa, 1916.

Hogarth, G. *Memoirs of the Opera in Italy, France, Germany, and England*, 2 vol., London, 1851.

Ivanov, F. *Uno scenografo romantico veneziano, Francesco Bagnara*, Venice, 1940.

Jemolo, A. *Il dramma di Manzoni*, Florence, 1973.

Levi, P. *Un attore, un fattore*, Rome, 1897.

Lippmann, F. *Vincenzo Bellini und die italienische Opera Seria seiner Zeit*, Cologne, 1969.

Mancini, L. *Le tragedie di Silvio Pellico avanti la prigionia*, Sinigaglia, 1898.

Manzi, A. *Gustavo Modena, il governo e la Compagnia Reale Sarda*, Genoa, 1936.

Manzoni, A. *Lettere*, Verona, 1970.

_____. *Opere*, Verona, 1970.

Marcazzan, M. *Foscolo, Manzoni, Goethe*, Brescia, 1948.

Marigo, A. *Il romanticismo di Silvio Pellico e la "Francesca da Rimini,"* Como, 1905.

Mario, T. *Della vita di Giuseppe Mazzini*, Milan, 1886.

Martini, F. *Del teatro drammatico in Italia*, Florence, 1862.

Masi, E. *Il risorgimento italiano*, Florence, 1917.

Massé, D. *Un cattolico integrale del risorgimento*, Rome, 1959.

Mazzini, G. *Scritti*, Imola, 1938.

Meldolesi, C. *Profilo di Gustavo Modena*, Rome, 1972.

Momigliano, A. *Alessandro Manzoni*, Messina, 1948.

Monaco, V. *La repubblica del teatro*, Florence, 1968.

Moncalvo, G. *Autobiografia del vecchio artista Moncalvo*, Milan, 1858.

Montanari, B. *Della vita e delle opere d'Ippolito Pindemonte*, Venice, 1834.

Monti, V. *Epistolario*, 6 vol., Florence, 1928-1931.

Mussi, U. *Teatri fiorentini*, Florence, n.d.

Muzzi, S. *Notizie intorno alla vita di Luigi Vestri*, Bologna, 1841.

Niccolini, A. *Cenno sul corse di studii della Reale Scuola di Scenografia,* Naples, 1832.

Notarnicola, B. *Saverio Mercadante*, Rome, 1949.

Orlandi, E. *Il teatro di Carlo Marenco*, Florence, 1900.

Orrey, L. *Bellini*, London, 1969.

Pacini, G. *Le mie memorie artistiche*, Florence, 1865.

Pagani, G. *Del teatro in Milano, avanti il 1858*, Milan, 1884.

_____. *Notizie storiche sulla località della Cannobiana*, Milan, 1892.

Paglicci-Brozzi, A. *Sul teatro giacobino ed antigiacobino in Italia 1796-1805*, Milan, 1887.

Paschetto, G. *Felice Romani*, Turin, 1907.

Pastura, F. *Vincenzo Bellini*, Turin, 1959.

Petracchi, A. *Sul reggimento dei publici teatri,* Milan, 1821.

Piozzi, H. *Glimpses of Italian Society*, London, 1892.

Pompeati, A. *Vincenzo Monti*, Bologna, 1928.

Radiciotti, G. *Gioacchino Rossini, vita documentata e influenza sull'arte*, 3 vol., Tivoli, 1927-1929.

Ravello, F. *Silvio Pellico*, Turin, 1954.

Razeto, A. *Silvio Pellico e i suoi tempi*, Geneva, 1904.

Rebora, R., and G. Cattanei. *Teatro e risorgimento*, Geneva, 1956.

Reforgiato, V. *Shakespeare e Manzoni*, Catania, 1898.

Regli, F. *Dizionario biografico dei più celebri poeti ed artisti melodrammatici, tragici e comica che fiorirono in Italia dal 1800 al 1860*, Turin, 1860.

Resarco, F. *Pietro Giacometti e il suo teatro*, Genoa, 1882.

Rinieri, I. *Della vita e delle opere di Silvio Pellico*, 3 vol., Turin, 1898.

Ritorni, C. *Commentarii della vita e delle opere coredrammatiche di Salvatore Viganò*, Milan, 1838.

Rognoni, L. *Gioacchino Rossini*, Milan, 1955.

Royer, A. *Histoire du théâtre contemporain en France et à l'étranger depuis 1800 jusqu'à 1875*, Paris, 1878.

Rudman, H. *Italian Nationalism and English Letters*, London, 1940.

Sanguinetti, L. *La Compagnia Reale Sarda*, Rocca San Casciano, 1963.

Sansone, M. *L'opera poetica di Alessandro Manzoni*, Milan, 1947.

Scalera, A. *Il Teatro dei Fiorontini dal 1800 al 1860*, Naples, 1909.

Scopel, S. *Sulla fortuna della tragedie foscoliane*, Valdobbiadene, 1905.

Scotti, C. *Simone Mayr*, Bergamo, 1903.

Solimene, G. *Verdi non ha vinto Mercadante*, Rome, 1955.

Stendhal. *Life of Rossini* (trans. R. Coe), New York, 1970.

_____. *The Private Diaries* (trans. and ed. R. Sage), New York, 1954.

_____. *Rome, Naples, and Florence* (trans. R. Coe), London, 1959.

Taddei, E. *Del Real Teatro di San Carlo*, Naples, 1817.

Tonelli, L. *Manzoni*, Milan, 1928.

Toye, F. *Rossini: A Study in Tragicomedy*, London, 1934.

Trevisani, C. *Delle condizioni della letterature drammatica italiana nell'ultimo ventennio*, Florence, 1867.

Ulloa, P. *Pensées et souvenirs sur la littérature contemporaine du royaume de Naples*, Geneva, 1860.

Valery, M. *Voyages historiques et littéraires en Italie*, Brussels, 1835.
Vannucci, A. *Ricordi della vita e delle opere di Gian Battista Niccolini*, Florence, 1886.
Vassalli, D. *Vincenzo Monti nel dramma dei suoi tempi*, Milan, 1968.
Verri, P. *Storia di Milano*, Milan, 1834.
Viganò, L. *Il teatro italiano*, Milan, 1857.
Viglione, F. *Sul teatro di Ugo Foscolo*, Pisa, 1904.
Visconti, A. *Vecchi teatri milanesi*, Milan, 1920.
Weinstock, H. *Donizetti and the World of Opera in Italy, Paris, and Vienna in the First Half of the Nineteenth Century*, New York, 1963.
_____. *Rossini: A Biography*, New York, 1968.
_____. *Vincenzo Bellini: His Life and His Operas*, New York, 1971.
Zendralli, A. *Tommaso Gherardi del Testa*, Bellinzona, 1910.

Late Nineteenth Century

Adami, G. *Librettisti e poeti verdiani*, Rome, 1941.
Albini, E. *Cronache teatrali, 1891-1925*, Genoa, 1972.
Alcari, C. *Il Teatro Regio di Parma nella sua storia dal 1883 al 1929*, Parma, 1929.
Altomare, L. *Il teatro di Roberto Bracco nella drammatica contemporanea*, Molfetta, 1930.
Antona-Traversi, C. *Eleonora Duse, sua vita, sua gloria, suo martirio*, Pisa, 1927.
_____. *La verità sul teatro italiano dell'ottocento*, Udine, 1940.
_____. *Vita di Gabriele d'Annunzio*, 2 vol., Florence, 1933.
Antongini, T. *D'Annunzio*, London, 1938.
Barbiera, R. *Vite ardenti nel teatro*, Milan, 1931.
Barbina, A. *Capuana inedito*, Milan, 1974.
_____. *Teatro verista siciliano*, Bologna, 1970.
Barsotti, A. *Giuseppe Giacosa*, Florence, 1973.
Basilea, S. *L'opera di Giuseppe Gallina nel teatro italiano*, Bologna, 1931.
Bellotti-Bon, L. *Condizioni dell'arte drammatico in italia*, Florence, 1875.
Bergin, T. *Giovanni Verga*, New Haven, 1931.
Bersezio, V. *La commedia piemontese*, Turin, 1887.
Boccardi, A. *Emilio Praga*, Milan, 1881.
Boglione, G. *L'arte della Duse*, Rome, 1960.
Bonavita, F. *Il teatro e l'arte di Ermete Novelli*, Forlì, 1905.
Bordeux, J. *Eleonora Duse: The Story of Her Life*, London, 1924.
Bozzetti, C. (ed.) *Il teatro del secolo ottocento*, Turin, 1960.
Bracco, R. *Nell'arte e nella vita*, Lanciano, 1941.
_____. *Tra le arti e gli artisti*, Naples, 1918.
Bush, H. *Verdi's Aida: The History of an Opera*, Minneapolis, 1978.
Capuana, L. *Gli "ismi" contemporani*, Catania, 1898.
_____. *Il teatro italiano contemporaneo*, Palermo, 1872.
Cattaneo, G. *Giovanni Verga*, Turin, 1963.
Carnor, M. *Puccini: A Critical Biography*, London, 1958.
Cauda, G. *Chiaroscuri di palcoscenico*, Savigliano, 1910.
_____. *Figure e figurine del teatro di prosa*, Chieri, 1925.
_____. *Nel regno dei comici*, Chieri, 1912.

Cenni, G. *Arte e vita prodigiose di Ermete Zacconi*, Milan, 1945.

Cervi, A. *Irma Gramatica*, Bologna, 1900.

Cesari, G. *Amilcare Ponchielli nell'arte del suo tempi*, Cremona, 1934.

Ciavarella, A. *Verga—De Roberto—Capuana*, Catania, 1955.

Corsi, M. *Le prime rappresentazioni d'annunziane*, Milan, 1932.

Costetti, G. *Confessioni di un autore drammatico*, Bologna, 1883.

Cuccetti, G. *Enrico Annibale Butti tra l'arte e la vita*, Milan, 1914.

Curato, B. *Sessant'anni di teatro in Italia*, Milan, 1947.

Curti, A. *Arte e teatro di Edoardo Ferravilla*, Milan, 1931.

Curti, P. *Adelaide Ristori*, Milan, 1855.

_____. *Ernesto Rossi*, Milan, 1858.

Damerini, A. *Amilcare Ponchielli*, Turin, 1940.

D'Ardenghi, B. *Il teatro neo-idealistico*, Palermo, n.d.

De Blasi, J. *Pietro Cossa e la tragedia italiana*, Florence, 1911.

De Cesare, R. *The Last Days of Papal Rome* (trans. H. Zimmern), Boston, 1909.

De Gubernatis, A. *Tommaso Salvini*, Florence, 1908.

De Mohr, A. *Felice Cavallotti*, Milan, 1898.

De Rensis, R. *L'"Amleto" di Arrigo Boito*, Ancona, 1927.

_____. *Franco Faccio e Verdi*, Milan, 1934.

_____. *Lettere di Arrigo Boito*, Rome, n.d.

Di Martino, G. *Adelaide Ristori, attrice drammatico*, Florence, 1908.

Dornis, J. *Le Théâtre italien contemporain*, Paris, 1903.

Duse, E. *Memorie e reliquie*, Milan, 1925.

Ferrari, V. *Paolo Ferrari, la vita—il teatro*, Milan, 1899.

Ferrigni, P. *Il teatro di Paolo Ferrari*, Milan, 1922.

Ferrone, S. *Il teatro di Verga*, Rome, 1972.

Field, K. *Adelaide Ristori: A Biography*, New York, 1867.

Fiocco, A. *Teatro italiano di ieri e di oggi*, Rocca San Casciano, 1958.

Flori, E. *Il teatro di Enrico Annibale Butti*, Milan, 1902.

Forgione, M. *La vita e l'arte di Marco Praga*, Padua, 1944.

Folani, F. *Hamlet rappresentato da Enrico Rossi*, Trieste, 1874.

Fusero, C. *Eleonora Duse*, Milan, 1971.

Gandolfo, A. *Enrico Annibale Butti*, Palermo, 1928.

Garaio-Armò, L. *Il teatro di Giuseppe Giacosa*, Palermo, 1925.

Gatteschi, G. *Stanislao Morelli*, Florence, 1892.

Gatti, C. *Verdi*, 2 vol., Milan, 1931.

Gatti, G. *Vita di Gabriele D'Annunzio*, Florence, 1956.

Greppi, A. *Risorgera Milano*, Milan, 1953.

Guerrieri, G. *Eleonora Duse e il suo tempo*, Treviso, 1974.

Guetta, C. *Ernesto Rossi: Appunti e ricordi*, Leghorn, 1906.

Gullace, G. *Gabriele D'Annunzio in France*, Syracuse, 1966.

Harding, B. *Age Cannot Wither*, Philadelphia, 1947.

Hingston, E. *Adelaide Ristori: The Siddons of Modern Italy*, London, 1856.

Incagliati, M. *Il Teatro Costanzi*, Rome, 1907.

Infessura, S. *Diario della città di Roma*, Rome, 1890.

Knepler, H. *The Gilded Stage*, London, 1968.

Lelièvre, R. *Le Théâtre dramatique italien en France 1855-1940*, La Roche-sur-Yon, 1959.

Levi, C. *Autori drammatici italiani*, Bologna, 1922.

_____. *Profili di attori*, Milan, 1923.

Lyonnet, H. *Le Théâtre en Italie*, Paris, 1900.

MacClintock, L. *The Contemporary Drama of Italy*, Boston, 1920.

McLeod, A. *Plays and Players in Modern Italy*, London, 1912.

Manca, S. *Tommaso Salvini*, Palermo, 1904.

Mapes, V. *Duse and the French*, New York, 1898.

Martin, G. *Verdi: His Music, Life and Times*, New York, 1963.

Martini, F. *Al teatro*, Florence, 1895.

Marzot, G. *Battaglie veristiche dell'ottocento*, Messina, 1941.

Masci, F. *La vita e le opere di Gabriele D'Annunzio*, Rome, 1950.

Mason, T. *The Othello of Tommaso Salvini*, New York, 1890.

Monaco, G. *Pietro Cossa*, Vercelli, 1931.

Monaldi, G. *Giacomo Puccini e la sua opera*, Rome, n.d.

_____. *Iconografia verdiana*, Bergamo, 1913.

Mongelli, L. *Cenni artistico-biografici su Fanny Sadowsky*, Naples, 1899.

Montazio, E. *Adelaide Ristori*, Paris, 1855.

_____. *Ernesto Rossi*, Trieste, 1865.

Muret, M. *La Littérature italienne d'aujourd'hui*, Paris, 1906.

Nardi, P. *Vita di Arrigo Boito*, Milan, 1942.

_____. *Vita e tempo di Giuseppe Giacosa*, Milan, 1949.

Navarria, A. *Giovanni Verga*, Catania, 1964.

Nicastro, L. *Confessioni di Eleonora Duse*, Milan, 1946.

Novelli, E. *Foglietti sparsi narranti la mia vita*, Rome, n.d.

Ojetti, N. *Tommaso Salvini*, Florence, 1916.

Orsi, D. *Toselli e il teatro piemontese*, Turin, 1898.

Palmieri, E. *Teatro in dialetto*, Turin, 1960.

_____. *Il teatro veneto*, Milan, 1948.

Panzacchi, E. *Soliloqui artistici*, Rome, 1885.

Pardieri, G. *Ermete Novelli*, Bologna, 1965.

_____. *Ermete Zacconi*, Bologna, 1960.

Parisi, P. *Roberto Bracco. La sua vita. La sua arte. I suoi critici*. Palermo, 1923.

Pellizzari, A. *Il pensiero e l'arte di Luigi Capuana*, Naples, 1919.

Personà, L. *Il teatro italiano della "Belle époque,"* Florence, 1972.

Piccini, G. *Memorie di un impresario fiorentino*, Florence, 1892.

Pleasants, H. *The Great Singers*, New York, 1966.

Policastro, G. *Il teatro siciliano*, Catania, 1924.

Pompeati, A. *Arrigo Boito poeta e musicista*, Florence, 1919.

Pompei, E. *Pietro Mascagni nella vita e nell'arte*, Rome, 1912.

Pullini, G. *Marco Praga*, Bologna, 1960.

_____. *Teatro italiano fra due secoli*, Florence, 1959.

Radicotti, G. *Teatro e musica in Roma nel secondo quarto del secolo XIX*, Rome, 1905.

Raymond, C. *Un Comédien français en Italie*, Paris, 1900.

Rheinhardt, E. *The Life of Eleonora Duse*, London, 1930.

Rhodes, A. *The Poet as Superman: A Life of Gabriele d'Annunzio*, London, 1959.

Ricci, C. *Arrigo Boito*, Milan, 1919.

Righetti, C., *et al. Ferraville e compagni,* Milan, 1890.

Rinaldi, M. *Musica e verismo*, Rome, 1932.

Ristori, A. *Memoirs and Artistic Studies* (trans. G. Mantellini), New York, 1907.

Rolandi, V. *Libretti e librettisti verdiani,* Rome, 1941.

Rossi, E. *Quarant'anni di vita artistica,* 3 vol., Florence, 1887-1889.

_____. *Riflessioni sul teatro drammatico italiano,* Leghorn, 1893.

_____. *Studi drammatici e lettere autobiografiche,* Florence, 1885.

Roux, O. *Infanzia e giovinezza di illustri italiani contemporanei,* Florence, 1909.

Ruberti, G. *Storia del teatro contemporaneo,* Bologna, 1928.

Russo, L. *Giovanni Verga,* Naples, 1920.

Ruta, P. *Cinquant'anni di vita teatrale,* Bologna, 1913.

Salvini, C. *Tommaso Salvini nella storia del teatro italiano e nella vita del suo tempo,* Rocca San Casciano, 1955.

_____. *Le ultime romantiche,* Florence, 1944.

Salvini, T. *Discours en commémoration d'Adelaide Ristori,* Paris, 1907.

_____. *Leaves from the Autobiography* (trans. anon.), New York, 1892.

Sartori, C. *Puccini,* Milan, 1958.

Scaglia, R. (ed.) *Virginia Marini,* Alessandria, 1928.

Scalia, S. *Luigi Capuana and His Times,* New York, 1952.

Scarpetta, E. *Dal San Carlino al Fiorentini,* Naples, 1899.

Scarpetta, M. *Felice Sciosciammocca, mio padre,* Naples, 1950.

Sciuto, S. *Giuseppe Giacosa e la sua opera,* Acireale, 1910.

Signorelli, O. *Eleonora Duse,* Rome, 1955.

Silvestre, A., *et al. Notes et souvenirs sur Tommaso Salvini,* Paris, 1878.

Simoni, R. *Teatro di ieri,* Milan, 1938.

Sodini, A. *Ariel armato,* Milan, 1931.

Soldatini, G. *Alamanno Morelli e l'arte sua,* Milan, 1879.

Symons, A. *Eleonora Duse,* London, 1926.

Trapadoux, M. *Mme. Adelaide Ristori,* Paris, 1861.

Traversa, V. *Luigi Capuana, Critic and Novelist,* The Hague, 1968.

Trevisani, C. *Gli Autori contemporanei,* Rome, 1885.

Trevisani, G. (ed.) *Teatro napoletano,* Modena, 1958.

Tonelli, L. *L'opera di Giovanni Verga,* Catania, 1927.

_____. *La tragedia di Gabriele D'Annunzio,* Milan, 1913.

Verdi, Giuseppe. *Letters* (trans. C. Osborne), New York, 1971.

Verdinois, F. *Profili letterari napoletani,* Naples, 1882.

Vergani, L. (ed.) *Eleonora Duse,* Milan, 1958.

Vincieri, M. *Il teatro dannunziano,* Udine, 1940.

Walker, F. *The Man Verdi,* New York, 1962.

Weld, C. *Florence: The New Capital of Italy,* London, 1867.

Winwar, F. *Wingless Victory,* New York, 1957.

Zabel, E. *Die italienische Schauspielkunst in Deutschland,* Berlin, 1893.

Zacconi, E. *Ricordi e battaglie,* Garzanti, 1946.

Index

Acting, vii, 8-10, 23, 24, 38, 103, 104, 121, 128, 130, 142, 145, 153, 154, 163, 166, 170, 173, 179, 185-89, 193, 195, 196

Albergati, Francesco, 43

Alberto, Adamo, 102, 137, 139, 152

Alfieri, Vittorio, v, vi, 19-24, 33, 37, 38, 40, 45, 46, 48, 51, 55, 57, 62, 64, 65, 71, 72, 74, 75, 82, 105, 120, 122, 149, 150, 152; *Agamemnone*, 24, 76; *Antigone*, 22,78; *Bruto Primo*, 24, 41; *Bruto Secondo*, 104; *Filippo*, 21, 24, 78; *Misgallo*, 24; *Mirra*, 40, 78, 128, 129; *Oreste*, 22, 41, 71, 76, 104, 119, 141, 179; *Ottavia*, 78; *I poeti*, 20; *Polinice*, 21, 78; *Rosmunda*, 78, 83; *Saul*, 23, 24, 71, 76, 89, 104, 120, 137, 138, 143, 148

Alione, Giovan, 169

Aliprandi, Alfonsina, 137

Aliprandi, Luigi, 114

Andò, Flavio, viii, 179, 180, 182, 185, 188, 189, 190, 193, 196

Anelli, Angelo: *Dalla beffa al disinganno*, 40; *L'Italiana in Algeri*, 40; *Ser marcantonio*, 40

Antoine, André, 180, 188

L'antologia, 68, 73, 88, 89

Antona-Traversi, Camillo: *Danza macabre*, 187; *Il signor Lecocq*, 189

Arisoto: *La scolastina*, 16

Arrivabene, Adelia, 93, 94

Aristotle, 17, 65

Astolfi, Giuseppe, 120, 121

Avelloni, Francesco: *Bianca e Fernando*, 100; *Carlo XII di Svezia*, 71

Auber, Esprit, 139; *La muette de Portici*, 60

Augier, Emile, 139, 141, 161, 163, 164, 175, 184; *Gabrielle*, 182

Bagnara, Francesco, 51, 61, 94

Barbaja, Domenico, 34, 47, 54, 60

Baretti, Eraldo: *I fastidi d'un grand om*, 171

Baretti, Giuseppe, 12, 64, 65

Barlaffa, Francesco, 77

Battaglia, Carlo, 18, 20, 40, 42, 163
Battaglia, Giacinto, 95, 113; *La famiglia Foscari*, 95; *Vittorina*, 95
Bazzi, Anna Maria, 75, 100, 103
Bazzi, Gaetano, 52, 74, 75, 94, 103
Beauharnais, Eugène de, 34, 50
Beaumarchais, P.A.C. de, 43, 74, 189; *The Barber of Seville*, 78
Bellini, Vincenzo, 1, 51, 59, 60; *Il pirata*, 60, 109; *I puritani e i cavalieri*, 109; *La sonnambula*, 108
Belloni, Antonio, 42, 43, 63, 74, 81, 82
Bellotti-Bon, Luigi, viii, 94, 121, 141, 161-68, 182, 183, 185, 188, 189
Berchet, Giovanni, 62, 63; *Lettera semiseria*, 62, 55
Bergamo, 44, 102
Bernhardt, Sarah, 135, 176, 180, 189, 193-97
Bersezio, Vittorio: *Fratellanza artigiana* 174; *Le miserie d'monssù Travet*, 170
Berti, Filippo: *Gli amanti sessagenari*, 118
Bettinelli, Saverio: *Gli eroi ateniesi*, 18
Bettini, Amalia, 56, 101-103
Bettini, Giovanni and Lucrezia, 42, 55, 101
Bettoli, Parmenio: *Il Boccaccio a Napoli*, 150; *Le idee della signora Aubray*, 150
Blanès, Pellegrino, 40-43, 56, 69, 75, 79, 89
Boccomini, Giovanni, 75, 78, 79
Boito, Arrigo, 156-59, 181, 189, 193, 194; *Mefistofele*, 156-69; *Le sorelle d'Italia*, 156
Bologna, 18, 20, 34, 46, 55, 90, 98, 102, 118, 121, 135, 157, 174
Bon, Francesco Augusto, 75, 77, 100, 105, 113, 117, 137, 163, 171; *Addio alla scene*, 103; *Dietro le scene*, 100; *Ludro e la sua gran giornata*, 77, 137, 163; *Il matriomonio di Ludro*, 77, 100; *Niente di male*, 77; *Pietro Paolo Rubens*, 113; *S'io fossi ricco*, 100; *La vecchiaia di Ludro*, 77, 100
Bonazzi, Luigi, 94
Booth, Edwin, 136, 145, 148
Borghi, Giovan, 75, 77
Bozzo, Michele, 134, 135, 138
Bracco, Roberto, viii, 162, 175, 188, 189, 198; *Don Pietro Caruso*, 189; *Maschere*, 188
Brofferio, Angelo, 107
Butti, Enrico, viii, 162, 186; *La corsa al piacere*, 190; *La fine d'un ideale*, 190; *Gli Atei*, 190; *Lucifero*, 191; *Una tempesta*, 191; *L'utopia*, 186, 187
Byron, George Gordon, Lord, 57, 60, 69, 144, 150

Cajani, Cosimo, 71
Calini, Orazio: *Zelinda*, 19
Caminer, Elisabetta, 20; *L'onesto colpevole*, 13
Camarano, Salvatore, 115
Canna, Pasquale, 53
Capuana, Luigi, 161, 177, 178, 191, 192; *Giacinta*, 178, 182, 183

Carasale, Angelo, 26, 28

Carbonari, 55, 56, 86, 89, 90

Carducci, Giosuè, 192

Carlo Alberto, 76, 95, 104

Carrer, Luigi: *L'ultimo colloquio di Antonio Foscarini*, 70

Carrera, Valentino: *Quaderna di Nanni*, 165

Casa di Goldoni, 189

Castagna, Giuseppe, 134

Cavalletti, Carolina, 42, 55, 57

Cavallotti, Felice, 167, 168; *Agnese*, 167; *Alcibiade*, 167; *I pezzenti*, 167; *La sposa di Mènecle*, 167

Cavona, Antonio, 63

Cavour, Camillo Benso, Count di, 86, 97, 98, 117, 126, 129, 131, 133, 170

Cazzola, Clementina, 120, 121, 137, 139, 184

Censorship, 45, 46, 50, 51, 55, 58, 62, 63, 72, 73, 78, 87, 90, 91, 99-101, 104, 105, 111, 113, 115, 116, 119, 130, 138, 164, 177

Cerlone, Francesco, 28

Cerrito, Fanny, 112

Chatterton, F.B., 143, 144, 153

Checchi, Teobaldo, 180, 185

Chekov, Anton, 196; *The Cherry Orchard*, 191

Chiari, Pietro, 7, 11-13; *La schiava chinese*, 8; *La scuola delle vedove*, 6, 7

Chiossoni, David: *La donna del popolo*, 129

Chizzola, Charles, 142

Ciceri, P.L.C., 60, 176

Cima, Camillo: *El zio scior*, 172

Cimarosa, Domenico, 30, 46, 58, 59; *Il matrimonio segreto*, 30

Colbran, Isabella, 54

Coletti, Francesco: *Quel che l'occhio non vede il cuor non crede*, 150

Colomberti, Antonio, 81, 90, 120

Colomberti, Isabella, 79, 81, 106

Comédie Française, vi, 44, 52, 128, 131, 151, 182

Commarano, Vincenzo and Filippo, 47

Commedia dell'arte, v, 1, 2, 4, 6, 7, 12, 14, 20, 28, 34, 40, 43, 47, 112, 172, 173

Compagnia Drammatica della Città di Roma, 185, 189

Compagnia Drammatica Lombarda, 114, 115, 138, 163

Compagnia Nazionale Toscana, 71, 72, 81, 82, 89

Compagnia Reale di Parma, 81-83

Compagnia Reale Italiana, vi, 34, 40-43, 55

Compagnia Reale Sarda, vii, viii, 52, 57, 74-81, 86, 95, 98-107, 118, 119, 126, 128, 130, 131, 138, 144, 149, 150, 163, 166, 178

Il Conciliatore, 62, 63, 68

Conti, Antonio: *Giulio Cesare*, 18

Corneille, Pierre, 2, 16, 18, 64, 150; *Le Cid*, 151; *Stilicon*, 17

Cossa, Pietro: *I Borghia*, 167; *Cola di Rienzo*, 167; *Nerone*, 152 153, 167, 177, 187, 189; *Plauto e il suo secolo*, 167

Costetti, Giuseppe: *I dissoluti gelosi*, 165; *Il dovere*, 165; *Il figlio di famiglia*, 165; *La morte del conte di Montecristo*, 165

Cottellini, Gaetano, 119
Crescimbeni, Giovan, 17
Cuccetti, A.M.: *Carlo in Sciaffusa*, 45

Dall'ongaro, Francesco: *I dalmati*, 95; *Danae*, 95; *Il fornaretto*, 93;
     Guglielmo Tell, 95
D'Annunzio, Gabriele, viii, 162, 192-99, 201; *La città morta*, 194, 195, 197,
     198; *La figlia di Iorio*, 198; *Francesca da Rimini*, 198; *Il Fuoco*, 195,
     196, 198; *La gioconda*, 197, 198; *La gloria*, 197; *Sogno d'un mattino
     di primavera*, 195, 197
Dante, 22, 33, 69, 88, 92, 99, 131, 141
Darbes, Cesare, 6, 13
David, Domenico, 17
De Gubernatis, Angelo: *Buddha*, 150; *De Nala*, 150; *Don Rodrigo*, 150;
     Mâyâ, 150; *Pier delle Vigne*, 150; *Re Desarata*, 150
Delfino, Giovanni: *Cleopatra*, 19
Della Valle, Cesare: *Giuliette e Romeo*, 77, 78; *Ifigenia in Aulide*, 55; *Ip-
     polito*, 55; *Medea*, 55, 129
De Marini, Giuseppe, 41, 55, 74, 75, 93, 101
Denina, Carlo, 64
Destouches, P.-N., 76, 79
Dialect drama, 113, 162, 169-76
Diderot, Denis, 43; *Le Père de famille*, 42
Di Giacone, Salvatore: *'O voto*, 174
Domeniconi, Luigi, 81, 87, 91, 102, 103, 105, 108, 119, 149
Dondini, Cesare, 94, 117, 121, 137, 139, 149, 150, 166
Donizetti, Gaetano, 1, 44, 51, 60, 87, 110; *Anna Bolena*, 108; *Chiara e
     Seratina*, 60; *Don Pasquale*, 40, 109; *L'elisir d'amore*, 108; *Marin
     Faliero*, 109
Dottori, Carlo: *Aristodemo*, 15
Ducis, J.F., 65, 71
Dumas, Alexandre, vii, 94, 105, 106, 114, 127, 128, 150, 165, 175
Dumas, Alexandre, *fils*, 139, 150, 161, 163, 164, 175, 176, 179, 185, 187, 196;
     La Dame aux camélias, 121, 138, 173, 179, 184, 189, 193, 195, 196; *La
     Femme de Claude*, 179, 195, 196; *Le Fils naturel*, 165; *La Princesse de
     Bagdad*, 179
Duse, Eleanora, vii, viii, 52, 162, 166, 176, 178-80, 182, 183, 185, 188, 189,
     192-99

Elssler, Fanny, 112
Emanuel, Giovanni, 178, 180

Fabbrichesi, Salvatore, 40, 42-45, 52, 55-57, 63, 75, 77, 78, 89, 102, 106
Faccio, Franco, 159, 181; *Amleto*, 156; *I profughi fiamminghi*, 156
Fagiuoli, Giovan: *Gl'inganni iodevoli* , 15; *Gli sponsali in maschera*, 15
Fauriel, Claude, 63, 69

Federici, Camillo and Carlo, 43, 46, 77
Ferdinand IV, 34, 47, 50, 54, 55, 96
Ferrari, Paolo, 87, 117-21, 139, 150, 152, 161, 164-67, 171, 182, 191; *Amici e rivali,* 164; *Amore senza stima,* 164; *Baltromeo calzolaro,* 118; *La bottega del cappellaio,* 149; *Il duello,* 164; *Goldoni e le sue sedici commedie nuove,* 117, 121, 164; *Il ridicolo,* 164; *La satire e parini,* 121; *Il Tartufo moderna (prosa),* 118, 120, 149, 164; *Gli uomini seri,* 164
Ferrario, Carlo, 158, 159
Ferravilla, Edoardo, 172-74
Ferri, Camillo, 79, 80, 99, 102, 185, 188
Ferri, Domenico, 53
Florence, 15, 22-24, 34, 40, 41, 52, 64, 66, 68-74, 88, 90, 98, 105, 115, 118, 119, 124, 125, 131, 134, 138, 140-42, 145-50, 155, 157, 163-65, 174, 177, 178, 184
Fortis, Leone, *Cuore e arte,* 114
Foscolo, Ugo, 45, 46, 63, 65, 66, 76, 89, 111; *Aiace,* 45; *Ricciarda,* 46; *Tieste,* 45
Fumagalli, Amalia, 119

Galliari, Bernardino, 21
Gallina, Ercole, 72, 89
Gallina, Giacinto, 171, 172; *Le barufe in famegia,* 171; *La mama no mor mai,* 171; *Una famegia in rovina,* 171
Galuppi, Baldassare, 2, 8, 29, 30; *L'arcadia in Brenta,* 29
Garelli, Federico, 169; *Guera o pas?,* 170
Garibaldi, Giuseppe, 86, 97, 117, 124, 131, 138, 152
Gautier, Théophile, 127, 128
Gazes, Francesco, 187
Gemelli, Enrico, 171
Genoa, 14, 34, 50, 76, 88, 89, 91, 102, 134, 156
Gherardi del Testa, Tommaso, 67, 105, 179; *Il berretto bianco da notte,* 106; *La carità pelosa,* 165; *Le coscienze elastiche,* 165; *Ludovico Sforza,* 105; *Le scimmie,* 106; *Il sistema di Giorgio,* 105; *Una folle ambizione,* 105; *Il vero blasone,* 165
Ghirlanda, Giovanni, 78, 79, 102
Giacometti, Paolo, vii, 87, 106, 107, 152, 163, 171, 198; *La benefattrice,* 106; *Camilla Faà de Casale,* 106; *Carlo II, re d'inghilterra,* 106; *La donna,* 107; *Elisabetta regina d'inghilterra,* 117, 132, 133, 135, 136; *Fieschi e Fregosi,* 106; *La gioventù di Carlo II,* 106; *Giuditta,* 129, 132; *L'indomani dell'ubbrico,* 164; *Isabella de Fiesco,* 106; *Maria Antoinetta,* 134, 135; *La morte civile,* 139, 143-46, 152, 187, 189; *Il poeta e la ballerina,* 106; *Quattro donne in una casa,* 106; *Reneta di Francia,* 135; *Siamo tutti fratelli!,* 104; *Sofocle,* 139; *L'ultimo dei duchi di Mantova,* 150
Giacosa, Giuseppe, viii, 161, 167, 168, 178, 180, 182-84, 190, 191, 193, 198; *A can che lecca cenere non gli fidar farina,* 167; *Come le foglie,* 162, 188, 191; *Diritti dell'anima,* 187; *Il fratello d'armi,* 168; *Luisa,* 182; *Il più forte,* 191; *La signora di Challant,* 189; *Il trionfo d'amore,* 168; *Tristi amori,* 168, 182, 183, 184; *Una partita a scacchi,* 167

Giraud, Giovanni, 48, 72, 106, 108; *L'Ajo nell'imbarazzo*, 48, 77; *La ciarliera indispettito*, 48, 74; *Regalie per Capo d'Anno*, 100

Gluck, Christoph Willibald, 29, 30, 44; *Artaserse*, 35; *La clemenza di Tito*, 29

Goethe, J.W. von, 37, 38, 66, 67, 150; *Faust*, 89

Goldoni, Carlo; v, vi, 1-4, 6-12, 14-17, 19, 20, 28, 35-37, 40, 42, 43, 45, 46, 48, 68, 72, 76, 82, 83, 106, 108, 113, 117, 150, 164, 166, 168, 171, 188, 189; *Amalasonte*, 3; *L'amante militare*, 9; *Belisario*, 4; *La buona figiola*, 30; *Il burbero beneficio*, 71; *La casa disabitata*, 83; *I due gemelli veneziani*, 6; *Gondoliere veneziano*, 4; *La locandiera*, 8, 83, 193, 195, 197; *La massère*, 8; *Pamela mariata*, 10; *Pamela nubile*, 10, 42, 90, 105, 138; *La putta onorata*, 6; *Il servitore di due padrone*, 12; *La sposa persiana*, 8; *La sposa sagace*, 119; *Il vecchio bizzarro*, 9; *La vedova spiritosa*, 10

Gotthardi, Giovan, 99, 100, 104

Gozzi, Carlo, 1, 11-14, 20, 37, 40, 137, 171; *L'amore delle tre melarance*, 12; *Il corvo*, 12; *Le droghe d'amore*, 13; *Il montanaro don Giovanni Pasquale*, 37; *Re cervo*, 12; *Turandot*, 12

Gramatica, Irma, 198

Grasso, Giovanni, 175

Grau, Maurice, 132, 134, 142, 144, 152

Gravina, Gian, 17

Greppi, Giovanni: *Teresa*, 46

Grisi, Giulia, 109

Gritti, Francesco: *Amleto*, 65

Guerrazzi Francesco: *L'assedio di Firenze*, 115; *I bianchi e i neri*, 88; *Priamo*, 88

Halm, Friedrich: *Ingomar*, 143, 144, 146

Home, John: *Douglas*, 69, 70

Howells, W.D., 66, 148

Hugo, Victor, vii, 59, 60, 94, 99, 106, 114, 150, 167, 176; *Angelo, Tyran de Padoue*, 181; *Cromwell*, 68; *Hernani*, 83, 94, 156, 157

Ibsen, Henrik, viii, 162, 185-89, 198; *A Doll's House*, 185, 186, 199; *An Enemy of the People*, 188; *Ghosts*, 186, 187, 189; *Hedda Gabler*, 186, 199; *The Lady from the Sea*, 199; *Little Eyolf*, 187; *The Master Builder*, 186, 189; *Rosmersholm*, 186, 187, 199; *The Wild Duck*, 189

Iffland, A.W., 43, 56, 76, 150

Internari, Carolina, 56, 82, 83, 89, 102, 107, 119, 126, 127, 138

Ivon, Emma, 173, 174

Janin, Jules, 127-29

Job, Anna, 119

Jomelli, Niccolò, 29, 44

Kean, Edmund, 79, 144

Kotzebue, A. von, 43, 76; *Graf Benjowsky*, 90

Lablache, Luigi, 109
Lamartine, Alphonse de, 126-28
Lampugnani, Giovanni, 35, 36; *Artaserse*, 36
Leghorn, 88, 129
Legouvé, Ernest, 127-29; *Beatrix*, 131; *Médée*, 129, 130, 132, 133, 135
Leigheb, Claudio, 189
Leigheb, Giovanni, 105, 149
Leoncavallo, Ruggero, 161; *I Pagliacci*, 181
Leoni, Mario: *I mal nutrì*, 171
Leoni, Michele, 65
Leopardi, Giacomo, 68
Liveri, Barone di, 28
Lombardi, Francesco, 56, 119
Lorenzo, Tina di, 190

Machiavelli, 33, 69; *Mandragola*, 155
Maeterlinck, Maurice, 196; *L'Intruse*, 187
Maffei, Scipione, 19; *Merope*, 16, 17, 76
Maggi, Andrea, 148
Magnani, Gerolamo, 158, 159
Magnocavallo, Ottovio: *Conrad*, 19; *Roxana*, 19
Majeroni, Achille, 138, 139, 141
Manin, Daniele, 95
Manzoni, Alessandro, 51, 63-69, 76, 79, 88, 99, 117, 169, 170; *Adelchi*, 67; *Il cinque maggio*, 111; *Il conte di Carmagnola*, 63, 65-67; *Lettre à M. Chauvet*, 68; *I promessi sposi*, 68, 69, 94, 98, 178, 181
Marenco, Carlo, 79, 99, 105, 167, 168; *Adelia*, 99; *Buondelmonte e gli amidei*, 77, 79; *Manfredi*, 99; *Pia dei Tolomei*, 79, 99, 100, 119, 121, 128, 129, 133, 166
Marenco, Leopoldo: *Celeste*, 166; *Il falconiere di Pietra Ardena*, 167; *Giorgia Gandi*, 166; *Marcellina*, 166; *Piccardo Donati*, 166; *Saffo*, 166
Marchionni, Angelo, 43
Marchionni, Carlotta, 43, 74, 78, 80-82, 98-101, 103, 117
Maria Luisa of Parma, 77, 81, 111
Marini, Virginia, viii, 139, 184-89
Mario, Giovanni, 109
Martelli, Pier, 16
Martini, Vincenzo: *Il misantrope in società*, 107; *Una donna di quarant'unni*, 107
Martini, Virginia, 162
Martino, Giuseppe de, 173
Mascagni, Pietro, 161, 180, 181; *L'amico Fritz*, 181; *Cavalleria rusticana*, 181, 185, 193, 195, 196, 198; *I Rantzau*, 181
Mascherpa, Romualdo, 52, 81, 82, 102, 103, 108, 117, 120
Mayr, Johann Simon, 44, 47, 48, 58; *Adelaide di Guesclino*, 44; *Che originali*, 44; *Lodoiska*, 44; *Medea in Corinto*, 60; *La rosa bianco e la rosa rossa*, 60; *Saffo*, 44

Mazzini, Giuseppe, 86-92, 98, 107, 109, 111, 115
Medebac, Girolamo, 4, 8, 9, 19
Medebac, Theodora, 7, 40
Medrano, Giovanni, 26
Menadier, Eugène and Hippolyte, 162, 163, 169
Meraviglia, Ferdinando, 43
Mercadante, Saverio, 51, 59; *Amelete*, 59; *I briganti*, 59, 109; *Elise e Claudio*, 59; *Il giuramento*, 59
Merelli, Bartolomeo, 110, 111
Merelli, Felippo, 17
Metastasio (Pietro Trapassi), 17, 19, 20, 23, 24, 28, 29, 35, 60; *Achille in Sciro*, 27; *Didone abbandonata*, 17; *Guistino*, 17
Meyerbeer, Giacomo, 59, 60, 109, 139, 140
Milan, 3, 20, 34-48, 50, 51, 55-63, 68, 92, 94-98, 102, 108-15, 120, 122, 125, 149, 156, 162, 163, 167, 170-75, 178, 183, 184, 188
Milone, Tancredi, 171
Miutti, Francesco, 75
Modena, 16, 20, 73, 76, 90, 98, 120
Modena, Giacomo, 89, 91
Modena, Gustavo, vii, 56, 86, 89-98, 104, 105, 111, 113, 117-19, 128, 138, 145, 149, 150, 163, 169, 176
Molière, 1, 2, 16, 48, 64, 76, 113, 189
Moncalvo, Giuseppe, 100, 112, 113, 172; *Il dialogo fra Radetzki e Metternich con Meneghino locandiere*, 113; *Meneghino, medico per forze*, 113; *Meneghino schiavo in Turchia*, 113
Montaignani, Achille: *Adalberto all'assedio della Roccella*, 104
Montanelli, Giuseppe: *Camma*, 133
Monti, Luigi, 138
Monti, Pietro, 102
Monti, Vincenzo, 22, 37-41, 45, 55, 58, 60, 63, 65, 76, 120; *Aristodemo*, 37, 39; *Caio Gracco*, 38, 39; *Galeotto Manfredi*, 38, 39; *I pittagorici*, 39; *Il ritorno di Astrea*, 58; *Teseo*, 39
Morelli, Alamanno, viii, 94, 114, 141, 162-66, 185
Morelli, Stanislao: *Arduino d'Ivrea*, 141
Marlacchi, Francesco, 48
Moro Lin, Angelo, 171, 172
Moro Lin, Marianna, 170, 171, 174
Morrochesi, Antonio, 56, 64, 71, 114
Mozart, W.A., 36, 44, 47, 58; *Ascano in Alba*, 36; *Lucio Silla*, 36; *Mitridate*, 36
Murat, Joachim, 34, 50
Musset, Alfred de, 150, 176

Naples, vii, 3, 12, 17, 24-31, 33, 34, 41, 42, 46, 47, 50-57, 63, 68, 75, 81, 95, 98, 102, 109, 115, 116, 126, 130, 134, 138, 139, 141, 152, 162, 168, 173-75, 178, 179, 198
Napoleon, 24, 31, 33-35, 39, 40, 42, 46, 50, 70, 117
Nardelli, Gaetano, 102
Niccolini, Antonio, 47, 53

Niccolini, Giovan Battista, 51, 62, 69-73, 76, 79, 81, 105, 120, 150; *Antonio Foscarini*, 70, 72, 81; *Arnaldo da Brescia*, 73; *Beatrice Cenci*, 73; *Della imitazione drammatica*, 72; *Edipo nel bosco delle Eumenidi*, 69; *Filippo Strozzi*, 73; *Giovanni da Procida*, 72; *Ino e Temisto*, 69; *Lodovico Sforza*, 72, 73; *Matilde*, 69; *Medea*, 69, 129; *Nabucco*, 70; *Polissena*, 41, 69; *Rosamunda d'Inghilterra*, 73; *I sette a Tebe*, 69

Nota, Alberto, 43-45, 72, 78, 101, 105, 107, 108; *Allessina*, 77; *L'atrabiliare*, 57, 77; *L'ammalato per immagionazione*, 77; *La fiera*, 78, 101; *La novella sposa*, 78

Novelli, Augusto, 174

Novelli, Ermete, viii, 175, 188, 189

Noverre, J.G., 58

Nozzari, Andrea, 54

Pacini, Giovanni, 40; *L'ultimo giorno de Pompei*, 61

Padua, 3, 42, 90, 93, 113

Paisiello, Giovanni, 30, 31, 47, 54, 59; *Il barbiere di Siviglia*, 30; *Nina*, 30; *I pittagorici*, 39; *La vedova di bel genio*, 30

Paladini, Francesco, 83

Parma, 18, 37, 68, 73, 81, 82, 108, 158

Patti, Adelina, 140

Pavesi, Stefano: *Ser Marcantonio*, 40

Pellandri, Anna Fiorelli, 40-43, 56, 69, 75

Pellico, Silvio, 51, 62, 63, 66, 98-100, 120, 150; *Ester d'Engaddi*, 98; *Corradino*, 99; *Francesca da Rimini*, 62, 76, 78, 80, 82, 90, 99, 100, 105, 119, 127, 129, 131, 138, 141, 169; *Iginia d'Asti*, 103; *Le mie prigioni*, 63, 98; *Tommaso Moro*, 99

Pelzet, Ferdinando, 82

Pelzet, Maddalena, 72, 81, 82, 119, 138

Perabò, Antonio: *Valsei*, 19

Perez, Davide, 29, 44

Pergolesi, Giovanni: *La serva padrona*, 26

Perotti, Gaetano, 75

Pertica, Luigi, 56

Petitio, Antonio, 173

Pezzana, Giacinta, 166, 170, 178, 198

Piamonti, Isolina, 141-44

Piave, Francesco Maria, 116, see also Verdi

Piccini, Giulio, 194

Piccini, Niccolò: *La cecchina*, 30

Pieri, Gaspare, 119-21, 163

Piermarini, Giuseppe, 36

Pietracqua, Luigi, 170

Pindemonte, Giovanni: *Baccanali*, 104; *Discorso sul teatro italiano*, 73; *Ginevra di Scozia*, 78; *Lucio Quinzio Cincinnatio*, 41

Piomarta, Gustavo: *L'avventure di Meneghia Peccenna*, 43

Pirandello, Luigi, 192, 202

Pius VII, 34, 47, 50

Pius IX, 95, 96, 124, 125
Politeama Fiorentino, 140, 141
Polvaro, Carlotta, 90, 91
Ponchielli, Amilcare: *La Gioconda,* 181; *I promessi sposi,* 181
Praga, Emilio, 156, 161; *I profughi fiamminghi,* 156
Praga, Marco, 184; *Alleluja,* 189; *La moglie ideale,* 189; *Le virgini,* 184
Prepiani, Giovan, 57, 102
Puccini, Giacomo, 161, 182, 183; *La Bohème,* 182; *Manon Lescault,* 182; *Tosca,* 1, 182; *Le villi,* 181

Rachel, Elisabeth, 127-33, 144, 176
Racine, Jean, 15, 55, 64, 76, 131, 188; *Britannicus,* 153; *Phèdre,* 128, 130, 132
Rafstopulo, Antonio, 72, 82, 89, 90
Ramirez, Giuseppe: *Giulietta e Romeo,* 65
Rasi, Luigi, 198
Re, Vincenzo, 27
Renzi, Francesco de: *Un baccio dato non e mai perduto,* 150
Ricci, Teodora, 13
Riccoboni, Luigi, v, 15, 16
Ricordi, Giulio, 158, 159
Righetti, Carlo, 172
Righetti, Domenico, 75, 100
Righetti, Francesco, 80
Righetti, Vincenza, 75, 78, 100, 103, 106, 107
Ristori, Adelaide, vii, 52, 87, 98, 100-108, 112, 117, 119, 121, 125-37, 141-43, 149, 151, 152, 155, 162, 163, 166, 175, 176, 193, 195
Robotti, Antonietta, 100, 105
Romagnoli, Carlo, 94, 144
Romagnoli, Luigi and Rosa, 75, 100
Romani, Felice: *Chiara e Serafina,* 60; *Medea in Corinto,* 60; *Il pirata,* 60; *La rosa bianca e la rosa rossa,* 60; *Il Turco in Italia,* 60
Rome, 8-10, 16, 17, 22, 34, 37, 44, 51, 54, 55, 57, 74, 80, 95-97, 102, 111, 115, 119, 124-26, 136, 147, 152, 164, 168, 173, 175, 178, 182, 183, 189
Rosapina, Carlo, 196
Rossi, Cesare, 178-80, 182, 183, 185, 189, 193
Rossi, Ernesto, vii, 52, 87, 98, 104, 105, 121, 122, 125, 126, 128, 130, 131, 136, 137, 139, 141, 144, 146-55, 162, 163, 175, 176, 188
Rossini, Gioacchino, vii, 44, 46-48, 54, 55, 59, 60, 87, 108, 109; *Il barbiere di Siviglia,* v, 54; *La cambiale di matrimonio,* 46; *La cenerentola,* 54; *Demetrio e Polibo,* 48; *La donna del lago,* 59; *Elisabetta,* 54; *La gazza ladra,* 54, 59, 63; *L'italiana in Algeri,* 40; *La pietra del paragone,* 46; *Otello,* 54; *Semiramide,* 54; *Il turco in Italia,* 60
Rostand, Edmond: *Cyrano de Bergerac,* 148, 190
Roti, Giovanni Battista, 13
Rovetta, Gerolamo, 161, 184, 189, 190, 192; *I disonesti,* 184; *Realtà,* 188; *Romanticismo,* 162, 190; *Trilogia di Dorina,* 184
Rubini, Giovan, 109

Sacchi, Antonio, 12-14, 40
Sadowsky, Fanny, 93-95, 112, 114, 117, 120, 138, 151, 152, 176
Salieri, Antonio, 36
Salvini, Alessandro, 93, 142
Salvini, Giuseppe, 93
Salvini, Tommaso, vii, 52, 87, 93, 94, 119, 120, 125, 126, 131, 136-55, 162,
    163, 175, 176, 178, 184, 185, 188, 189, 195
Sanquirico, Alessandro, 51, 59-61, 158, 176
Sardou, Victorien, 141, 152, 163, 184, 185
Scarpetta, Eduardo, 173, 174; *Don Felice*, 173
Scenery and costume, 28, 53, 59-61, 120, 134, 147, 151, 158, 187
Schiller, Friedrich von, 69, 81; *Don Carlos*, 78; *Kabale und Liebe*, 116;
    Maria Stuart, 90, 119, 128, 129, 132, 133, 135, 136; *Die Räuber*, 59;
    Wilhelm Tell, 39
Schurmann, Joseph, 193, 195
Scott, Sir Walter, 60; *The Fair Maid of Perth*, 88
Scribe, Eugene, 75, 94, 105-107, 114, 120, 127, 128, 141, 150; *Adrienne
    Lecouvreur*, 114, 134, 184; *Verre d'Eau*, 93
Selvatico, Riccardo: *La bozéta de l'ogio*, 171
Shakespeare, William, 38, 39, 41, 51, 60, 64-67, 69, 72, 87, 91, 141, 143-45,
    149, 151-55, 166, 179; *Antony and Cleopatra*, 122, 189, 194;
    Coriolanus, 39, 122, 147-49; *Hamlet*, 38, 56, 59, 64, 65, 71, 114, 121,
    122, 133, 138, 143, 144, 146, 148-55, 179; *Julius Ceasar*, 39, 122, 155;
    King Lear, 122, 147, 149, 152-55; *Macbeth*, 101, 122, 132, 135, 146,
    144, 146, 147, 149, 153; *The Merchant of Venice*, 122, 149, 189;
    Othello, 38, 39, 56, 120-22, 137, 139, 142-49, 151, 154, 155, 159, 179,
    189
Shaw, George Bernard, 92, 193
Sicily, 34, 119, 175, 177, 191
Signorini, Telemaco, 177
Sografi, Simeone Antonio, 42, 43, 46, 77; *Le convenienze teatrali*, 42;
    Lucrezia Dondi Orologio-Obizzi, 42; *Il matrimonio democratico*, 42;
    Ortensia, 42; *Il padre di famiglia*, 42; *La putta di sentimento*, 42;
    Tom Jones, 42; *Verter*, 42
Solera, Temistocle, 110, 111
Somigli, Mariano, 71
Staël, Germaine de, 61, 62; *Corinne*, 82
Stanislavsky, Constantin, 145, 146
Sudermann, Hermann: *Magda*, 193, 195
Suñer, Luigi: *I gentiluomini speculatori*, 164, 165; *I legittimisti in Italia*, 165;
    L'ozio, 165; *Una piaga sociale*, 165

Taddei, Luigi, 103, 138
Taglioni, Maria, 112
Taine, Hippolyte, 177, 184
Talli, Virgilio, 191
Tamburini, Antonio 109
Tana, Gaimbattista: *'L cont Piôlet*, 169, 170

Tasso, Torquato, 16, 22, 69
Teatro Alberti (Rome), 8, 9
Teatro [d']Angennes (Turin), 74, 76, 169
Teatro Apollo (Rome), 48, 116, 136
Teatro Apollo (Venice), 94
Teatro Argentina (Rome), 8, 9, 48, 54, 114, 115
Teatro Bellini (Palermo), 197
Teatro Borgognissanti (Florence), 71, 140
Teatro Brunetti (Bologna), 135
Teatro Cannobiana (Milan), 36, 43, 108
Teatro Capranica (Rome), 8, 9, 10
Teatro Carcano (Milan), 44, 108, 113
Teatro Carignano (Turin), 20, 21, 74, 75, 107, 150, 178
Teatro Carlo Fenice (Genoa), 134
Teatro Cocomero (Florence), 70-72, 105, 106, 131, 140, 141, 148
Teatro Costanzi (Rome), 181, 182
Teatro [della] Dame (Rome), 30
Teatro [del] Dondo (Naples), 130
Teatro Drammatico Nazionale (Rome), 182, 183
Teatro Ducale (Milan), 3, 35, 36
Teatro Ducale (Parma), 18, 108
Teatro Falcone (Genoa), 14
Teatro [La] Fenice (Venice) 42, 44, 46, 47, 54, 61, 79, 114, 116, 117
Teatro Fiando (Milan), 172
Teatro Filodrammtici (Milan), 39, 185
Teatro [dei] Fiorentini (Naples), 26, 30, 55, 94, 102, 119, 130, 134, 137-39, 144, 151, 152, 166, 178, 179, 184
Teatro [del] Fondo (Naples) 41, 47, 54, 134, 138, 139, 151, 152
Teatro Gerbino (Turin), 150
Teatro Goldoni (Florence), 70, 141
Teatro Goldoni (Venice), 117
Teatro Granari (Rome), 8
Teatro Grande (Trieste), 114
Teatro Lentasio (Milan), 92, 113
Teatro Leopoldo (Florence), 140
Teatro Lirico (Milan), 198
Teatro [alla] Logge (Florence), 141, 147
Teatro Manzoni (Milan), 182-84, 186, 187, 191
Teatro Nuovo (Naples), 26, 30, 55
Teatro Nuovo (Padua), 42
Teatro [della] Pace (Naples), 26
Teatro [della] Pace (Rome), 8
Teatro Pagliano (Florence), 140
Teatro [della] Pallacorda (Florence), 70, 140
Teatro [La] Pergola (Florence), 70, 109, 114, 134, 140, 141, 158, 181
Teatro Re (Milan), 92, 94, 108, 114, 118, 120, 121, 137, 149
Teatro Regio (Turin), 74, 181
Teatro [di] San Agostino (Genoa), 76
Teatro [di] San Angelo (Venice) 2, 4, 7, 8, 13, 14, 20, 29, 45

Teatro SS Apostoli (Venice), 2
Teatro [di] San Benedetto (Venice), 117
Teatro San Carlino (Naples), 173
Teatro San Carlo (Naples), 27-29, 47, 52-54, 59, 60, 79, 114, 116, 134, 138
Teatro [di] San Cassia (Venice), 2
Teatro [di] San Fantin (Venice), 2
Teatro SS Giovanni e Paolo (Venice), 2
Teatro [di] San Giovanni Grisostomo (Venice), 2, 14, 18, 20
Teatro [di] San Luca (Venice), 8, 12, 16, 20, 46
Teatro [di] Santa Maria (Florence), 71, 141, 175
Teatro [di] San Moise (Venice), 46
Teatro [di] San Salvador (Venice), 2, 13, 14
Teatro [di San Samuel (Venice), 2, 4, 6, 8, 12, 14, 171
Teatro [di] Santa Radegonda (Milan), 43
Teatro [alla] Scala (Milan), 34, 36, 41-48, 53, 57-60, 79, 108-12, 114, 156-59, 181, 182
Teatro Scribe (Turin), 169
Teatro Tordinona (Rome), 8-10, 48
Teatro Valle (Rome), 8, 9, 37, 38, 48, 54, 57, 74, 119, 136, 141, 148, 187, 197
Teatro [del] Verme (Milan), 181
Tessari, Alberto, 42, 53, 57, 81, 163
Tessero, Adelaide, 170, 183
Testoni, Alfredo, 174
Tommaseo, Niccolò, 89
Torelli, Achille, 139, 161, 165, 166, 174, 182; *I mariti*, 165, 166
Toselli, Giovanni, 169-72, 174; *Cichina 'd Moncalè*, 169
Trieste, 37, 56, 102, 147, 149, 163
Trissino, Giovan, 16; *Sofonisba*, 15
Tritto, Giuseppe: *Nicaboro in Jucatan*, 31
Tolstoi, Leo, 198; *The Power of Darkness*, 186, 187
Turin, vii, viii, 20, 21, 34, 52, 55, 74-81, 87, 88, 94, 98, 107, 117, 118, 122, 124, 126, 136, 149, 150, 156, 162, 163, 165, 169-71, 174, 178, 179, 183, 184, 190

Varano, Alfonso: *Giovanni di Giscala*, 18
Vendramin, Antonio and Francesco, 8, 13
Venice, 2-8, 11-17, 20, 24, 29, 33, 34, 42-46, 50, 51, 54, 56, 57, 70, 89, 94-96, 102, 117, 118, 121, 122, 124, 129, 149, 162, 164, 171, 172, 193
Venier company, 42, 71
Ventura, Giovanni, 79
Verdi, Giuseppe, v, vii, 44, 87, 107, 108, 110-12, 114-17, 155-59, 181; *Aida*, 155, 157-59; *Alzira*, 114, 134; *Attila*, 114, 115; *La battaglia di Legnano*, 114, 115, 139; *Il Corsaro*, 114; *Don Carlo*, 155; *I due Foscari*, iii; *Falstaff*, 199; *La forza del destino*, 155-57; *Giovanna d'Arco*, 114; *Inno delle nazioni*, 156; *Jersualem*, 114; *I Lombardi*, 110, 111, 114; *Luisa Miller*, 101, 115, 116, 134; *Macbeth*, 114, 157, 158; *I masnadieri*, 114; *Nabucco*, 110, 111; *Oberto*, 108, 110; *Otello*, 156, 159, 181; *Rigoletto*, 116, 140; *Simon Boccanegra*, 159; *La traviata*, 157; *Il trovatore*, 116; *Un ballo in maschera*, 116, 117, 149; *Un giorno di regno*, 110

Verga, Giovanni, viii, 161, 175, 177, 182, 184, 192, 198; *Cavalleria rusticana*, 178, 180-83; *In Porteneria*, 182, 183; *I malavoglia*, 178
Vernini, Pietro, 134
Verona, 57, 101, 102
Verri, Alessandro: *Amleto*, 64, 71; *Le congiura di Milano*, 38
Vestri, Angelo, 94, 138
Vestri, Gaetano, 94, 105
Vestri, Luigi, 56, 71, 74, 80, 82, 100, 101, 103, 121
Viganò, Salvatore, 58, 59, 63
Vigny, Alfred de, vii, 114, 176; *Chatterton*, 91; *Le Maréchal d'Ancre*, 93, 94
Visetti, Giovane, 57
Vitali, Bonafede, 4
Vitaliani, Italia, 185
Vittorio Emmanuele I, 50, 74
Vittorio Emmanuele II, 96, 97, 104, 111, 117, 124, 125, 141, 156, 165
Voltaire, 11, 12, 17, 18, 48, 65, 76, 122; *Semiramide*, 20; *Zaïre*, 90, 94, 120, 137, 138

Wagner, Richard, 156, 157, 188, 196
Woller, Gaetano, 106

Young Italy, 89, 91

Zacconi, Ermete, viii, 162, 175, 185-89, 197, 198
Zago, Emilio, 172
Zamarini, Carlo, 114
Zanazzo, Giggi, 174
Zeno, Apostolo, 17, 24, 26
Zingarelli, Nicola, 47, 48, 54
Zola, Emile, 145, 161, 176, 177, 178; *Thérèse Raquin*, 166, 179
Zoppis, Giovanni, 170, 171